FREAKING OUT

ALSO BY JOSHUA WOODS

Feudal America: Elements of the Middle Ages in Contemporary Society
—Vladimir Shlapentokh and Joshua Woods

America: Sovereign Defender or Cowboy Nation?
—Edited by Vladimir Shlapentokh, Joshua Woods, and Eric Shiraev

RELATED TITLES FROM POTOMAC BOOKS

Generation's End: A Personal Memoir of American Power After 9/11
—Scott L. Malcomson

The "Ugly American" in the Arab Mind: Why Do Arabs Resent America?
—Mohamed El-Bendary

American Avatar: The United States in the Global Imagination
—Barry A. Sanders

FREAKING OUT

A DECADE OF LIVING WITH TERRORISM

JOSHUA WOODS

Potomac Books
Washington, D.C.

Published in the United States by Potomac Books, Inc. All rights reserved. No part of this book may be reproduced in any manner whatsoever without written permission from the publisher, except in the case of brief quotations embodied in critical articles and reviews.

Library of Congress Cataloging-in-Publication Data
Woods, Joshua.
 Freaking out : a decade of living with terrorism / Joshua Woods. — 1st ed.
p. cm.
 Includes bibliographical references and index.
 ISBN 978-1-59797-666-4 (hardcover : alk. paper)
 ISBN 978-1-59797-888-0 (electronic edition)
 1. Terrorism—United States—Public opinion. 2. Terrorism—Government policy—United States—Public opinion. 3. September 11 Terrorist Attacks, 2001—Personal narratives. 4. United States—Foreign relations—Public opinion. I. Title.
 HV6432.W66 2011
 363.3250973—dc23

                                             2011023386

Printed in the United States of America on acid-free paper that meets the American National Standards Institute Z39-48 Standard.

Potomac Books
22841 Quicksilver Drive
Dulles, Virginia 20166

First Edition

10 9 8 7 6 5 4 3 2 1

CONTENTS

ACKNOWLEDGMENTS

This book benefited from several agents of inspiration and edification. Stan Kaplowitz, Toby Ten Eyck, Fred Fico, and Vladimir Shlapentokh at Michigan State University deserve first mention. I am fortunate to have experienced their expertise, intellectual curiosity, and willingness to support the work of others. Jill Higgins, my wife and a talented wordsmith, provided both technical and substantive support to the book. Chris Oliver at the University of Kentucky deserves my gratitude for his constructive criticism. A big thanks to Brad Love, University of Texas at Austin, for supporting the research effort behind this book. I would like to thank Hilary Claggett of Potomac Books. Her initial support and consistent backing thereafter were essential to the timely completion of this project. I also benefited from the excellent editorial support of Aryana Hendrawan, Amanda Irle, and Elizabeth Norris.

Many thanks go to Corey Colyer and Margaret Stout at West Virginia University for providing needed comments on some parts of the manuscript. I wish to convey gratitude to West Virginia University and the Department of Sociology and Anthropology for offering me the opportunity to work on this book. The faculty and staff in the Department of Sociology at Michigan State University also merit my thanks for their excellent teaching and mentoring.

Above all, my gratitude goes to family and friends, especially Roberta Gabier and Thell Woods, mom and dad, who taught me to value ideas. I also extend thanks to Russ Gabier, a wise and inquisitive conversationalist; Miriam Downey, for her support and editorial help; and Joe and Pat Higgins, for their encouragement.

PREFACE

Good news. At least a decade has passed since 9/11 and you have not been killed by a terrorist. You escaped the wrath of the "shoe bomber" and the "underwear bomber," as well as other dangerously accessorized evildoers. You are alive. The question is, how much did you worry about your chances? If you're like most Americans, you worried quite a bit. In fact, for ten consecutive years following 9/11, roughly half the population thought that an attack on the United States was likely to occur in the "next several weeks," and nearly the same amount worried about being victimized by terrorism.[1]

Whether we like it or not, 9/11 is still with us. To some extent it *is* us. The images of airliners, crumbling towers, ash-covered faces, flames, and firefighters are fixtures in our memories and imaginations. On 9/11, we created a new place for these extraordinary thoughts and feelings to settle and take root. Years later, the events of 9/11, according to psychologists, were still remembered in greater detail and by more Americans than any other event in recent history, including the assassinations of President Kennedy and Dr. King, the attacks on Pearl Harbor, the 1969 moon landing, the fall of the Berlin Wall, the explosion of the *Challenger* space shuttle, and the O. J. Simpson verdict.[2]

While almost all of us remember 9/11, the specific meanings we attach to this day, and the type of reasoning we use to explain it, are very different. For the evangelical Christian pastor Jerry Falwell, the attacks were a manifestation of God's judgment of America, a punishment for "throwing God out of the public square," a response to the "pagans, and the abortionists, and the feminists, and the gays and the lesbians who are actively trying to make that an alternative lifestyle, the A.C.L.U., People for the American Way, all of them who have tried to secularize America."[3] The path forward would, presumably, require atonement, redemption, and a renewed belief in Falwell's rendering of Christian values.

For the muckraking filmmaker, Michael Moore, 9/11 was the result of massive blunders by a failed-businessman-turned-president named George W. Bush, whose family's connections to the House of Saud obfuscated his duties to protect the nation.[4] The only suitable response was to boot the president and his cronies out of office and put an end to their oil ambitions, wartime profiteering, and cynical manipulation of the terrorist threat.

The views of Falwell and Moore, though extreme and unrepresentative of mainstream thinking, exemplify the diverse ways of interpreting 9/11 and the threat of terrorism. As the Twin Towers crumbled to the ground, as the flames poured out of the Pentagon, as the smoke rose from the Pennsylvania countryside, Americans from all walks of life set about the task of making sense of what happened and how to react. In the next years, the nation would continue to emote and denote the meaning of 9/11. We would ask why this attack occurred and what should be done about it. We would watch as the United States mobilized its response, united its people, and changed the world.

In time, we would look back and examine the ensuing developments of that fateful day, including the outpouring of support for the victims of 9/11, the rise in patriotism and civic engagement, and the renewed public interest in global affairs. We would also account for the interminable wars in Afghanistan and Iraq, the long-term surge in defense spending, the Patriot Act, the increase in security measures everywhere, the tightening of immigration policies, the demonization of Islam, the missing WMD, the secret CIA prisons in Eastern Europe, extraordinary rendition, the torture question, the unending detention of terrorism suspects at Gitmo, the prisoner abuses at Abu Ghraib, the thousands of dead American soldiers, and the tens of thousands of civilian casualties.

This is a story about one group's attempt to understand why these events took place. While the reactions of everyone from evangelical preachers to leftist filmmakers are important to this narrative, it will be told from the perspective of social scientists. Given the extraordinary nature of the attacks and the subsequent shifts in U.S. policies, the intellectual curiosity of many scholars—psychological distress notwithstanding—kicked into overdrive. For the anxious empiricist, 9/11 was a window of opportunity, a giant unsolved puzzle, a natural experiment for investigating both classic and newly discovered social, political, and psychological questions. As a result, in the years following the attacks, a flood of scientific research poured out of universities and other research centers.

Some scholars examined the social construction of terrorism, scrutinizing the political rhetoric and media coverage associated with 9/11. Others investigated the public's elevated worries about terrorism and the effect of these concerns on public opinion. Still others elucidated the post-9/11 changes in U.S. foreign and domestic policies, homeland security, civil rights, the economy, globalization, technology, and social movements. The objective of this book is to unite these areas of research, interweaving the sociology, psychology, and political science of terrorism to create a fuller, more compelling explanation of what 9/11 meant to Americans, and how it influenced a range of social developments over the next decade.

Before discussing my plans for compressing these diverse social scientific narratives into one story, the title of this book requires a brief explanation. It was inspired, in part, by a series of commentaries produced by the *Daily Show with Jon Stewart*. Functioning as a nationally televised "22-minute editorial cartoon," the show's host, Mr. Stewart, regularly swings his ironic sword at the traditional news media and political establishment.[5] Remarkably, the critical edge of Stewart's commentary remained at least somewhat sharp after 9/11. While the 24-hour news networks offered a continual stream of terrifying visual imagery and dramatized the American military's response to the attacks, the *Daily Show* openly criticized the mass media and public officials for exploiting the country's emotional vulnerabilities. In one episode, for instance, Stewart hosted a mock awards ceremony for the "Most Useless News Channel Dramatic War Graphic."

At a time when the major news channels were parroting the president and dutifully airing the Department of Homeland Security's terror alerts, Stewart questioned the terrorist threat, made light of it, lampooned it, told jokes about al Qaeda, and gave us a chuckle about the danger of anthrax and bioterrorism. Speaking before his nearly 2 million viewers not long after 9/11, he not only censured those who would use the terrorist threat to pursue political aims, he also proposed a more benign version of reality—a world, for instance, where Osama bin Laden dressed his pets in costumes for Halloween.

Much of this material, which ran in a special series for years after 9/11, was televised under the satiric banner "America Freaks Out." The parallel title of this book was not intended, however, to suggest that the nation's response to 9/11 was somehow funny, or that the terrorist threat should be taken lightly, ignored, or understood narrowly as a product of political machinations. The point is not to dismiss the threat but rather to emphasize the uniqueness of Stewart's perspective on it, as well as the scarcity of alternative American interpretations of 9/11 and the danger of future attacks.

Although modern society has devised numerous clever ways to inform people about looming perils, from road rage and killer bees to the transport of radioactive materials, it has not created an infrastructure to quell our concerns, promote careful cognition, and convert anxiety into prudent action. The *Daily Show* deserves to be highlighted because it stands as an exception, albeit a flawed and inadequate one, to the rule.

The question that really struck me as I watched the "America Freaks Out" series was, how did the show get away with it? At a time when Bush's press secretary, Ari Fleischer, was issuing public warnings to dissenting voices—Bill Maher in particular—to "watch what they say, watch what they do," how did Stewart manage to say almost anything he wanted? One answer, I suppose, is simple: He was funny. He made us laugh as he knocked the status quo. As experts have delineated for years, from Plato to the producers of *Saturday Night Live*, criticism veiled in humor is difficult to dispute and sometimes serves as a powerful political tool.

But the *Daily Show*'s take on 9/11 represents more than a comic critique of mainline politics. In fact, the uniqueness of Stewart's post-9/11 contribution can be found less in his political ideology, which is scattered and incohesive (probably by design), than in his implicit understanding that humor may be one of the few effective antidotes to fear and moral panic. Scientific research on the functions of humor is well charted. We know that laughter releases tension physiologically, exercising our hearts, lungs, and muscles while boosting immunity.[6] Humor can also serve as a source of courage and a tool for remaining focused on the task at hand amid an otherwise terrifying set of circumstances. It is often used, for instance, by people in high-stress or dangerous occupations, from ambulance drivers to crab-boat fishers on the Bering Sea. Humor, in this context, operates as a sort of countermadness that subsumes anxiety, which may, in turn, make it easier to dress an ugly wound on a four-year-old child or scale a wall of icy crab pots in rough seas.

Charlie Chaplin, a comic genius who sailed through his share of troubled waters, described humor as a means of survival. He once remarked, rather early in his career, that humor is a "gentle and benevolent custodian of the mind which prevents one from being overwhelmed and driven to the point of insanity by the apparent seriousness of life."[7] Chaplin provided laughter and relief to the public through some of the toughest periods in history, as the world came apart during World War I, through the gloom and doom of the Great Depression, and the terrifying rise of Hitler. Still, nearing the end of his career, his philosophy had not changed: "Humor," he said, "heightens our sense of survival and preserves our sanity. Because of humor we are less overwhelmed by the vicissitudes of life."[8]

While jesting about the terrorist threat may seem revolting to some, it may also, nevertheless, serve as a formidable psychological defense against terrorism itself, and, more important, our inevitable response to it—whether it be a sense of helplessness and immobility, or a reckless call to arms. What the ambulance driver knows too well is that working through crises requires quick, careful thinking and conscientious action. On 9/11, we all took a ride in the ambulance. The task at hand is to explain our response to this terrible voyage— the stories we told, the leaders we celebrated, the groups we formed, and the sacrifices we made in order to feel a little more comfortable in our seats.

My plan for telling this story begins with chapter 1, "The War on [Insert Enemy Here]." This chapter places the events of 9/11 and the threat of terrorism in historical context, juxtaposes the problem of terrorism with previous international threats, and offers a concise review of the post-9/11 shifts in foreign and domestic policy. It briefly chronicles both major government actions and less visible changes, such as those affecting immigration policies, the use and abuse of homeland security funding by local and state governments, and several others.

Chapters 2, 3, and 4 take aim at the minds of individuals after 9/11, when concerns about terrorism escalated and key social attitudes and behaviors changed. As witnessed throughout American history, wars and other national threats have united the nation, promoted civic engagement, and empowered communities. But they have also encouraged dogmatism, prejudice, violence, and a willingness to trade civil liberties for greater security. These chapters will attempt to determine which of these tendencies proved to be more powerful in the first post-9/11 decade.

The goal of chapters 5 and 6 is to bridge the psychological with the social, and reveal how changes in an individual's attitudes and beliefs were shaped by deeper social undercurrents. I consider the relationship between media coverage of terrorism and the public's perceptions of the threat. Do all news stories and popular images of terrorism generate the same response? What is it about this coverage that really scares us? Why are we more concerned about being blown up by Islamic radicals than homegrown terrorists à la Timothy McVeigh? Why does the motive matter? How do certain news frames trigger strong emotions and cloud our judgment? If chapter 5 clarifies why some portrayals of terrorism scare us more than others, chapter 6 explains when and under what circumstances these thoroughly frightening images and ideas appear on television and movies, in newspapers, and on the Internet. Who controls the fear factory, for what purpose, and by what means? Did the press emerge as a watchdog or a lapdog in the wake of 9/11? Did the politics of fear change when President Barack Obama stepped into office in January 2009? Did the incoming president create a new paradigm for understanding the threat of terrorism and what to do about it?

To situate 9/11 and the U.S. response to it in a global context, chapters 7 and 8 analyze public opinion and press coverage of the attacks in seven foreign countries: China, Colombia, Egypt, Germany, India, Lithuania, and Russia. Comparisons are drawn between these socioeconomically and politically diverse nations to demonstrate that the images and understandings of terrorism have materialized in different forms across the world. Given the great range of interpretations, it is worth considering how the various styles of government, economic systems, and culture in these nations shape the public discussion of terrorism via the mass media. Chapter 8, in particular, examines whether democratic countries, as conventional wisdom holds, have facilitated an open, pluralistic discussion of the terrorist threat and other vital issues surrounding this global concern.

The September 11 events altered the thoughts, feelings, and behaviors of public officials, the press, and the people. The reactions of these groups are interrelated, but the study of them has remained isolated and compartmentalized across academic disciplines. Policy experts have told us much about the Patriot Act, the political maneuvers behind the Iraq War, and many other government actions, but their stories often ignore the mass media, public opinion, the psychology of terrorism, and culture. Political scientists and social psychologists have covered public opinion and explained the cognitive and affective processes involved with reading or consuming messages about terrorism, but they have left the social antecedents of these messages unattended. Sociologists and communication scholars have investigated the social, political, and cultural factors that influence the public discourse, but often treat the effects of this content as foregone conclusions. Without bringing these different perspectives together, the puzzle of 9/11 will remain unsolved. This work will, with a bit of luck, address this concern.

1

THE WAR ON
[INSERT ENEMY HERE]

The "war on terrorism" was born at 8:30 p.m. on September 11, 2001, as a solemn President Bush made his first major address to the nation following the attacks. He told us that our freedom was in jeopardy, that the perpetrators were evil, that our vital institutions remained strong, and that we would stand together and win the war on terrorism.

In the next two weeks, between the 12 and 25 of September, the president referred to the ongoing crisis as a "war" at least once each day in his public statements. Looking back on these speeches, the president's repetition of this term seems at once intentional and a bit ridiculous. He described the situation as a war during a photo op with his national security team, in a telephone conversation with New York mayor Rudy Giuliani, in the National Cathedral on the Day of Prayer and Remembrance, at the Islamic Center of Washington, in his first post-9/11 radio address, at Camp David, on the South Lawn, in the Rose Garden, at the Pentagon (and, presumably, on a boat, with a goat, in the rain, on a train, in a box, with a fox, here and there, and anywhere). Before trick-or-treaters hit the streets in October, President Bush, if not by careful explication, made it clear to nearly everyone on earth that the United States was now at war.

But what did this war on terrorism mean? What, exactly, were we up against? And how should we respond? At the time, these questions were debated by numerous journalists, scholars, and politicians, and would occupy observers for years thereafter. The first item of business in such a discussion is usually the task of defining the term "terrorism" itself.[1] After examining the

1

countless speeches, interviews, articles, chapters, and entire books devoted to exploring the legal, institutional, and moral definitions of terrorism, I made two notable discoveries. First, this discussion is not particularly interesting. And second, there is really no way to traverse this lexicographic landscape without becoming pinned down by ideology.

By accepting a single, narrow definition of terrorism, one must follow a predetermined ideological path and eschew any chance for nuanced, objective reasoning on the matter. On the contrary, by keeping an open mind, one is likely to keep an empty one, as accepting all definitions limits one's ability to distinguish between any two objects, events, or actions. Collectively, the available definitions suggest that "terrorism" refers to any type of violence or threat of violence against any target for any reason—a definition that squarely defeats the purpose of definitions.

Unfortunately, even if we corral our understanding of terrorism within the two or three "official" definitions (the FBI, the State Department, and the Defense Department each has its own designation), we still may end up more frustrated than edified. The FBI, for instance, defines terrorism as "the unlawful use of force or violence against persons or property to intimidate or coerce a Government, the civilian population, or any segment thereof, in furtherance of political or social objectives."[2] By this definition, mass murders and naughty teenagers belong in the same category, given the fact that "unlawful intimidation" has been used for "social objectives" by al Qaeda, the McVeigh and Nichols partnership, Harris and Klebold, the KKK, the New York City Mafia, the Los Angeles Police Department, the union busters at River Rouge, the 1989 Detroit Pistons, and a group of bullies who terrorized my elementary school.

It may be a wiser step, for this reason, to focus not on what terrorism is, but on what particular terrorist groups, such as al Qaeda, have in common with our enemies of the past. Drawing historical comparisons between the threats of today and yesterday may tell us more about terrorism than any universal definition.

A New Cold War?

Several scholars have suggested that the war on terrorism is similar to the Cold War, which pit the United States against the Soviet Union. While some authors stress the similarity in magnitude between the Soviet threat and the dangers posed by international terrorists, others sidestep the debate over the nature of the two threats, but nonetheless argue that the confrontations led to comparable social, economic, and geopolitical circumstances.[3] To serve it up in a single sentence, my argument disputes the first group of scholars and supports the second.

With all of its powers, real and otherwise, al Qaeda (or even the "international terrorist network" as a whole) was never the Soviet Union. Unlike the USSR, terrorist groups such as al Qaeda are not controlled by a powerful, centralized government. The destructive potential of these groups, as one expert claims, is "unbridled by the interests, form and structure of a state."[4] In the 1990s, al Qaeda looked more like a loosely coupled, multinational business alliance than a typical, top-down organization. Authority was not concentrated at the top; it was scattered, and the framework became even more fragmented as the official war on terrorism began in the wake 9/11.[5]

After squaring off against slow-moving bureaucracies for much of the twentieth century, the United States now faced its first enemy "adhocracy." Henry Mintzberg used this term to describe a decentralized organization that operates in a fast-changing environment and produces unique outputs within multidisciplinary teams.[6] In short, as an *organization,* al Qaeda at the start of the twenty-first century had more in common with a high-tech startup in Silicon Valley than with the Soviet Union. The dynamic nature of its adhocracy may have helped it, in some ways, to disrupt and harm the United States, but it was not the ideal structure for pursuing a long-term offensive aimed at ending U.S. statehood, or even confronting its dominance in the world.

As a second contrast to the Soviet threat, terrorist activities are not motivated by a clear and cohesive ideological or religious position. As argued by Daniel Byman, an expert on security studies at Georgetown University, even before Osama bin Laden's death in 2011, al Qaeda had not been able to unify the jihadist movement. Groups such as Hamas and others within the hardcore jihadist community rejected al Qaeda's leadership, disagreed on basic objectives, and denounced some al Qaeda operations, particularly in Iraq, as "a foolish war, not jihad" that led to great suffering among fellow Muslims.[7] Following bin Laden's death, the in-fighting and disorganization was thought to increase.

Terrorism involves a variety of diverse stakeholders, groups, and social movements. Robert Pape develops this idea in his book *Dying to Win,* an extensive study of suicide terrorism.[8] Based on an analysis of 315 suicide attacks, he refutes, quite convincingly, the popular notion that terrorist organizations are driven primarily by religious zealotry or some form of otherworldly ambition. Among other things, he notes that the world leader in suicide terrorism is the Tamil Tigers of Sri Lanka, a non-Muslim secular group, which is bent not on aligning the world with its brand of religious faith, but on securing land and creating an independent state in a rather small and remote region of the world.

It's about territory, not transcendence, according to Pape: "The targets of modern suicide terrorist campaigns have been democratic states which have stationed heavy combat troops on the territory that the terrorists view as their national homeland."[9] Many of the organizers of terrorist activities are logical, determined individuals motivated by specific, localized political and economic goals.

If international terrorism was facilitated by a large, clandestine organization with a unified set of fervent, idealistic beliefs, it would, perhaps, pose an even greater threat to the United States than did the Soviet Union. Given its shadowy existence and its reliance on suicide attacks, the strategy of deterrence, which proved effective during the Cold War, would not have the same effect on such an organization. However, after a careful consideration of numerous terrorist events around the world, one can see, as Pape argues, that the raison d'être of most terrorist groups and individuals is more local and pragmatic than it is global and idealistic.

In fact, the ideological inconsistency of international terrorism has been reflected in the Bush administration's official statements about the threat. In the first days after 9/11, President Bush framed the conflict in religious terms. He referred to the perpetrators as "Islamic extremists" and the war on terrorism as a "crusade."[10] In the next months, however, he seemed to curtail some of his references to Islam and relied more on phrases such as "good versus evil" or described the enemy as "haters of freedom." The president later invoked the term "Islamic fascists," while other members of his administration used the label "Islamofascism." Although his rhetoric contained emotional and moral substance, it lacked a consistent intellectual framework and failed to indicate the ideological pattern of the enemy.

As the war on terrorism spread across the Middle East, the administration's statements about the enemy remained mostly devoid of conceptual and ideological refinement. It suffices to point out that, while the term "terrorism" is difficult to define, the Bush administration's favorite catchword "terror" is even vaguer. Based on a search of the White House website one year prior to President Bush's departure from office, the phrase "war on terror" appeared in roughly three times more articles, press briefs, and speeches than the alternative phrase, "war on terror*ism.*"

Terrorism has been around for centuries, generating an abundance of detailed explanations and public knowledge, but the "war on terror" suggests that the enemy is something new, amorphous, and indefinable, if no less menacing. As discussed in chapter 6, one of the central political advantages of this frame lies in its flexibility. The less Americans understand, in specific terms, about the enemy, the easier it is for officials to shift their explanation of the threat and their plans for confronting it. As a highly adaptable rhetorical device, the threat of terror has been used to justify and promote any number of public policies, private endeavors, and special interests, from war plans in Iraq to oil drilling in the Arctic National Wildlife Refuge in Alaska.

Now let's step back to the previous conflict. During the Cold War, government officials clearly denoted the dangers of communism and its proliferation throughout the world. Setting aside the controversy surrounding the Soviets' real intentions toward international communist organizations, there is no denying that communism itself was understood by most Americans as a global movement orchestrated and propelled primarily by the Soviet Union and determined to destroy capitalism, democracy, and the American way of life. As confirmed by Gallup polls, the "threat of communism" ranked highly on the list of America's "most important problems" throughout the 1950s and 1960s.

The Soviets' ideological predilections were a regular topic of discussion for the principal Cold Warriors, from Winston Churchill and John F. Kennedy to Margaret Thatcher and Ronald Reagan. In the last year of his presidency, Reagan was still quoting the *Communist Manifesto* in his diatribes on the Soviet threat. For instance, in May 1988, during an interview at the White House with a Soviet journalist, Reagan made a reference to "the declarations of Karl Marx," and suggested, speaking for the Soviets, that "Communism could only succeed when the whole world had become Communist." He went on to proclaim that "every General Secretary but the present one [Gorbachev] . . . reiterated their allegiance to that Marxian theory."[11] Though scholars on Marx would scoff at Reagan's lack of sophistication and simplistic analysis, his iterations on the enemy fell within a logical framework; they clearly contained more definitive, intellectual substance than President Bush's contentions that we face "a monumental struggle of good versus evil," "a different kind of enemy that hides in the shadows," a foe that is willing to sacrifice everything, because, of course, "they hate our freedoms."[12]

The third distinction lies in what is known about the probability and potential consequences of a Soviet versus a terrorist strike. While there is still fervent debate about the general level of safety of American citizens during the Cold War, there is little disagreement about the technical capacity of the Soviet Union to unleash its nuclear arsenal and cause massive death and destruction in the United States.[13] The basic premise of nuclear deterrence rested on each side's ability to make the threat of mutual destruction well known and credible to its opponent. The supposed realness of the Soviet threat, according to the distinguished professor of international relations, Joseph Nye, explains, in part, why the United States was able to maintain good relations with many foreign countries during the Cold War, or at least recover quickly from its unpopular policies.[14]

The available information on the terrorist threat is far less conclusive. Estimating the risk of terrorism has always been difficult, and the extraordinary events of 9/11 only intensified the uncertainties surrounding the danger. At the end of the first decade of the twenty-first century, a cloud of ambiguity still hovered over the probability and potential magnitude of a future attack, the intent and identity of the possible perpetrators, and the type of assault they might carry out. In contrast to the centralized danger posed by the Soviets, the number of terrorist-attack scenarios (including one, don't forget, where nothing happens at all) is virtually limitless.

As suggested by Paul Slovic, a leading expert on risk assessment, 9/11 represented a "new species of trouble," an unbounded threat that could not be assessed with quantitative risk analysis.[15] Unlike natural hazards such as hurricanes and earthquakes, the threat of terrorism has no fixed geography. And unlike common, everyday hazards such as crime, car accidents, and illnesses, the number of major terrorist attacks in U.S. history is so small that robust statistical estimates are simply not possible.

While a number of security advisers, unnamed U.S. officials, and a notable vice president have made absurdly precise (and inaccurate) predictions about impending attacks, several other government agencies, university research groups, and private-sector analysts have noted the inherent difficulty of producing accurate terrorism risk assessments.[16] In a report on the threat to the food supply, the U.S. Food and Drug Administration stated plainly, "It is difficult for the FDA to predict with any certainty the likelihood that an act of food terrorism will occur."[17] In the wake of 9/11, Congress asked the National Academy of Sciences to assess the risk of a terrorist attack on the spent-fuel pools of nuclear reactors. Its report indicated that "the probability of terrorist attacks on spent fuel storage cannot be assessed quantitatively or comparatively," and that assessing the risk is problematic because the number of scenarios is limitless and the risk ultimately depends on "impossible-to-quantify factors such as terrorist motivations, expertise, and access to technical means."[18]

In a key study on the threat of al Qaeda, congressional research staffer Kenneth Katzman suggested, "There is no consensus among experts in and outside the U.S. government about the magnitude of the threat to U.S. national interests posed by the Al Qaeda organization."[19] The Monterey Institute of International Studies, the largest NGO devoted to combating the spread of WMD, issued a statement on the threat of bioterrorism that repeatedly stressed the difficulty of assessing the intent and capabilities of terrorist groups that wish to mount biological attacks.[20] In its otherwise assertive report on the risk of terrorist events, the RAND Corporation noted similar problems.[21] Gordon Woo, a top private-sector risk analyst, has produced an intricate mathematical model for predicting terrorist acts, but still concedes, "Nobody can predict the precise timing of the next major terrorist attack."[22]

Although some economists regard financial institutions—insurance companies in particular—as the most reliable prognosticators in the world, these institutions have also had trouble estimating the risk. Is it possible for 9/11 to be repeated? If so, what are the chances? How can an insurance company carry out such an assessment? What should terrorism insurance cost? Answers to these questions have proved to be utterly elusive. As explained in an official statement by Treasury Secretary Paul O'Neill in October 2001, "At the moment, there are no models, no meaningful experience, no reasonable upper bound on what an individual company's risk exposure may be."[23] The best actuaries and financial analysts in both the public and private sectors were, in a word, stumped.

To solve their problem, they would turn to the federal government, not the market. A new law called the Terrorism Risk Insurance Act skated through Congress and received the president's stamp of approval in November 2002. While the free market's true believers protested, an overwhelming majority of our nation's top leaders supported the legislation, which made the government responsible for a potentially large portion of the losses incurred by future terrorist attacks. The risk of terrorism was now pooled in the seemingly bottomless pockets of U.S. taxpayers.

For many observers, the creation of the law had not been a surprise. The government had served a similar function during World War II when it provided property owners with insurance protection against loss from enemy attacks. More remarkable was the continued inability of insurers to find their footing and allow market mechanisms to take charge. Initially passed as a temporary fix, Congress extended the Terrorism Risk Insurance Act for two years in December 2005 and then, in 2007, reauthorized it for another seven years. The brightest minds in business, government, and science were unable to formulate a meaningful explanation of the terrorist threat. The extent of America's most important problem would remain equally unknowable and seemingly catastrophic. In the final analysis, our understanding of the threat would rely, at least in part, on our imaginations.

Under these conditions, three interrelated developments, functioning within a complex set of social and organizational circumstances, transformed American society in the decade following 9/11. First, an unprecedented level of fear swept the country. Americans from all walks of life appeared to be far more adept at imagining worst-case than best-case scenarios. Significantly elevated concerns about the danger lingered, as discussed in detail in chapter 2, for at least a decade after the attacks.

Meanwhile, the lack of clear information about the threat only amplified the public's demand for it, which brings us to the second development. After 9/11 and for years to come, the media produced and disseminated countless reports, commentaries, images, interviews, and documentaries on all aspects of the danger, from the nation's porous international borders and the vulnerability of the food and water supply to the weakness of security everywhere. The sage advice of Scottish poet and novelist Robert Louis Stevenson to "keep your fears to yourself but share your inspiration" was entirely lost on the post-9/11 news media.

As for the third development, the government responded to the new situation by creating or changing several foreign and domestic policies, bureaucratic procedures, and aspects of law enforcement. The remainder of this chapter offers a brief discussion of these changes, leaving the first two developments, and their bearing on the third, for later chapters.

The Day Things Changed

The threat of terrorism, in spite of the vagueness of the danger, served as the impetus for several far-reaching changes in state policy and practice, including military engagements, state-sponsored assassinations, increased military spending, a hardening of the security apparatus, expanded powers of surveillance, secret courts and prisons, the targeting of ethnic communities, and the degradation of civil liberties and human rights. Here, perhaps, is where the war on terrorism bears the most resemblance to the Cold War.

In response to 9/11, the Bush administration initiated military campaigns in Afghanistan and Iraq. As these conflicts grew into protracted wars, they claimed the lives of thousands of American soldiers and tens of thousands of civilians in foreign lands. By the summer of 2011, according to the Department of Defense, more than 6,000 U.S. troops had been killed in either Iraq or Afghanistan.[24] Almost no one had stood in the way of America's march to war. The U.S. Congress rallied around the flag after 9/11 and showed widespread support for the wars. Within three days of 9/11, Congress approved a resolution authorizing the president to take military action. This decision was unanimous in the Senate. Among the 420 representatives in the House, only 1 member dissented. California Democratic Representative Barbara Lee cast the opposition's lone vote—a "vote of conscience," she called it—which was subsequently greeted by a barrage of hate mail and telephone messages, including threats against her life (otherwise known as "terrorism," according to the FBI).[25]

A few weeks later, when the bombs began dropping in Afghanistan, dozens of lawmakers put out strong endorsements of the president's actions. A special joint statement was issued by a bipartisan group of Republican and Democratic leaders who commended Bush for his decision and said, "We stand united with the president and with our troops."[26] One year later, congressional support for the administration's solution persisted as lawmakers authorized the war in Iraq (in the Senate by a vote of 77 to 23, and in the House by 296 to 133). The president responded to the vote by declaring that "America speaks with one voice."[27] And, for the most part, he was right. Aside from a few distant rumblings from the ivory tower and the aging peaceniks of California, Americans rallied around their president and his crushingly violent solution.

The same could not be said about the international community. Similar to the Vietnam War, the wars in Iraq and Afghanistan were initially built on strong popular support, which later dissolved. It left in its path numerous casualties, a high level of insecurity throughout the conflict regions, lost and coerced allies, and new enemies. At a time when the United States needed international cooperation most, its military and political responses to the attacks coincided with a significant drop in the country's favorability ratings in most foreign countries, among both our allies and enemies.[28] As discussed in chapter 7, many foreign elites disagreed with a range of notions that were accepted as conventional wisdom in the United States, including the designation of the perpetrators of 9/11, the motives for carrying out the attacks, and the proper response to them. Even in countries where the people's sympathy and solidarity flooded the news media, there were numerous commentators, journalists, and politicians who openly (and ardently) disagreed with the basic precepts of the war on terrorism.

As America's image in the world deteriorated, so too did the U.S. federal budget. Between 2001 and 2003, U.S. defense expenditures increased by 26 percent, from $335.9 billion to $422.5 billion (in constant 2005 dollars).[29] By 2007, the defense budget reached $481.4 billion, levels not seen since the Reagan-era buildup of the 1980s.[30] Between 2001 and 2009, an additional estimated $860 billion were spent on funding the wars in Iraq and Afghanistan.[31] At decade's end, even as the troops began leaving Iraq, the cost of war increased as President Obama added 30,000 reinforcements to Afghanistan at a White House–estimated cost of $30 billion per year, or about $1 million per soldier or Marine.[32] By summer 2011, there were roughly 100,000 troops in Afghanistan and in spite of the president's plan for a withdrawal of troops by July 2011, top commanders were still asking for more frontline infantrymen who could go on combat missions and keep the Taliban at bay.[33]

After a decade of war, Taliban suicide bomber attacks remained common, and the enemy showed no signs of giving up.[34] Underscoring the Taliban's continued strength, five hundred fighters escaped from Afghanistan's largest prison in April 2011. Providing their comrades with a Hollywood-like escape route, Taliban leaders dug a three-foot-wide tunnel that ran for more than half a mile, passing beneath security posts, the prison's tall concrete walls, a highway, and finally emerging under the floorboards of a nearby house.[35]

The Afghan government continued to struggle in its efforts to provide basic services to its people. Mismanagement, fraud, and corruption plagued the public and private sectors of Afghan society throughout the first decade of war. In early 2011, roughly $900 million simply disappeared from Afghanistan's largest financial institution, prompting worries that the bank, which was deemed "too big to fail," could collapse and spread chaos across the country's economic system.[36] Moving to another absurd disappointment, the *New York Times* published a story in May 2011 about a costly unfinished highway project funded by the United States in southeastern Afghanistan, which, in the end, may rival Alaska's fabled "road to nowhere." Initiated in 2007 with an estimated price tag of $69 million, the cost of the sixty-four-mile highway reached $121 million by May 2011 and was expected to drain another $55 million in tax revenues before completion. At a cost of $43.5 million, the provision of security was one of the project's biggest expenses. Most disturbingly, some military officials suspected that the individuals and groups that provided the security had links to the Taliban and were staging attacks on the highway in order to extort more money for protection.[37]

Afghanistan also failed in various ways to meet international human and civil rights standards. Children in particular suffered under illegal practices and systemic exploitation. According to the Human Rights Council at the United Nations, young boys were often recruited into the Afghan National Police force and participated in the armed conflict.[38] It wasn't until January 2011 that the government signed a formal agreement with the United Nations to halt underage recruitment. The sexual abuse of children has been another major concern. An April 2010 *Frontline* episode detailed the common practice of *bacha bazi* (literal translation: "boy play"), which involves the use of boys as sex slaves.[39] Dressed as girls and made to dance before male audiences, the boys are then sold in auctions for sexual purposes, often to elites within the military and the police, according to Afghan and United Nations officials.[40]

The bad news from Afghanistan was, at times, farcical if no less troubling. For years, a thriving trade in the streets of Kabul was the sale of military and police uniforms. Struggling with their low incomes, many active soldiers would sell their extra uniforms, while deserters cashed in completely. Although unauthorized uniforms were commonly used by militants to impersonate security forces and carry out attacks, the government proved ineffective at cracking down on the sales.[41]

While the U.S. response to 9/11 led to chaos and instability overseas, there were significant social, political, and economic reverberations at home as well. Government waste and mismanagement were not, as it turned out, limited to Afghan society. According to a report released in May 2011 by the Government Accountability Office, a congressional watchdog, billions of dollars in defense spending have been wasted by the Pentagon. Pointing to "management failures," the auditors estimated that $70 billion were lost over a two-year period. Much of the problem arose as the Pentagon purchased large weapons systems before the designs were fully tested, leading to unforeseen costs down the line. Even Robert Gates, the defense secretary, conceded that the Pentagon had "lacked discipline" as spending skyrocketed after 9/11 and continued to increase for nearly a decade.[42]

The events of 9/11 did not lead to an immediate economic crisis in the United States, but they did influence long-term economic growth, insofar as resources that may have increased productivity were now being spent on security. As suggested by Gail Makinen, a specialist in economic policy for the Congressional Research Center, "since it will take more labor and capital to produce a largely unchanged amount of goods and services, this will result in a slower rate of growth in national productivity, a price that will be borne by every American in the form of a slower rate of growth of per capita real income."[43]

In spite of the dragging economy, the massive increase in federal spending produced a number of big winners. The Bush administration created the Department of Homeland Security, focused the nation's fiscal attention on countering terrorism, and increased domestic spending on police, firefighters, medical first responders, and a host of new technologies and procedures to prevent nuclear and biological terrorism, secure the borders, and improve security at the nation's numerous points of critical infrastructure. Among the main benefactors were private-sector defense contractors and security firms. As one financial analyst estimated, the deluge of funding boosted stocks in the defense industry by 114 percent between January 2001 and June 2006.[44] As public concerns about terrorism persisted, the task of keeping Americans safe remained a lucrative and politically popular enterprise. Millions of businesspeople, bureaucrats, and public agencies came to depend, directly and indirectly, on this fast-growing industry for their livelihoods.

In the first four years after 9/11, Congress doled out $10 billion for homeland security, much of which went to local police and emergency crews, in spite of recommendations by the 9/11 Commission to allocate the money primarily to large urban centers and high-profile symbolic targets. Although the funding helped retool some first responders that sorely needed it, the expenditures generated criticism from all corners of the political landscape and became fodder for late-night talk show hosts.

Why did Tiptonville, Tennessee—a city of fewer than 2,500 people in the middle of nowhere, whose major social event of the year is the Blue Suede Shoes BBQ Cook-Off—receive $183,000 in homeland security money? Did Converse, Texas, have a sufficient need for its high-tech homeland security trailer, aside from using it to transport riding tractors to its annual lawnmower races? Should Columbus, Ohio, be using federal funds to buy bulletproof dog vests for its canine corps? Why should any fire department in the country pay $63,000 for a decontamination unit that no one knows how to use? Did Newark, New Jersey, need to spend a quarter million dollars on air-conditioned garbage trucks to keep its people safe? These were only a few of the pertinent questions asked in a *60 Minutes* interview with Representative Chris Cox, chairman of the House Homeland Security Committee, in April 2005.[45]

Much of the new security spending allowed for the purchase and installation of surveillance systems, smart cameras, and high-tech software dedicated to watching the general public. Aided by a $5.1 million federal grant, the city of Chicago, for instance, spent $8.6 million on expanding and modernizing its system with sophisticated new computer programs that sound an alarm any time someone is viewed by one of its 2,250 cameras behaving "suspiciously" near buildings and other potential terrorist targets. Suspicious behavior, as reported by Stephen Kinzer in the *New York Times*, includes wandering in circles, lingering outside public buildings, pulling a car onto the shoulder of a highway, or putting down a package and walking away from it.[46] In the new age of security, we are being watched more than ever. Just "hanging out" on a street corner may result in police officers being immediately dispatched to the scene.

It should be kept in mind that for every big winner in the appropriations game there is usually a big loser. During the post-9/11 spending frenzy, the losers were those Americans who relied on domestic programs that were reduced or eliminated altogether as the Bush administration placed terrorism at the top of its agenda and shaped the outlays of the federal budget accordingly.

Other significant policy changes emerged as officials struggled to balance the country's security concerns with the need to preserve the rights and liberties of people living in the United States. In October 2001, the administration, led by Attorney General John Ashcroft, introduced the USA PATRIOT Act, which passed in the Senate by a vote of 98 to 1, and by 357 to 66 in the House. Although the legislation enjoyed strong presidential and congressional support and was renewed by Congress in March 2006, the bill generated a great deal of controversy among scholars, civil rights advocates, and ordinary people.

A few of the act's provisions proved especially contentious: one allowed law-enforcement agencies to search private residences without informing the owners (known as "sneak-and-peek" searches); a second permitted "roving wiretaps" that gave investigators the ability to follow suspects who switched phone numbers or providers; another allowed federal authorities to access the library and bookstore records of anyone connected to a terrorism investigation; and a fourth permitted the prolonged detention and deportation of noncitizens suspected of links to 9/11 without due process.[47] When some of these provisions came up for renewal again in 2011, civil liberties advocates were confident that greater limits on these powers would pass into law. Nevertheless, on May 19, 2011, with the support of the Obama administration, Congress extended the Patriot Act's most controversial provisions without any changes for four additional years.[48]

There is ample evidence that the Federal Bureau of Investigation took advantage of its expanded counterterrorism and surveillance powers. In its initial investigation of 9/11, the FBI cast its dragnet far and wide, detaining 762 people, most of them of Arab or Asian origin, and holding them for months without charging them with a crime or notifying their families. These irregularities and abuses were outlined in a government report by the Office of the Inspector General, which found that: (1) the delay in being officially charged "affected the detainees in several ways, from their ability to understand why they were being held, to their ability to obtain legal counsel, to their ability to request a bond hearing," (2) officials lied about whether specific detainees were being held at the high-security facility, (3) the detainees were confined "under highly restrictive conditions," and (4) the prisoners were subjected to "a pattern of physical and verbal abuse."[49] By the end of the investigation, none of the 762 detainees were charged as terrorists. In spite of the investigation's failure, Ashcroft defended the Justice Department's treatment of the suspects, stating that "we make no apologies for holding suspects as long as necessary to determine whether they had links to terrorism."[50]

Throughout the first post-9/11 decade, the FBI found itself at the center of a number of law-enforcement controversies. According to a study by the Center on Law and Security at the New York University School of Law, the majority of criminal convictions in high-profile terrorism cases in the United States relied on sting operations and informants.[51] In some of these cases, legal experts raised concerns over whether the agents crossed the line into entrapment, using various enticements to lure penniless men and sometimes teenagers into highly sophisticated plots they never could have handled (or even dreamed of) on their own. One defendant, Hemant Lakhani, agreed to sell missiles to an undercover FBI agent who was posing as a terrorist. When it became clear that Lakhani had no access to such weapons, another undercover agent sold him a fake version of the arms so that he could, in turn, make the illegal sale. During the transaction, incidentally, Lakhani appeared to test the weapon by placing it on his shoulder pointed in the wrong direction. His entrapment defense failed and he received a forty-seven-year prison sentence. In another sting operation, the defendant, James Cromitie, agreed to carry out an attack after being offered $250,000 by the undercover agent. Cromitie's entrapment defense, like all the others in the ten years following 9/11, also failed, prompting legal experts to suggest that juries may be weighting these cases differently than other entrapment cases, given the dramatic events of 9/11 and the constant media spotlight on terrorism.

The FBI's search for al Qaeda in America also influenced private business operations. Every year, thousands of "national security letters" were issued to businesses without judicial review. These letters allowed the FBI to secretly attain confidential records on consumers from all kinds of private firms, such as telephone companies, Internet service providers, banks, and credit card companies. An investigation by the inspector general of the Justice Department found that the use of such letters increased significantly after 9/11 (from 8,500 in 2000, to 39,000 in 2003; 56,000 in 2004; and 47,000 in 2005) and suggested that the letters were used improperly, and sometimes illegally.[52] In March 2007, the FBI director himself admitted that the bureau had used the Patriot Act inappropriately to obtain information about people and businesses. As stated plainly by one expert, the letters "generated thousands of leads that, when pursued, have led nowhere."[53]

The National Security Agency also received greater latitude in its efforts to seek out terrorists. Before 9/11, its mission had been to spy only on international communications. Court approval was required whenever an investigation involved people living in the United States. In the wake of 9/11, the NSA received secret authorization from President Bush to eavesdrop on Americans without a warrant. In 2008, a congressional revision of the Foreign Intelligence Surveillance Act essentially legalized this practice. As a senator at the time, Barack Obama supported the new legislation, and continued as president to rely heavily on the NSA's warrantless surveillance techniques. According to a report by the *New York Times,* the NSA was likely listening to the telephone conversations or reading the emails of up to five hundred people in the United States at any given time.[54] Though much remained unknown about the NSA's activities, its new power to spy on Americans with little oversight represented a noteworthy post-9/11 shift in domestic intelligence-gathering practices.

In what ranked among the most morally questionable and longstanding U.S. counterterrorism measures, the Bush administration declared, not long after 9/11, that the enemy soldiers captured in Afghanistan and other regions of its boundless war on terrorism were "unlawful combatants" and therefore unprotected by the Geneva Convention. As a result, hundreds of people were imprisoned without a trial and tortured at the newly created Guantánamo Bay Detention Camp in Cuba.[55] The Bush administration claimed that the camp was outside U.S. jurisdiction and that the prisoners could be held indefinitely.

The Supreme Court later ruled that the detainees were, in fact, entitled to some protections specified in the conventions. More definitively, in June 2008, the court ruled 5 to 4 that the prisoners had a constitutional right to go to federal court to challenge their continued detention.[56] In January 2009, only days following his inauguration, President Obama signed an executive order to close the camp within one year, but congressional wrangling over the relocation of the prisoners and other details of the closing would extend the camp's existence for the foreseeable future. The president signed two other orders on the same day, which instructed the CIA to dismantle its network of secret prisons for terrorism suspects and prohibited the use of torture in interrogations.[57] In 2011, WikiLeaks, an antisecrecy organization, disseminated several hundred classified military documents, which provided evidence that many innocent men had been jailed for several years and often subjected to abuse and torture. Among the 779 detainees at Guantánamo, 409 were considered by intelligence specialists to be "low-level guerrillas," 150 were innocent of their charges, 7 men died in captivity, and only 16 were deemed "high-value detainees."[58]

During both the Bush and Obama periods, terrorism suspects and enemy combatants were not the only groups targeted by the nation's tightening security apparatus. Given the fact that 9/11 exposed what seemed like frightening weaknesses in immigration practices, the nation's welcome mat to the world quickly lost its luster. In the immediate aftermath, there were calls for severe restrictions on immigrant admissions, greater enforcement of preexisting immigration laws, and heightened security at the borders. Although the hard-liners on immigration reform were unsuccessful in fully carrying out their agenda, a number of key changes had a profound influence on immigrant communities in the United States, according to senior analysts at the Immigration Policy Center.[59] Unauthorized immigrants in particular became targets of the government's counterterrorism frenzy. According to a research group at Syracuse University, the federal prosecutions for immigration violations more than doubled between 2001 and 2004.[60]

Contrary to expectations, when President Obama arrived in office, immigration enforcement efforts, still driven by the threat of terrorism, only intensified through a program called Secure Communities. In spite of strong resistance from several state governments, the program led to a record number of deportations (almost 800,000 between May 2009 and May 2011).[61] Overall, in the decade following 9/11, the new administrative and legislative steps led to millions of immigrants remaining illegal, not to mention being increasingly frightened by the police and more vulnerable to exploitation.

The post-9/11 shifts in immigration policy coincided with a decline in the admissions of foreign graduate students in American universities. The National Science Foundation's statistics division reported that the number of full-time foreign graduate students on temporary visas studying science and engineering dropped by 19 percent between 2001 and 2004.[62] Sociologists Susan Brown and Frank Bean argue that much of this falloff resulted from tougher visa review processes. As an interesting side note, they suggest that "the imposition of 'hard' national security measures can erode 'soft' power and thus in turn the very security such measures were designed to enhance."[63] In other words, alienating a generation of elite international graduate students was probably not the best formula for winning the hearts and minds of the global community.

In concluding this brief and admittedly incomplete review of post-9/11 policy shifts, one can reasonably reflect on the corresponding lack of attention we gave other pressing issues. According to Gallup polls, as the threat of terrorism shot to the top of America's list of "most important problems," other issues that had been gradually rising in importance were suddenly forgotten. For instance, education, mentioned by 11 percent of respondents in May 1999 and by 16 percent in March 2000, dropped to 3 percent in November 2001. In the next three years, the importance of education would never move above 6 percent, less than half of its pre-9/11 level. Similar trends were seen in the cases of Medicare, Medicaid, and Social Security.[64]

For years terrorism preoccupied much of our social system, including two presidential administrations, the state and federal legislatures, the judiciary, the FBI, the CIA, the NSA, the IRS, the Departments of State, Defense, Homeland Security, Treasury, Justice, Interior, Agriculture, Commerce, Transportation, and Energy, not to mention numerous organizations in the private sector. In the next years, other serious problems, such as the shady operations of Wall Street banks and the unchecked deepwater oil drilling in the Gulf of Mexico, were undoubtedly brewing, but with our eyes fixed on terrorism, these issues would surprise most of us when they materialized. Any assessment of how terrorism changed America should account not only for the things we put in motion, but also for the things we set aside—that is, for the opportunity cost of placing terrorism at the forefront of the national agenda.

Conclusion

This chapter began with the essential question, what is terrorism? After some deliberation, it became clear that the Bush administration declared war against a rather ambiguous noun, one that was both highly evocative and difficult to define. Most definitions of the term seem to be driven more by the political interests of the definer than by careful, empirically grounded deliberations. Although creating a universal classification of terrorism would be unwise, the task of gaining knowledge about organizations such as al Qaeda is no less important, particularly if we intend to develop public policies to confront it.

When compared with the Soviet Union, our major enemy of the past, the current foe begins to take shape. By the end of the first post-9/11 decade, al Qaeda, even without its infamous leader, Osama bin Laden, may have still had the power to cause terrible destruction in the United States and elsewhere. As happened in the Cold War, our confrontation with terrorist groups has resulted in significant policy shifts at home and abroad. But unlike the Soviet Union, the "international terrorist network" is a loosely coupled system, a fragmented organization that does not have a clear, overriding objective or a cohesive ideological orientation.

Also contrasting with the Cold War paradigm, we do not have a reliable understanding of the danger that al Qaeda and other groups pose to the United States and the world. Our most talented analysts in both the public and private sectors have failed to provide meaningful information about the risk of future attacks. And in another comparison with the Soviet Union, there is also far less agreement among our foreign allies about the nature and extent of the threat.

This uncertainty is one of the most intriguing aspects of the war on terrorism. We didn't know then and we still don't know what we're up against, and yet we have responded in decisive ways to whatever we imagined it to be. In the years following 9/11, as if a new Cold War had begun, we united as a nation and bounded headlong into military engagements overseas, upgraded our security apparatus, poured money into the defense industry, targeted the supposed enemies among us (all minority groups), held terrorism suspects indefinitely, trampled on the idea of due process, established secret prisons, tortured detainees, and generally degraded civil liberties and democratic values. Much of this trend flowed unbroken into the first years of the Obama administration.

It may be tempting to pass a negative judgment on these developments and place blame on the founders of the "war on terror," President George W. Bush and his administration. Many intellectuals have done just that—from Hollywood luminaries such as Robert Redford and Sean Penn, to the influential political theorist Noam Chomsky and the Nobel Prize–winning economist

Paul Krugman. To do so, however, is to overemphasize the significance of individual social actors. Blaming Bush obscures, and perhaps forgives, the personal responsibility of American citizens (like me and you), and neglects the systemic social and psychological processes that, in fact, deserve much of the "blame" (if it must be laid) for shaping these developments. My goal in the next chapters is to chart these circumstances, connecting the government's decisive policy shifts to the attitudes and behaviors of individual citizens, to the media's endless amplification of the terrorist threat, to risk entrepreneurs, to the terrorism industry, to the politics of fear, and to the culture of war.

2

SOLID FEAR

In Zygmunt Bauman's discussion of modernity, he associates the threat of terrorism with something he calls "liquid fear."[1] Today, suggests Bauman, we live in a state of constant worry about dangers too numerous and complex to count or fully comprehend. We perceive our fragmented, commercialized, globalized existence as unstable and uncertain. Traditional social bonds and notions of community are wearing thin. Meanwhile, the state is in the process of outsourcing its traditional functions, bequeathing its old-school duties to you and me, the *individual*. According to a number of scholars, the task of securing life and property, once the primary job of the state, has been increasingly left to private citizens, their pocketbooks, and the many corporations set up to exchange these purses for peace of mind.[2]

While the state walks with a new lightness of stride, we as citizens feel less at ease as we face the complicated, technical, specialized, multitudinous hazards of our everyday lives. I myself have no idea how microprocessors work; what to do if I get a virus (electronic or otherwise); whether to eat or protest genetically modified food; how to prevent carpet mites, black mold, radon, showerhead bacteria, and gingivitis; or what to do about the spiny green vine that is choking its leafy companions in my backyard. Adding to the menace, we live within a social system—the great hamster wheel known as capitalism— that constantly reminds us that dangers lurk around every corner and precautions (paid for in full or in three easy payments) must be taken. Such a plight, Bauman contends, is all the more distressing for those who lack the financial resources needed for solving their twenty-first-century challenges.

Running amuck with worry and flying solo in a fast-paced society, we have seen our fears become detached from their original sources and blended together. The fear that defines modern times, according to Bauman, is "diffuse, scattered, unclear, unattached, unanchored, free floating with no clear address or cause," a soupy uncertainty blended with "insecurity" (an awareness that multiple threats are *out there*) and "vulnerability" (a sense that there's no escaping harm).[3] This is where Bauman's "liquid fear" comes in. Picture a stew made with all the items in your refrigerator. My stew at least—a warm pool of beer, milk, Dijon mustard, leftover Chinese takeout, blue-cheese dressing, and pickled jalapeños—would certainly not be solid, nor would it be possible to fully identify or separate its ingredients. The task of carefully examining and understanding any particular part of the stew would be as onerous and unlikely as the task of eating it.

Bauman's liquid fear, while necessary for comprehending the general anxiety of modern times, does not, however, fully capture the essence of the terrorist threat or the effect 9/11 had on American minds. The fear of terrorism is, in several respects, special. To the extent that it departs from liquid fear, and it doesn't entirely, I suggest that the perceived threat of terrorism is, for lack of a more inventive contrasting modifier, something "solid."

First, terrorism is an equal-opportunity danger, generating concerns among rich and poor alike. None of the accoutrements of wealth—hefty gates, walls, security alarms, doormen, mammoth SUVs, world-class physicians, Ivy League educations, scorching cups of cappuccino—can fend off a terrorist strike (and they may, in fact, attract them). Though not an ideal common ground for civilization, the perceived threat of terrorism was in fact one of the few mental constructs that most Americans shared in the decade following 9/11. Hardening against Bauman's melting, fragmented, ambiguous modernity, the events of 9/11 and subsequent attacks directly influenced millions of Americans simultaneously, leading many of us down the same path, toward a similar state of mind and into a unified stream of history.

Second, while the war on terrorism has involved plenty of private enterprises, the state reemerged as the main provider of security and the organizing force behind the nation's response to 9/11. Straying from Bauman's view and reviving Weberian notions of the modern state, the U.S. military and other government agencies led the way in shaping the post-9/11 security framework overseas and in all areas of the critical infrastructure at home. As discussed in the previous chapter, even private insurance companies refused to enter the terrorism risk market, which means that the government became the primary underwriter of skyscrapers, apartment buildings, football stadiums, and other capital investments. Whether taxpayers like it or not, they are *united,* at least fiscally, in the war on terrorism.

Third, the danger has not, as in the case of liquid fear, been decoupled from its putative cause. As demonstrated later in the book, for at least a decade large percentages of Americans associated the threat with radical Islamic groups such as al Qaeda. Over roughly the same period, one in four related news articles published in the opinion-leading press linked terrorism to extreme forms of Islam.[4] While these assumptions may be misguided, they are no less real and potentially consequential.

Finally, the threat, particularly in light of 9/11, is not blurry, unclear, or hidden. For most Americans, 9/11 is still crystal clear—a tragedy frozen in the collective mind. The attacks killed 2,992 people, left a smoldering crash site in the Pennsylvania countryside, severely damaged one section of the Pentagon, and wrought enormous destruction in New York City. It took six years and eight months to build the World Trade Center and one hour, forty-two minutes to destroy it.[5] According to a report by the Federal Reserve Bank of New York, 30 million square feet of office space in Lower Manhattan were demolished.[6] The character and magnitude of these events had no precedent in the history of the United States. This was not a dream. This was not a movie. Airliners crashed into buildings. Massive steel structures collapsed. People fell from the sky. Our memories of 9/11 may be flawed and our interpretations may vary, but the basic plot of that fateful day still exists as a sturdy (if not entirely "solid") shared experience for millions of Americans.

The Perceived Threat of Terrorism Before and After 9/11

Although it is not surprising that many of us were worried about further aggression in the days following 9/11, the extent and permanence of these concerns are worthy of careful consideration. Academics, as you might have gathered, rarely use the term "freaking out" when describing the public's response to terrorism. Even the word "fear" is frowned upon by some. Most social scientists apply a more refined set of labels to our psychological reactions to danger. Responding to hazards, we experience reactions that are emotional (worry, fear, anxiety) and cognitive (beliefs about the characteristics of a danger and the probability of being harmed). In most cases, these two components go together. On the one hand, a resident of Florida's east coast may, for instance, believe that the chance of being disassembled by a bull shark while swimming in the ocean is quite high. The same person may also worry, often and intensely, about the danger, especially if he or she is fond of swimming. On the other hand, a citizen of Akron, Ohio, may fully agree with the Floridian's risk assessment of shark attacks, but have no concern about them whatsoever.

It is also important to distinguish between threats to individuals versus groups. After 9/11, many people not only perceived an increased threat to their personal safety, but also to their families, friends, neighbors, communities, the citizens of their state, and, perhaps, the nation as a whole. Social scientists refer to our thoughts about the danger to collectivities as "sociotropic" threat perceptions and to personal vulnerabilities as "egocentric."

A final distinction should be drawn between physical threats versus symbolic ones. People are attentive not only to the prospect of bodily harm, but also to incoming dangers to their self-esteem, status, and identity. When asked, for instance, to perform an elaborate dance step at a wedding, a reluctant performer is likely to perceive a greater threat to her self-image than her physical safety (though exceptions to this rule may apply). In the case of 9/11, given the symbolic nature of the attacks, some people sensed an increased threat to their well-being, as well as to their identity as Americans. Of course, as the U.S. military and security apparatus mobilized after the attacks, many people at home and abroad, Arabs and Muslims in particular, sensed a similar set of threats.

The reasons for making these distinctions are twofold. First, social scientists almost always denote these differences in their research. If, as suggested in the preface, this book is going to tell their story, it ought to demonstrate some familiarity with their chosen voice. Second, and more important, social scientists have found that people's behavioral responses to threats often depend on the type of psychological phenomena experienced (emotional/cognitive), the perceived target (egocentric/sociotropic), and the type of vulnerability (physical/symbolic). At the same time, when the need for simplicity outweighs the demand for specificity, the term "perceived threat" will be used here as a sort of family name for this complicated assortment of thoughts and feelings.

Now that I've established what *perceived threat* means, I can consider how much of it we experienced in the case of terrorism and for how long. Although thoughts about terrorism were nothing new to most of us, the effects of 9/11 were exceptional in this respect. Previous attacks in the United States, including the first assault on the World Trade Center in February 1993 and the Oklahoma City bombing in April 1995, certainly captured our attention, but the issue of terrorism did not become an enduring narrative in the media, or a permanent fixture in the minds of most Americans.[7] According to national surveys carried out by the Gallup Organization, the percentage of respondents who were very or somewhat worried about being personally victimized by terrorism peaked at 42 percent after the Oklahoma City attacks, dropped to 35 percent one year later (April 1996), and remained at this level until declining even further to 24 percent in April 2000.[8]

The response to 9/11 was quite different. With the wreckage still shifting in New York City, 58 percent of Americans said that they were very or somewhat worried about being personally victimized by terrorists. A greater percentage (66 percent) believed that a new attack was very or somewhat likely. Almost half the population thought that "Americans have permanently changed the way they live" (49 percent). Large percentages reported being less willing to "fly on airplanes" (43 percent), "travel overseas" (45 percent), "go into sky-scrapers" (35 percent), and "attend events where there are thousands of people" (30 percent).[9] Tensions ran so high that television talk shows on the East Cost had trouble filling their couches for months after the attacks as movie stars and other celebrities cancelled their flights.[10]

Personal concerns about "opening mail" and "food safety" also increased.[11] In the two decades prior to 9/11, "terrorism" never made the list of America's most important problems; after 9/11, terrorism became a top concern (mentioned in response to an open question by 46 percent of respondents in October 2001) and stayed on the list for several years.[12]

While the intensity of people's emotional and cognitive responses to 9/11 diminished in the years after the attacks, the threat of terrorism did not disappear. In the first three years, rather than declining uniformly as in the case of the Oklahoma City bombings, the percentage of those who were very or somewhat worried fluctuated, falling 23 points by November 2001, only to rise 13 points by February 2003. One year later, the level of worry assumed a steady upward trend. Between 2005 and 2007, worry levels exceeded the peak rating after the Oklahoma City bombings. These sustained concerns may have resulted from the tumultuous events of the times, including the start of the war in Iraq (March 2003), the Madrid train bombings (March 2004), and the London bombings (July 2005). In July 2007, 47 percent of Americans were very or somewhat worried about being personally harmed by terrorists; 40 percent believed that a new assault was very or somewhat likely.[13] By the end of the decade, worries about terrorism stood at 42 percent, which was near the average (41 percent) seen on this Gallup measure since September 11, 2001.[14] After the killing of Osama bin Laden in 2011, however, worries were on the rise once again, as were people's beliefs that a new attack was imminent. Overall, according to a May 2011 poll, 62 percent thought an act of terrorism was either very or somewhat likely to occur in the next several weeks.[15]

Survey questions that measured sociotropic threat also showed stability over time. According to a series of nationally representative panel studies, political scientist Darren Davis found that the percentage of Americans who were very or somewhat concerned that "the United States might suffer another terrorist attack in the next three months" stayed in a tight range (80 percent to 85 percent) between November 2001 and November 2004.[16]

The considerable increase in self-reported fears was reflected in indicators of the nation's mental and physical health after 9/11. Early on, some experts warned that a vast number of Americans would suffer from post-traumatic stress disorder (PTSD). Although such warnings overestimated actual levels of psychological distress, several studies showed that the effects on mental health were not trivial.

New York City residents were found to be particularly susceptible to psychological harm. Roughly 8 percent of Manhattan residents and 20 percent of those living near the World Trade Center suffered from PTSD.[17] Public health officials reported that people's mental health needs in the state of New York increased significantly after 9/11.[18] Parents and health officials were especially concerned about the effects on children. A study of New York City public school students found an association between students' exposure to the 9/11 events and mental disorders, including agoraphobia, separation anxiety, and PTSD.[19] Other studies on New York City youth supported these findings.[20]

Aside from children, certain subpopulations were shown to be particularly vulnerable to psychological trauma as a result of 9/11, including people with previous psychiatric illnesses, those who had been victims of crimes or other distressing events in the past, refugees who had been traumatized in their native countries, people with pessimistic outlooks, and those suffering from depression.[21]

The heightened stress was also shown to increase the number of heart attacks, as well as the use of cigarettes and alcohol.[22] Holman and her colleagues found that stress responses to 9/11 were associated with a significant increase in cardiovascular ailments over a three-year period following the attacks, even after controlling for pre-9/11 health status factors and demographic variables.[23]

Although psychological distress was shown to be more prevalent in New York City than elsewhere,[24] several studies found that 9/11 had at least some effect on mental health across the nation. Based on a nationally representative sample, 44 percent of adults and 35 percent of children reported one or more substantial symptoms of stress due to 9/11, which included "feeling very upset," having "disturbing thoughts," "trouble falling asleep," or "angry outbursts."[25]

Other national studies confirmed these results. Based on a national cross-sectional study with comparison groups before and after 9/11, the percentage of young adults who reported "sadness at least some of the time in the past 7 days" increased significantly for both males and females; female respondents experienced a significant increase in psychological distress.[26]

Mental health researchers also demonstrated that the various symptoms of psychological harm, particularly at the national level, diminished substantially within six months of the attacks.[27] Nevertheless, as social scientists pointed out, millions of Americans were now storing these traumatic events and emotional experiences in their memories. When recalled, they could have renewed effects on mental health, as well as influence other attitudes, beliefs, and behaviors.

Conclusion

In the aftermath of 9/11, many Americans felt that their lives would never be the same, that a dark line had been drawn across history, that the attacks would not be forgotten. The fears evoked by 9/11 and subsequent attacks around the globe were great enough to produce physical and psychological aliments in the short term, and elevate public worries and risk perceptions above the pre-9/11 levels for at least a decade. In spite of living for ten years without experiencing another major attack on U.S. soil, more Americans accepted the plausibility of the terrorist threat in May 2011 than at any time since the start of the Iraq War in 2003.

In the next two chapters, I'll explain why these high and prolonged concerns matter. The aim is to show how the perceived threat of terrorism galvanized society and how a united nation, in turn, contributed to the social, political, and economic consequences that were discussed in chapter 1. Our fears of terrorism are not only "solid," they are attached to other solid aspects of a broader mental structure, a way of seeing the world that led to significant changes—some tragic, some promising—in many people's lives.

3

A COUNTRY UNITED . . .
SORT OF

One aspect of fear is not frightening at all. In fact, it's rather pleasant. Anyone who has shared an even mildly threatening experience with other people knows that, at times, freaking out and friendship go hand in hand. A new sense of togetherness or social bond seems to emerge in almost any group, big or small, as it squares off against a mutually perceived threat from outside. After 9/11, a number of social scientists believed that a renewed sense of togetherness might emerge from the wreckage, that people would now grasp their civic duties, friendships, and social responsibilities more firmly and with greater purpose. This chapter attempts to reveal whether this happened, why, to whom exactly, and for how long.

Individualism and the Pre-9/11 Niche Society

To appreciate the extent to which people and communities came together after 9/11, I should begin by describing the nation's level of civic engagement and collective spirit before the attacks. Americans have never been known as a collectivistic, community-oriented lot. Individual pursuits and the desire to further one's personal interests were more familiar to many of us than the inclination to join groups and promote the common good. While it may be argued that American society has recently reached new heights in this respect, such a contention is anything but novel. Alexis de Tocqueville, for instance, had no problem spotting American individualism during his famous tour of the United States in 1831.[1] From the time it was coined in the early nineteenth century, "individualism" has been thought of as a uniquely American inclination. When the term came into use in the United States, it took on a positive connotation, whereas most Europeans had seen it in a negative light.[2] As pointed out by sociologist Robert Bellah, individualism took root in America prior to the arrival of industrial capitalism. After the Civil War, as industrialists began their march, and particularly later in the twentieth century during the era of capitalist development, individualism was further reinforced in American culture, gaining the status of a secular religion and easily comingling with the popular ideas of free enterprise, personal liberty, and the individual pursuit of happiness.[3]

Though embraced by many, individualism has certainly had its critics. In 1970, Philip Slater voiced his criticism plainly in *The Pursuit of Loneliness.* America was a competitive, individualistic society, he argued, one in which "an enormous technology seems to have set itself the task of making it unnecessary for one human being ever to ask anything of another."[4] Bellah and his colleagues, in their contemporary classic, *Habits of the Heart,* echoed some of Slater's claims and questioned whether individualism has any redeeming qualities.[5] One of the most famous recent renditions on the subject is *Bowling Alone* by political scientist Robert Putnam. Writing before 9/11, he suggested that we have become increasingly disconnected from various groups and social structures, that "social capital" is on the decline, and that now more than ever we are "bowling alone."[6]

Part of this tendency may be accounted for by the fact that many Americans have figured out ways to live, prosperously enough, without relying on or engaging with large assemblages of other people. Aside from piquing the interest of several academics, the novelist David Lodge flirted with this idea from a rather unique perspective. In a novel called *Thinks,* one of his characters, a professor of cognitive science, mentions to a colleague that we as a people—as Westerners in particular—have gotten "beyond the four Fs." The inquisitive colleague asks, "What are they?" and the character responds, "Fighting, fleeing, feeding and . . . mating."[7]

To some extent, Lodge's character offers a valid point. Given the socioeconomic, political, and technological circumstances of contemporary society, most Americans have gotten beyond the need for large-scale social involvement for securing their basic needs. Once the engine of collective activity, the "four Fs" are now taken for granted by many of us. When it comes to the war on terrorism and other international conflicts, responsibility for the first two Fs—"fighting" and "fleeing"—has been placed in the hands of a relatively small group of professional soldiers and military experts. Without conscription, the racial and socioeconomic composition of the armed forces has become less representative of the general population.[8] War, under such conditions, does not generate the same level of communal interest and collective spirit.

As for "feeding," the United States is one of the most overweight and wealthy countries in the world. Though poverty lurks in many areas, providing oneself with the essential nutrients for survival is not a concern for most Americans. In step with the armed forces, the act of gathering food has lost its collective character as well. Large corporations now control the lion's share of U.S. farmland, and new technologies have displaced workers from the fields. Solitary individuals wander the aisles of supermarkets, carefully avoiding the shopping carts of other humans. With self-serve checkout lanes, even the purchase of groceries can be completed without social interaction.

"Mating," no less than the other Fs, has become increasingly driven by individual choices rather than by social institutions. Few social scientists deny, for instance, that the role of marriage in society has changed over the last decades. A study by Martin and her colleagues found that a majority of adolescents indicated that they would engage in sexual intercourse before marriage, or already have.[9] A similar number of adolescents held positive attitudes toward cohabitation.[10] For many Americans, the institution of marriage is no longer a primary guide for sexual behavior.

Having moved beyond the "four Fs," we now have more time, energy, and desire for a sort of fifth F—finding yourself—which leads to an increase in self-involvement and a further decrease in social involvement. The best way to pursue the fifth F is to withdraw from the anonymous, indifferent multitude and join a smaller group that consists of people more like one's self. "You gotta find your niche" is not only a popular saying in business, but also a social strategy that defines, at least in part, contemporary American culture.[11] The use of this strategy is apparent in almost all areas of life, from sports and recreation to academics, religion, and family life. To find your niche is to find a narrower social environment where the potential for praise and adoration is far greater than in society at large. According to numerous studies in social psychology, simply becoming a member of a small group can enhance one's self-esteem.[12] To do the opposite—to join the broader community—is to invite disillusion, identity crisis, and low self-esteem.

Before 9/11, there just wasn't much in the way of social infrastructure to counteract the prevailing winds of American individualism and egotism. As Putnam suggested prior to the 9/11 attacks, it would take something really big—"a palpable national crisis, like war or depression or natural disaster"—to recharge the nation's collective impulse.[13] As discussed in the next sections, determining the extent to which 9/11 produced such an effect would occupy social scientists for at least a decade.

The Social Functions of Freaking Out

Georg Simmel, an influential German scholar of the late nineteenth century, was one of the first sociologists to hash out the idea that conflicts and crises increase "social cohesion" in groups.[14] The American sociologist Lewis Coser piggybacked on Simmel's work in his book *The Functions of Social Conflict*.[15] Coser's contribution was to show that the relationship between external conflict and internal cohesion depends on the group's level of togetherness prior to the outbreak of conflict or external aggression. Group members, he suggested, must see the threat as something that concerns "us." As an illustration, Coser described the different effects that World War II had on French and British societies:

> The Nazi attack appreciably increased the internal cohesion of the British social system, temporarily narrowing the various political, social and economic fissures that existed in British society. In France, on the other hand, these fissures were widened to the point of a breakdown in consensus even concerning the most basic question of all: whether France was to continue as an independent national unit.[16]

Social psychologists have added to this perspective, suggesting that the social tendencies described by Simmel and Coser should be understood as something "in-built" or structured in the minds of individuals. British social psychologist Henri Tajfel and his student, John Turner, developed a theory of intergroup conflict, which argues that higher levels of perceived threat strengthen in-group solidarity, as individuals develop more favorable attitudes toward "insiders," take steps to protect and affirm their values and social identity, and reinforce their ties to the in-group.[17]

Terror management theory offers a different explanation of how people process threats, but makes similar predictions about the effects.[18] Developed by a team of experimental social psychologists, the theory proposes that violent attacks, such as those seen on 9/11, heighten our awareness of "the inevitability and potential finality of death."[19] This heightened "mortality salience," in turn, encourages positive reactions to in-groups and promotes other pro-social behaviors aimed at validating one's worldview or cultural orientation. In essence, death freaks us out, and showing support for family, friends, and allies lessens these disagreeable thoughts and feelings. To use the words of terror management theorists, "Providing help to those in need, especially those who are deemed praiseworthy of help within the culture, is one example of how meeting cultural standards of value provides individuals with a sense of personal value."[20]

Political scientists have offered their take on this topic as well. An extreme external danger may operate as a "galvanizing crisis" that generates increased levels of social capital and civic engagement.[21] It may also encourage us to put greater trust in our local, state, and federal governments, and "rally around the flag" in support of the president.[22]

Vivid examples of increased social cohesion in the face of perceived peril are not hard to find in American history. In the latter part of the eighteenth century, the perceived threat from British soldiers was high in the minds of the American colonists. The press was filled with stories about the brutish occupiers harming and harassing colonists. Accounts of physical abuse and even rape were commonly found in the pages of the *New York Journal* and *Boston Evening Post*.[23]

The dangers posed by British troops were, seemingly, confirmed on March 5, 1770, when soldiers fired on a civilian mob in Boston, killing five people. Radicals seized on the event to highlight the threat of British tyranny and unify public sentiment against it. Paul Revere, a craftsman and anti-British propagandist, produced his historic engraving, which provoked the colonists' anger, dismay, and sense of common purpose. Whether the "Boston Massacre," as it came to be known, was really a *massacre* matters less than the simple fact that many colonists came to see it that way. These perceptions, combined with the public's reaction to a series of other key events, would radicalize moderate thinking, unite the colonists, and move them toward rebellion. As John Adams wrote, "On that night, the foundation of American Independence was laid."[24]

Americans reacted in a similar way to the bombing of Pearl Harbor in December 1941. Not unlike in their response to 9/11, Americans were horrified and shocked by the events. Under the guidance of a stalwart and increasingly popular president, Franklin Roosevelt, the country finally lifted its heels and united with its allies in the common cause of World War II. Putnam, along with many others, drew this comparison in an op-ed piece published shortly after 9/11 in the *New York Times*.[25] He wrote about the feelings of pride, citizenship, and community, as well as the heightened anxiety and perceived threat, that were evoked by the attack on Pearl Harbor. As examples, he cited the sacrifices people made in everyday life—the victory gardens, war bonds, and personal support of the troops—as well as civic engagement at the institutional level:

> The Civilian Defense Corps grew to 12 million Americans in mid-1943, from 1.2 million in 1942. In Chicago, 16,000 block captains in the corps took an oath of allegiance in a mass ceremony; they practiced first aid, supervised blackouts and planned gas decontamination. Nationwide, Red Cross volunteers swelled to 7.5 million in 1945, from 1.1 million in 1940. By 1943, volunteers at 4,300 civilian-defense volunteer offices were fixing school lunches, providing day care and organizing scrap drives.[26]

We should keep in mind (and this will be hashed out in detail in the next chapter) that historical examples of increased group solidarity in the midst of perceived dangers do not always result in such widely celebrated outcomes as the birth of our nation and the emergence of the "greatest generation." As one dramatic example, the infamous witch trials in Salem, Massachusetts, in the seventeenth century were in part the product of a formidable perceived threat—a supernatural one in this case. As God's chosen people, the community believed that "God visits terrible judgments upon His wayward people," and that it was their duty to confront by all means the evil within, as well as outside, themselves.[27] Conformity to these beliefs brought concerted action on the part of the Royal Governor of the Colony, the courts, the 34 accusers, the 84 witnesses, and the entire community, resulting in the arrest and imprisonment of roughly 165 people on charges of witchcraft.[28] In the end, at least 19 villagers from Salem were carted up to Gallows Hill and hung. One man was pressed to death under heavy stones. Many others languished in prison for months without a trial.[29]

Pro-Social Tendencies

There were several post-9/11 changes in American society that might fall under the title "Coming Together." These shifts can be broken into at least two subcategories: rally effects and pro-social tendencies. Rally effects include increased levels of presidential approval, trust in government, and patriotic sentiment. Pro-social tendencies include helping behavior, social trust, civic engagement, and collectivism. One question of interest is, which of these trends were more prominent in the wake of 9/11? Should the early 2000s be remembered as a time of renewed interest in world affairs and increased charity, volunteerism, and membership in community groups, or as a time of patriotic fervor, hero worship, and growing support for powerful political figures?

Helping Behavior and a Positive Outlook on Life

There were clear signs of pro-social tendencies in the immediate aftermath of 9/11. Countless people attended memorial services for the victims, as well as posted memorials online to pay their respects. According to a survey of 3,512 residents of Connecticut, New Jersey, and New York, 50 percent of the respondents attended a funeral or memorial service.[30] Cash and other gifts, estimated to be worth $1.4 billion, were donated to the victims of 9/11 and their families.[31]

Americans were more likely to volunteer in the post-9/11 period as well.[32] A study by Penner and colleagues confirmed the previous studies and further suggested that people gave their time to all types of charities, not only those related to 9/11.[33] Both studies, however, also showed that the boom in volunteerism lasted only three weeks. A research team led by Traugott posted the most optimistic estimate: their two-wave panel study suggested that volunteering rates remained elevated for up to six months.[34]

Using a variety of measures, other social scientists showed that people were more likely to perform "altruistic behavior" and show kindness, love, and friendship toward others.[35] There was also a slight increase (4 percent) in the percentage of Americans who believed that "there is much goodness in the world which hints at God's goodness."[36] Overall, however, 9/11's good

Samaritan effect lacked staying power. It should also be noted that much of the supporting evidence was based on self-reported data, as opposed to independently verifiable indicators of behavioral change.

Social Trust

Trust happens all the time. Trust makes it possible for you to leave your kids with a teenage babysitter, journey by car through congested roadways at high speeds with other anonymous travelers, enter a baseball park using a ticket purchased online from a complete stranger, crowd together with other people of unknown ethical, health, and hygienic circumstances, and buy a bag of peanuts from Bob, a vendor who tosses the salty projectile to you from thirty feet away and expects the cash payment to be passed down the aisle and through the self-interested hands of a dozen fellow spectators.

People's trust in other people (let's call it "social trust") varies across countries, as does the level of trust in any given society over time.[37] After 9/11, there seemed to be a significant increase in social trust according to several self-reported indicators. National surveys showed that the number of respondents who thought that "most people are helpful" and that "most people try to be fair" rose by 21 percent and 12 percent, respectively.[38] Putnam discovered similar increases in trust of various forms, including trust in the "people running my community" (8 percent increase), "neighbors" (7 percent), "local news media" (7 percent), and "friends" (8 percent).[39]

Americans were also more confident that their local communities would cooperate in collective actions, such as efforts to conserve energy or water.[40] While the increased level of social trust was shown to remain steady for several months,[41] there was a gradual return to pre-9/11 levels within about one year.[42]

Civic Engagement, Social Capital, and Collectivism

While trust is an essential component of any well-functioning society, it does not guarantee that people will come together, solve problems, build communities, perform their civic duties, or deliver soup to a sick neighbor. Some scholars thought that 9/11 would not only stimulate trust but also bring forth a string of corresponding actions. People would become citizens again, connect with their local and national leaders and political parties, join the PTA, revitalize bowling leagues across America, and actually vote. As seen in public responses

to major conflicts of the past, such as the American revolutionary struggle and
World War II, a new era of civic engagement and citizen action would grow
from the ashes of the 9/11 disaster.

Several scholars have investigated this topic, but most would likely agree
that Putnam stands out in the crowd. As mentioned above, just one year before
9/11, Putnam had predicted that a civic revitalization could be motivated by a
serious national crisis.[43] Not long after the attacks, he and a coauthor, drawing
on their ongoing research, published several opinion pieces in major news outlets. The events of 9/11, they suggested, had "dramatically led us to rediscover
friends, neighbors, public institutions, and a shared fate."[44] We were witness-
ing, it seemed, a considerable rise in "social capital," a sort of catchall phrase
used by social scientists to refer to social networks, social ties, the norms of
reciprocity, and trust.

Much of the available research on this topic, however, does not wholly
confirm Putnam's claims. As it turned out, the public at large was not quite
ready to trade in an evening of reality TV watching for one devoted to discussing the pothole crisis at a town hall meeting. Although there were some attitudinal changes, notable shifts in behavior were harder to find. The events of 9/11
did not, for instance, increase church attendance or membership levels in community organizations and clubs. Americans were actually slightly less likely
to have friends over to visit and more likely to watch television, according to
Putnam's own data.[45] Carol Ford and her colleagues also found no significant
pre–post 9/11 differences in people's contact with friends.[46]

Theda Skocpol made this point even stronger, showing that the average
net increase in "civic attitudes" was 15 percent, while the average net increase
in "civic behavior" was only 4 percent.[47] Drawing on panel data collected
roughly a month after 9/11 and again five months later, Schmierbach, Boyle,
and McLeod argued that the "civic surge" after 9/11 had been "temporary and
superficial."[48]

Other measures of civic engagement placed the "resurgence" further in
question. As Althaus suggested, if Americans were more involved in civic life
after 9/11, they did not show it by paying more attention to current events.[49]
Judging by the size of the TV news audience, the honeymoon of civic revitalization lasted less than one week. The size of the evening news audience had
more than doubled, from 13 percent of American adults in early September

2001 to more than 26 percent in the first five days following 9/11. Nielsen Media Research reported that 79.5 million people had watched the news on the night of the attacks (to put this number in perspective, roughly the same number of viewers watched the January 2001 Super Bowl).[50] Within one week, however, the evening news audience returned to near pre-9/11 levels.[51] A similar trend was seen in newspaper readership. According to some estimates, readership actually declined slightly in the first six months after the attacks.[52] Other studies showed that any increase in newspaper readership after 9/11 was quite modest (3 percent).[53]

Akin to civic engagement is the concept of collectivism. Some scholars supposed that 9/11 would soften American individualism and encourage people to see themselves as part of a common collective.[54] This conventional wisdom, however, was not confirmed by empirical research. A study based on surveys conducted before and after 9/11 (March and October 2001) found that the level of "collectivism" was slightly lower in the post-9/11 period.[55] The same study found that "cosmopolitanism" (a value orientation that suggests that all human beings belong to a single community) declined significantly between March 2001 and October 2001, and stayed at the same level until at least April 2002. These findings, as discussed in the next chapter, may reflect the relative strength of other, contradictory effects of 9/11 that led people to circumscribe their social identities and limit their collectivistic orientations.

"Bowling Together": The 9/11 Generation

If the spike in "community-mindedness" was generally short-lived, there was one subpopulation that seemed to buck the trend: young people. By the end of the decade, having conceded that the boom in social capital among adults had quickly busted, Putnam turned his attention to the youth. In the January 2010 issue of the *Journal of Democracy,* he and Thomas Sander outlined 9/11's generational effect. As the story goes, the "Greatest Generation" had lit the torch of civic engagement after WWII, which was later dropped by self-indulgent "Baby Boomers" and their progeny, "Generation X." After lying dormant for years, the "9/11 Generation"—those who had been in college or high school when the attacks occurred—raised the torch once more, ending decades of declining interest in politics and civic duties. As they entered college in 2002, they were more likely to "discuss politics" and were more interested in "keeping up to date with political affairs" than any freshman class since 1967.[56] For at least seven consecutive years following 9/11, voting rates among young people rose more than three times faster than for Americans over thirty years of age.[57] It would seem, according to these findings, the events of 9/11 had a more powerful and lasting effect on people who had experienced the tragedy during their impressionable adolescent years than just about everyone else.

Rally Effects

Few Americans would dispute the idea that pro-social tendencies represent a change for the better. The appeal of rally effects, to the contrary, is not universal. Given their pertinence to deep-seated partisan politics, I grouped them in a separate category.

Presidential Approval

Although American adults did not rally around each other to a great degree, they did rally around elected officials. President George W. Bush's approval rating increased dramatically after the attacks, rising from the mid 50s in the weeks before 9/11 to a record high rating of 90 percent during September 21–22, 2001.[58] Other polls showed that the swell of support for the president cut across party lines, even if it was higher among Republicans (96 percent) and Independents (76 percent) than among Democrats (66 percent).[59] The rally also included different racial and ethnic groups. As sociologist Neil Smelser noted, "Black Americans, who had given President Bush only 10 percent of their votes less than a year earlier, responded in public opinion polls that 75 percent were now supportive of him."[60] Members of Bush's cabinet, the U.S. Congress, as well as some local leaders, such as former mayor of New York City Rudy Giuliani, also received relatively strong increases in favorability after 9/11.[61]

Bush's approval rating did not return to its pre-9/11 level for roughly two years or more.[62] A number of social scientists were surprised by the length of this rally. Gaines, for instance, referred to it as "exceptional in magnitude and duration,"[63] while Collins called it "unusually prolonged."[64] Although the ratings of other major figures returned to baseline levels relatively quickly, Bush's post-9/11 boost held at 50 percent or higher well into 2005, which, according to some observers, accounted for his victory in the 2004 presidential election.[65]

It is worth noting that President Obama also received a terrorism-related boost in his approval rating. After the killing of Osama bin Laden in early

May 2011, national pride swept the country and Americans rallied around their leader once again. Overall, a majority now approved of his overall job performance and his handling of foreign policy. According to a *New York Times/ CBS News* poll, President Obama's job performance rating increased from 46 percent just before bin Laden's death to 57 percent after the news broke.[66] His elevated popularity was largely driven by a change of heart among Republicans and independents.

Trust in Government

Americans also united in support of the government as a whole. National polls showed that the public's "trust in government" more than doubled after 9/11, rising from 29 percent in March 2001 to 64 percent in late September 2001.[67] The number of Americans who were confident in the federal government's handling of both international and domestic problems rose by 15 percent and 17 percent, respectively.[68] Ford found that the elevated trust in government extended to the state and local levels as well.[69]

Based on data collected in twenty-three focus groups, Greenberg demonstrated that 9/11 stimulated public preferences for a greater government role in society. Among other things, he suggested that people wanted to delay the Bush administration's proposed tax cuts in order to "fund Social Security, rebuild after the terrorist attacks, help the unemployed, and increase support for education."[70] Greenberg, however, did not determine how long this attitude change lasted. Data collection, which took place within the first two months after 9/11, only represents the public's immediate reaction.

While the post-9/11 increases in trust and confidence in government were significant and remained high for three to five months, levels of trust faded faster than presidential approval, returning to pre-9/11 levels in about one year.[71]

Patriotism

The outpouring of support for individual leaders and government institutions coincided with a rise in national pride, along with various patriotic feelings, rituals, and acts.[72] There were dramatic increases in the percentage of people who reported being "very proud" of America for its advancements in "science and technology" (an increase of 26 percent), the "armed forces" (32 percent), "American history" (21 percent), "economic achievements" (32 percent), and "the way democracy works" (34 percent).[73] These elevated levels of pride were resilient for one year, if not longer.[74] Gallup trend data suggests that the elevation in patriotic sentiments lasted into the summer of 2005. No less than 61 percent (and as much as 70 percent) of Americans said they were "extremely proud" to be American in five post-9/11 polls, compared with only 55 percent in a January 2001 poll.[75]

According to at least two national surveys, a great majority of people (74 percent) said that they had displayed an American flag on their home, car, or person as a result of 9/11.[76] Flag display was equally prevalent in all regions of the country, though less so among blacks, as well as among younger and more educated people.[77] A study by Collins confirmed the high incidence of flag display after 9/11 with direct measures of this behavior. Collins also identified four distinct stages of flag display and other patriotic gestures: "(1) an initial, few days of shock and idiosyncratic individual reactions to the attack; (2) one to two weeks of establishing standardized displays of solidarity symbols; (3) two to three months of high solidarity plateau; and (4) gradual decline toward normalcy in six to nine months."[78]

The Appeal of "USA"

The post-9/11 patriotic fervor could be seen (sometimes in rather subtle forms) in the statements of political figures. In the 2004 presidential race, for instance, both frontrunners, George W. Bush and John Kerry, seemed aware of their word choices when referring to the nation. References to the "United States" were, perhaps, too sterile or plain. Candidates would fare better, it seemed, if they used a more devotional tone and spoke of "America," or better yet the "United States of America." According to the transcripts of the first six Democratic debates, the tag "United States of America" was used nineteen times in a discussion involving eight democratic candidates. John Kerry clearly led the pack by voicing almost half of these references.

While Kerry easily outstripped his Democratic cohort in this respect, he couldn't compete with Bush, who had made "USA" his mantra in the years after 9/11. A comparison between the six Democratic debates cited above and an equivalent number of Bush's public statements showed that the president employed the phrase "United States of America" almost three times more often than the Democrats.

While some may regard these factoids as incidental, a similar analysis of the mass media demonstrates that the labeling of our nation not only marks the ideological divide between politicians, but also between news sources. Most national newspapers use the acronym "U.S." when referring to the nation as a subject. You will never catch a journalist from the *New York Times* or *Washington Post* penning the letters "USA." The only national newspaper that uses the "USA" tag is the *USA Today,* the newspaper with the country's largest readership. Though the ideological leaning of this publication may be debatable, few would disagree that the *National Review,* which is loaded with "USA" references, has a conservative bent. Likewise, no one argues about the conservative stance of Bill O'Reilly or Rush Limbaugh, whose columns and websites are blazoned with this patriotic label.

Conclusion

Was America "a country united" after 9/11? According to social scientists, the answer is yes and no. Americans did rally around their leaders. They voiced greater support for the president, put more trust in government, reported higher levels of patriotism, and even revealed these feelings with actions, such as displaying the American flag, holding vigils, and singing the national anthem. With the exception of the 9/11 Generation, there is less evidence to suggest that Americans exhibited substantially more civic engagement, community involvement, long-term charitable work, or immersion in the major social issues of the day. Despite Putnam's hopeful pronouncements, the PTA, Lions Club, Rotary, and the bowling leagues were not overwhelmed with new members after 9/11. America's places of worship still struggled with declining memberships and attendance.

Although volunteering rates and charitable giving did increase substantially in the immediate aftermath of 9/11, in the long term America's coalescence materialized more so as political capital than as social capital. Americans rallied around their leaders, legislatures, and law enforcement, but did not line up in greater numbers to rebuild their communities, solve society's longstanding problems, or share in a common sacrifice. For months and even years, the White House was awash in trust and support from Congress, the people, and the press. As we put our faith in President Bush, the administration moved the nation in a new and considerably more violent direction.

But was it that simple? Should the American response to 9/11 be attributed solely to the public's support for an administration that happened to wage two wars, spend billions of dollars on national security, and diminish civil liberties? Is our only complicity in these developments to be found in our trust in government? Should the American public be remembered as a passive mechanism, a tool, a set of appendages wielded by political elites, or as a willing partner, as an inspiration in some cases, as the fuel of social and political transformation after 9/11? A number of social scientists have considered these questions. In the next chapter, I examine some of their answers.

4

THE AUTHORITARIAN
TURN

Here's a curious figure: $1,378,947.37. That's how much it costs to build a single Joint Air-to-Surface Standoff Missile (JASSM) (launching not included).[1] This is good news for Lockheed Martin, the corporation that produces the missile, bad news for the American people who pay for it, and really bad news for anyone on the ground when it explodes. The missile is about the size of a two-person canoe, weighs roughly 2,000 pounds, depending on the preferred warhead, and can be launched by a manned delivery platform that's located more than 200 miles from the target. A little airplane packed with advanced electronics and high-yield explosive, the JASSM is made to slice through the air on thin wings, autonomously, day or night, through good weather or bad, until it slams into something important. Essentially, it's a flying, computerized suicide bomber—an "unmanned kamikaze," as one weapons expert put it.[2]

Given its lofty price tag and specialized function as a destroyer of high-value targets, it might seem reasonable to limit production of the JASSM to a few dozen per year. In 2011, however, the Department of Defense requested 171 of these missiles, bringing our nation's annual JASSM tab to $235.8 million.[3] To put this in perspective, American taxpayers shell out roughly $6.5 million to build a typical elementary school. This means that instead of dropping our yearly quota of JASSMs on Afghanistan, we could bombard the country with thirty-six brand-new, American-made, brick-faced elementary schools each year (flagpoles included).[4] Of course, the JASSM is not the only weapon that's being funded by American taxpayers and hurled to oblivion by the military. The 2011 budget for weapons systems, which includes aircraft, ground programs, and shipbuilding, among others, is $214.7 billion—roughly a third of the total budget for national defense ($738 billion).[5]

Considering the trajectory of our military engagements abroad, we will likely be paying for many more bombs, missiles, warheads, and mines of all shapes and sizes. In 2011, the armed forces ordered 2,985 Small Diameter Bombs (SDB) at $111,390 each. Several SDBs can be snugly fastened to a fighter jet for those occasions when dropping only one bomb is undesirable. In the same year, we spent $252.6 million on our collection of Joint Direct Attack Munitions (JDAM), a guidance system that makes "dumb" bombs into "smart" ones, while our famous fleet of Tomahawk missiles came at a cost of $310.8 million.[6]

There are many other types of munitions, each with a special purpose, but almost all of them follow a general rule of thumb: they explode. And when they do, they often kill people. This may not seem surprising. And yet, as it turns out, there are several ways to die or be hurt in an explosion, some of which are quite remarkable. If you grew up in the age of TV shows like MacGyver and the A-Team, you probably expect, as I do, explosions to interact with human bodies by throwing them through the air, usually in slow motion across a back-drop of flame and smoke. According to experts on the physics and mechanisms of explosions, many deaths or wounds do actually occur as a result of bodies being thrown through the air.[7] Known as "tertiary blast injuries," the harm aris-es when the body, following its unexpected flight, strikes other objects, such as walls, cars, lampposts, kitchen countertops, filing cabinets, or other people.

A more likely scenario, however, is known as the "secondary blast injury," which happens when various items such as chunks of glass or cement whizz through the air and collide with people. In addition, there is an assortment of other blast-related injuries, including chemical and thermal burns; crush inju-ries and suffocation from collapsed buildings; toxic dust, gas, and radiation exposure; and a nasty blood disorder called methemoglobinemia, which, if acute, turns you blue, leads to a really bad headache, followed by seizures and finally death.[8]

As bad as some of these circumstances sound, nothing is quite like the "primary blast injury." When a JASSM or a Tomahawk or an SDB or an insur-gent's roadside bomb explodes, it creates a blast front—a massive wave of air that instantaneously increases the ambient pressure that surrounds us. Once the front passes by, it leaves a vacuum, a zone of underpressure, in its wake. To put it mildly, the experience is not very good for you. Given the fact that air is relatively easy to compress, but water is not, gas-containing organs such as lungs, ears, and bowels are particularly vulnerable. As the blast front strikes the body, these balloon-like organs compress, which causes them to bruise, tear, and, if the pressure change is great enough, fail completely and collapse.

If there is any reason to enumerate the gruesome consequences of war (not to mention the massive cost of waging it), it is to affirm a rather plain, though often neglected, point. U.S. military operations are really scary. We destroy buildings, obliterate critical infrastructure, kill lots of people, and frighten entire populations. In this respect, we are not altogether different from the "terrorists" we condemn. Terror, in fact, plays a part in our military strategy. We have a number of very smart people working for our government—members of the military leadership, analysts, consultants—who spend time thinking, studying, and imagining how a large-scale military assault may produce a strategic psychological influence on local populations. We saw the fruits of this labor, for instance, during the invasion of Iraq in March 2003. Our military leaders talked about a new type of military campaign, one that would produce "shock and awe" and thereby precipitate victory.[9]

There is another reason to reflect upon the brutality of war. Such a deliberation, as I hope and intend, makes the question *why* more imperative. Under what conditions is the use of overwhelming acts of violence backed by the public? What explains our support for war and the other harsh policies and law-enforcement procedures that emerged after 9/11? A second question is *what*? What exactly changed in the American mind-set and for how long did it stay that way? If there was an "authoritarian turn" in our views of the world, how long did it last?

Authoritarian Tendencies

While crowds of social scientists explored the pro-social tendencies and rally effects discussed in chapter 3, an even greater share focused on whether 9/11 was associated with an increased desire for security and a new harshness in the American mind-set. I use the term "authoritarian tendencies" here to loosely categorize a variety of social-psychological changes after 9/11, including general shifts in culture and values, as well as specific changes in public opinion.

Some of the theories discussed in the previous chapter also help to explain these tendencies. According to intergroup conflict theory, for instance, higher levels of threat are associated with increased out-group bashing, stereotyping, and attribution errors.[10] Perceived threat, as suggested by terror management theorists and other scholars, may also activate greater adherence to conventional values, conformity to group norms, submissiveness to moral authorities, identification with powerful figures, and rejection of outsiders.[11] Though I do not wish to make a case for a new "post-9/11 personality," these tendencies are similar to the personality traits famously described in 1950 by sociologist Theodor Adorno and his colleagues in their book *The Authoritarian Personality,* which attempted to explain anti-Semitism and public support for the Nazi regime.[12]

Culture and Values

Changes in culture and values are generally thought to occur gradually. Some scholars, however, have argued that large-scale, traumatic events can cause sudden shifts in values and cultural orientations.[13] For example, the Japanese and German cultures were thought to have shifted rather quickly in the aftermath of World War II toward a rejection of dictatorship and militarism. Several post-9/11 studies advanced this line of thinking. Based on a content analysis of letters to the editor—a sort of mass-mediated sphere of political culture— Andrew Perrin showed that the number of "authoritarian" cultural scripts in American newspapers increased after 9/11.[14] The letters revealed a greater willingness to punish others who violate conventional values, a greater preoccupation with power and toughness, and a greater certainty that the world is a dangerous place. National polls provided only modest support for these findings. For instance, there were small to moderate increases in the percentage of Americans who believed that the "world is filled with evil and sin" (3 percent) and "human nature is fundamentally perverse" (9 percent).[15]

A shift in values was also discovered in studies on the electorate's evaluation of political candidates. After 9/11, voters grew more receptive to leaders who emphasized the greatness of the nation, proclaimed their resolve to fight terrorism, and win a victory over "evil."[16] In an experimental study, psychologist Mark Landau and his colleagues demonstrated that reminding subjects (undergraduate college students) about the events of 9/11 increased their support for Bush and decreased their support for presidential candidate John Kerry.[17]

To induce thoughts of terrorism, the experimental subjects were asked, "Please describe the emotions that the thought of the terrorist attacks on September 11, 2001 arouses in you," while control subjects were asked parallel questions about an upcoming exam. "Support" for the candidates was measured with a composite index that included four survey questions, including one that asked the subjects directly about their intention to vote for the given candidate in the 2004 presidential election. The increase in Bush's appeal was found in both conservative and liberal respondents.[18] Data collection was conducted between October 2003 and May 2004, indicating that the perceived threat of terrorism likely had an enduring effect on political attitudes. This and several other studies suggested that Bush's patriotic rhetoric and emphasis on "ridding the world of evil" gave him an advantage with voters in the 2004 presidential election.[19]

The theory brought to light by these findings—that many of us seem to prefer leaders with stereotypical attributes of power, toughness, and resolve in times of crisis—may also explain the masculinization of post-9/11 popular culture and our preferences for male leaders. Researchers found, for instance, that the percentage of Americans who thought that "a woman president would do a better job" dropped from 25 percent in January 2000 to 15 percent in September 2003.[20] Jennifer Lawless uncovered similar pre–post 9/11 differences using several survey questions related to women and leadership.[21] Examining the gendering of the post-9/11 cultural milieu, Lorraine Dowler observed an influx of masculine imagery, the "masculination of New York City," the heroes of the attacks, and other aspects of the public discourse on the nation's response to 9/11.[22] Dowler's study, however, did not determine the length of this trend.

Among other cultural shifts, "safety, order, and stability in society" were valued more after than before 9/11, while the need for "excitement, novelty, and a challenge in life" declined significantly following the attacks.[23] These changes held for roughly five months before returning to near pre-9/11 levels.[24] There was also a shift in the way Americans valued equality. In the context of organizations, people tended to perceive the difference in power between employees and bosses as more acceptable after 9/11—a tendency that lasted at least six months.[25] According to a study that collected data before 9/11 (March 2001) and at two time points after the attacks (October 2001 and April 2002), this change was significant, substantial, and persistent.[26] In coming to this conclusion, the study's authors used several questions to measure "acceptance of hierarchy" in organizations; the items that showed the greatest increases in support were "a hierarchy of authority is the best form of organization" and "the hierarchy of groups in a society should remain consistent over time."[27] Several other studies offered interesting and important insights on 9/11's effect on American culture and values, authoritarian values in particular, though few of them offered pre–post 9/11 data to support their assumptions.[28]

Military Actions

Many specific changes in public opinion paralleled these general shifts in values. The most apparent among them was the country's nearly unanimous call for military reprisals. Public approval of using "military action against terrorism" hovered around 90 percent for no fewer than six months after the attacks.[29] According to a Gallup poll conducted in November 2001, 62 percent of Americans advocated the start of a "long-term war," and 31 percent of respondents backed "the punishment of specific terrorists"; only 5 percent said that the United States "should not take military actions."[30] A great majority of Americans (65–71 percent) approved a military response even if it resulted in "civilian casualties" and the use of "ground troops."[31]

Although a call to war had followed previous terrorist attacks, 9/11 proved to be a special case. Responding to comparable survey questions, 60 percent of the public supported a military response to the bombing of U.S. embassies in Kenya and Tanzania in August 1998, while 80 percent supported a military response to 9/11.[32]

National pollsters also found broad public support for war in the specific cases of Afghanistan and Iraq. Between September 11, 2001, and March 2002, approval of the war in Afghanistan ranged from 65 percent to 77 percent, even when questions mentioned military operations on the ground and potential casualties of American troops and innocent civilians.[33] Other sources of public opinion data showed that a wide majority of Americans backed the Afghan war for at least five years after 9/11. Asked whether they thought the military actions in Afghanistan were a "mistake," 89 percent said "no" in November 2001; this number stood at 93 percent in January 2002, and remained at 70 percent or higher until August 2007.[34]

Given the longstanding conflict between the United States and Iraq, much is known about public attitudes on this issue. In the decade prior to 9/11, aside from a few brief spikes in approval, only slight majorities of Americans supported war with Iraq.[35] In February 2001, just seven months before the attacks, only 52 percent of Americans were in favor of military actions. One month after 9/11, however, the number jumped to 81 percent. Approval rating fluctuated in the next months and years but remained in the high 60s and 70s until June 2004, when it dropped to 56 percent, still four points above the pre-9/11 level.[36]

The attacks on 9/11 also brought an increase in public support for the assassination of terrorist leaders. Based on roughly comparable survey questions, the number of Americans who approved the assassination of "known terrorists" or "individual terrorist leaders" rose from 54 percent in late 1998 to 77 percent in October 2001.[37] This change in mind-set could not be made any clearer than by the public's response to the assassination of Osama bin Laden in May 2011. When word of the killing flashed across television screens, Americans ran into the streets; celebrated in large, raucous crowds; and chanted "U.S.A., U.S.A" in front of the White House, at Times Square, and the World Trade Center site, as well as on numerous college campuses across the country. Exploring the online video footage of college kids dancing around bonfires, one finds not only concerted expressions of joy, but also harsher, more aggressive chants such as, "Fuck bin Laden!" Elated news anchors and commentators from across the political spectrum portrayed the killing in glowing terms.[38] Bill O'Reilly described it as "a great day for the U.S.A.," while Jon Stewart called it "a good night."[39] Columnist Maureen Dowd rebuffed those who raised concerns over the international legal implications of the assassination, suggesting, "Morally and operationally, this was counterterrorism at its finest. We have nothing to apologize for."[40] Even some ethics scholars supported the killing.[41]

In addition to the increased support for harsh antiterrorism tactics and the use of military force in the war on terrorism, Americans also shifted their views on U.S. defense spending. During much of the 1980s and 1990s, a plurality of Americans thought that "too much" was being spent on defense. After 9/11—and for the next five years—a plurality believed that the government was spending "about the right amount."[42] It was not until February 2007 that public sentiment shifted again, returning to the notion that "too much" was being spent.

The Marriage of Fear and Optimism in Political Rhetoric

In the years after 9/11, several authors criticized President Bush for exaggerating the danger posed by terrorism and overemphasizing our vulnerability to attacks. In the editorial pages of newspapers everywhere, from the *Los Angeles Times* to the *New York Times,* we were told that the administration promoted fear in society with the help of its terror-warning system, the Office of Homeland Security, and its strident campaign against international terrorism and weapons of mass destruction. Although describing these threats was certainly high on the Bush administration's agenda, fear was not the only sentiment being peddled after 9/11. Political rhetoric in the post-9/11 era also tapped into the public's new yearning for confidence, strength, reassurance, and hope.

In fact, in the first months following the attacks, the Bush team spent more time urging us not to fear terrorism than it did warning us about the danger. I found empirical support for this claim by carefully analyzing all of the president's speeches (forty-six in all) during two periods in late 2001 (September 11–25 and October 7–21). The president's first seven words to the nation following the attacks were, "I want to reassure the American people. . . ."[43] In the next weeks and months, the president flooded his public statements with reassurances: "They cannot dent the steel of American resolve,"[44] "We will hunt down and punish those responsible,"[45] "America is united,"[46] and "Good will prevail."[47]

Bush cemented this theme in his address to a joint session of Congress on September 20, 2001. "Fear can threaten the stability of legitimate nations," he said. "And you know what? We're not going to allow it." Applause erupted on both sides of the aisle, as Democrats and Republicans took to their feet. In closing the address, the president voiced what would become the mantra of his foreign policy in the next years: "Freedom and fear are at war. Our nation—this generation—will lift a dark threat of violence from our people and our future. . . . Freedom and fear, justice and cruelty, have always been at war, and we know that God is not neutral between them" [Applause].

Unlike many American and foreign commentators, Bush never described the perpetrators as "well organized," "meticulous," "intelligent," "educated," or "thorough." In his descriptions of the United States and the American people, he rarely discussed the country's vulnerability, weakness, or its failure to defend itself. On October 8, 2001, the president did mention, in a rare case, that "America is not immune from attack." But he followed this statement by declaring that the country is "equal to this challenge, make no mistake about it. They've roused a mighty giant."[48]

On three separate occasions during the two periods under study, the president referred to the United States as "the greatest nation on the face of Earth." The single-word descriptions of America used most frequently by Bush included: "strong" (82 mentions), "determined" (26), and "united" (21). As a comparison, references such as "peaceful" (3), "democratic" (3), "friendly" (2), and "forgiving" (0) were far less common. Neither the strength of the terrorists nor the vulnerability of the United States played prominently in the president's speeches in the first two months following the attacks. If anything, the president reestablished a foundation for optimism and determination in the public mind.

The emphasis placed on the nation's strength, resilience, and determination may offer some insight into the question of why the Bush administration enjoyed long-term support for its military campaigns and other elements of the war on terrorism. As shown in numerous studies, people don't always respond to threats by supporting aggressive actions to remove or diminish them. When faced with extremely frightening situations or messages, we often become defensive and seek ways to deny that the danger exists. In a successful fear appeal, the message must at once frighten us with a danger and assure us that we can avoid it by taking specific actions. If our level of confidence is low, we might revert to what psychologists call "fear control processes"—that is, we might choose to ignore the message, derogate its source, or simply adopt a fatalistic perspective. In other words, if a fear appeal doesn't include a light at the end of the tunnel, we may avoid the tunnel altogether.

This perspective offers a necessary clarification of the standard explanation of how fear works in political communication. Many commentators speak only of the external stimulants of fear and discount the relevance of our internal sense of control. They link our rising fears to the frightening news stories and images on television and the ominous speeches of politicians. While public officials have provided plenty of scary stuff about terrorism for us to ponder, they have also convinced us that we can overcome the challenge. Put differently, if the Bush administration should be blamed for fear mongering, it should be blamed for hope mongering as well. We were not only made to be "afraid of the wrong things," as Barry Glassner skillfully argued in *The Culture of Fear,* but perhaps also hopeful of the wrong things.[49] Part of the dominant cultural framework that the Bush administration tapped into and reinforced was American optimism—that powerful cultural trait which seems to lead us, perhaps more so than people in other cultures, to be hopeful, to observe the glass half-full, to see the donut, in all its doughy glazed perfection, not the hole.[50]

Civil Liberties, Privacy, and Security

Another notable attitude shift surfaced as policymakers struggled to balance the country's security concerns with the need to preserve the rights and liberties of the American people. As mentioned in an earlier chapter, the Bush administration, led by Attorney General John Ashcroft, introduced the USA PATRIOT Act in October 2001, and it passed in the Senate and House by large margins. Although the legislation was renewed by Congress in March 2006, it remains controversial to this day.

As a result, much research was conducted to gauge public attitudes toward civil liberties after 9/11. While less data is available from the pre-9/11 period, a clear pre–post comparison can be made. The most common national polling question asked Americans about their willingness to "give up some civil liberties" in order to "curb terrorism." Two variants of this general trade-off question measured the public's willingness to give up "personal freedoms" or "privacy" to fight terrorism. Each of these trade-off measures increased considerably after 9/11.

Although a similar trend was seen in the wake of the Oklahoma City bombing in 1995, the post-9/11 change was much greater. Willingness to make the civil liberties trade-off stood at 49 percent after the bombing in Oklahoma. Two years later, as the salience of terrorism diminished, the indicator dropped to 29 percent. After 9/11, public willingness to trade liberties for security reached 69 percent (or even higher according to some national polls).[51] Significant increases were seen in the public's response to the "security-freedoms" trade-off and the "security-privacy" trade-off. The public also became less concerned that the government's measures to combat terrorism would negatively affect civil liberties; such concern dropped from 65 percent before 9/11 to 56 percent after.[52]

The public's elevated trade-off willingness was quite stable over time, even if it gradually decreased. For instance, as late as July 2005, the public's willingness to make the trade-off stood at 11 percent above the pre-9/11 level (29 percent in April 1997 versus 40 percent in July 2005); support for the personal freedoms trade-off dropped only 6 percent in the eight months after the attacks and held just above the pre-9/11 level, fluctuating between 61 and 64 percent, until May 2006.[53] "Concern" about the effects of antiterrorism measures on civil liberties remained below the pre-9/11 levels through February 2006.[54]

Based on a series of nationally representative panel surveys, Davis provided further evidence that the public's increased trade-off willingness remained mostly stable over time.[55] Public responses on seven of Davis's nine civil liberties trade-off measures changed by no more than 5 percent over a three-year period. The public's favorable views on such matters as requiring people to carry a national identity card at all times, racial profiling, performing warrant-less search and seizures, wiretapping, and making it a crime to belong to any organization that supports terrorism remained quite high and stable from November 2001 to November 2004.[56] The two measures that demonstrated a slight exception—one regarding the indefinite imprisonment of noncitizen terror suspects, and the other on whether teachers should be allowed to criticize the government—shifted in the pro–civil liberties direction by only 10 percent and 15 percent, respectively, over the same period. Further evidence on the stability of the public's trade-off willingness was provided by Greenberg and company.[57]

Muslims and Arabs

The attacks on 9/11 resulted in a disturbing set of circumstances for many Muslims and Arabs living in the United States. The prevailing climate of fear and distrust encouraged a range of offenses, from name calling and illegal prohibitions against head scarves in the workplace to falsified police reports, violent harassment, and murder. According to the Federal Bureau of Investigation (FBI), the number of hate crimes against Muslims rose from 33 in 2000 to 546 in 2001.[58] These offenses decreased to 170 in 2002, rose again to 191 in 2006, and stood at 128 in 2009, which still greatly exceeded the pre-9/11 level.[59] Although these official data reveal the growing problems faced by Muslims and Arabs after 9/11, there is no way to know the actual number of hate crimes, because numerous cases go unreported or misreported.[60]

Another source reported that "over 700 violent incidents targeting Arab Americans, or those perceived to be Arab Americans, Arabs and Muslims" occurred in the first nine weeks following the attacks.[61] The same report also stated that within one year after 9/11, 80 people were removed from airplanes after boarding based on their perceived ethnicity, and there were 800 workplace discrimination cases involving Arab Americans, which represented a fourfold increase over the prior year.

Statistics compiled by the U.S. Equal Employment Opportunity Commission (EEOC) confirmed that discrimination against Arabs and Muslims jumped after 9/11 and continued to increase in the next years.[62] By the end of the decade, the unrelenting U.S. military actions in Muslim countries and growing anti-Islamic sentiment among many Americans coincided with record numbers of Muslim workers receiving discriminatory treatment. Between September 2008 and September 2009, Muslim workers filed 803 such claims, a 20 percent increase from the previous year and up nearly 60 percent from 2005, according to the EEOC as reported in the *New York Times*.[63] Following up on many of these complaints, the EEOC filed several high-profile lawsuits against the alleged offenders, including the meatpacking company JBS Swift, the clothing store Abercrombie & Fitch, a Sheraton hotel, and Disney.

In spite of the Bush administration's efforts to curb these negative impulses, the image of Arabs and Muslims deteriorated considerably in the years after 9/11. A report by political scientist Costas Panagopoulos summarized a number of national surveys related to American perceptions of Islam. In January 2002, for instance, 14 percent of Americans thought that "mainstream Islam encourage[d] violence against non-Muslims"; roughly two years later the percentage of Americans holding this belief had more than doubled (34 percent). This figure remained stable until the latest available survey in March 2006 (33 percent). A similar proportion of Americans (39 percent) believed that "the attacks on America represent the true teachings of Islam."[64] According to another report, roughly four in ten Americans admitted that they had an unfavorable attitude toward Muslim countries.[65]

While levels of intolerance toward other religious groups remained stable, views of Muslims continued to sour during the first post-9/11 decade.[66] In 2006, 22 percent of Americans said that they "would not like to have Muslims as neighbors," up from 12 percent in 1995.[67] In late 2009, according to a Gallup poll, roughly one-third of Americans described their opinion of Islam as "not favorable at all," a percentage that far exceeded the shares of negative views of other religions; the same study found that 43 percent of Americans acknowledged having at least "a little" prejudice toward Muslims (only 18 percent, 15 percent, and 14 percent said the same thing about Christians, Jews, and Buddhists, respectively).[68]

While there is no question that negative attitudes toward Arabs and Muslims became more pervasive in the post-9/11 period, it should be pointed out that prejudice, discrimination, and stereotypes aimed at these groups represented serious problems before the attacks as well. The post-9/11 backlash was built on a solid ideological foundation, a cultural framework that had been constructed long before 9/11. As Jack Shaheen found in a study of nine hundred Hollywood films, Arab people have almost always been depicted in movies with unsavory labels and imagery. The Arabs of Hollywood's motion pictures are most often portrayed as brutal religious fanatics, Kalashnikov-carrying terrorists, kidnappers, rapists, or oil-rich dimwits bent on world domination. Arabs appeared as normal, human characters in only 5 percent of their Hollywood movie roles, according to Shaheen's study.[69]

Immigrants

Public attitudes toward immigrants and immigration also hardened after 9/11. According to national polls, the number of Americans who believed that "immigration should be decreased" stood at 38 percent in September 2000. Roughly one year later, as the nation responded to the terrorist attacks on 9/11, this indicator rose to 58 percent.[70] This twenty-point jump is significant, given the steadiness of this indicator over the two years prior to the attacks. The indicator dropped six points between February 1999 and September 2000, rose five points in March 2001, and dropped again by only two points in June 2001.

Other polling questions produced similar results. The percentage of Americans who thought that "immigration is a bad thing for this country" increased from 31 percent in June 2001 to 42 percent in October of the same year. Both indicators remained above the pre-9/11 level until June 2006.[71] Americans were particularly worried about "illegal" immigrants. In April 2001, only 28 percent of respondents said that they were "greatly concerned" about illegal immigration; as late as April 2007, 45 percent of respondents reported the same thing.[72] Data from multiple polling firms and individual researchers illustrate a mild-to-medium backlash against immigrants in the first post-9/11 decade.[73]

A Summary of 9/11 Effects

Many scholars have argued that 9/11 fundamentally changed the way Americans see the world. Years later, however, some observers suggested that the rush to identify 9/11 as a turning point in American history was "born out of shock" and that very little has changed since the attacks.[74] Judging from a broad examination of pre–post 9/11 research, the former argument is more convincing than the latter, particularly when one ponders the massive scope and variety of small-to-moderate 9/11 effects, rather than the strength of any one change in the public mind.

To emphasize this point, allow me to backtrack for a moment and review these changes. In this chapter and in the two preceding it, I discussed several 9/11 effects and sorted them into four groups: perceived threat, pro-social tendencies, rally effects, and authoritarian tendencies. Chapter 2 outlined evidence that the perceived threat of terrorism increased substantially and remained elevated for no less than a decade. So traumatic were the 9/11 events that many people suffered from severe psychological distress, particularly those living close to New York City, as well as children and people who had experienced traumatic events in the past. Ten years after that fateful day, the majority of Americans still believed that a future attack was very or somewhat likely to occur in the next several weeks, a proportion that exceeded the pre-9/11 level by almost three times.

Chapter 3 covered pro-social tendencies and rally effects, both of which were correlated with the rising level of fear, with an examination of how Americans rallied around the flag and their president. Similar effects included increased levels of public trust in local, state, and federal governments and a rise in various patriotic feelings, rituals, and acts. Yet these variables returned to pre-9/11 levels within a shorter time frame of about nine months to one year.

Americans also rallied around each other, though to a lesser extent. Also noted in chapter 3, in the first weeks after 9/11, they showed increased kindness and support for their friends, families, and fellow citizens. The public attended countless funerals and memorial services for the 9/11 victims, donated more money to charities, and served as volunteers more often. For roughly one year, people also reported that they trusted each other more and felt greater confidence in their communities as sources of support and cooperation. Although the evidence is mixed, 9/11 also brought a brief renewal in the public's civic engagement. People reported being more interested in politics and more connected to their communities. There were also slight increases in various "civic behaviors," such as attending political meetings and reading newspapers. Overall, however, these changes ranked among the weakest and least permanent 9/11 effects. And as shown earlier, while the post-9/11 increase in civic engagement among adults fizzled in the short term, the shift appeared to be more lasting among young people, particularly those who were in their teens during the attacks.

As discussed in this chapter, a loose category, labeled here as authoritarian tendencies, represents the fourth and most prominent set of 9/11 effects. Researchers working in the aftermath of 9/11 discovered general shifts in American culture and values, as well as specific manifestations of these effects in public opinion. Americans showed a greater willingness to punish those who violate conventional values and were more attracted to leaders who displayed power, toughness, and an iron determination to confront the enemy. Faced with the threat of terrorism and guided by an administration that was determined to "stand, fight and win the war on terror," Americans were ultimately more interested in "paybacks" than "paying it forward." The nation's response to terrorism could, it seems, be summed up with Jon Stewart's twist on a famous adage: "The pen is mightier than the sword if it has been sharpened to a fine point, dipped in deadly poison and is thrown from ten feet away. But really, you're better off with a sword."[75] The increased support for the war in Iraq did not return to pre-9/11 levels until June 2004, but even then the war enjoyed a favorable rating from a majority of Americans. There was also an upswing in support for harsh antiterrorism tactics, while racial and religious tolerance declined.

One of the goals of these chapters was to highlight the diversity of 9/11 effects. On this, however, I must admit to coming up short. In the interest of parsimony, I ignored changes that didn't seem to fit in my four-category framework. I left out the social scientific research that showed how 9/11 affected travel, tourism, and other consumer behaviors;[76] the housing slump and mortgage mess;[77] job performance and career choices;[78] healthcare concerns;[79] low birth weights;[80] the fear of crime;[81] food safety concerns;[82] moods and self-efficacy;[83] and even mundane matters such as restaurant tipping[84] and Halloween trick-or-treating.[85]

Also neglected were the post-9/11 shifts in public attitudes toward global warming,[86] alternative energy sources and green technology,[87] biotechnology,[88] environmental groups and social movements,[89] gun control,[90] police and law-enforcement agencies,[91] border security,[92] missile defense,[93] and many others.

Although I briefly addressed social attitudes toward Arabs, Muslims, and immigrants in the United States, I did not consider how 9/11 influenced views toward other racial and ethnic groups,[94] foreign countries, or international organizations.[95] This review only covered shifts in public opinion on the most glaring foreign policy issues involving Iraq and Afghanistan, yet the terrorist threat is clearly relevant to public attitudes on numerous other aspects of international relations.[96]

Given my focus on major national issues, I also ignored how 9/11 affected public thinking at the local level, particularly local politics and security concerns involving the regional infrastructure, from the Mackinaw Bridge in Michigan to the New Mexico border. While some of these issues were trivial—for instance, the crusade by officials in Dover, New Jersey, to strengthen the city's gumball machines against the terrorist threat—others were taken quite seriously by locals.[97]

Conclusion

Aside from an interest in demonstrating the diversity and duration of 9/11 effects, the underlying reason for spending so much time examining the changing attitudes, beliefs, and behaviors of ordinary Americans was to demonstrate that the government policy shifts associated with the war on terrorism were quite popular, and not merely the products of arrant policymakers. Much of what materialized in foreign and domestic policy was backed by large shares of the American people. Countless pre–post 9/11 studies and voluminous polling data indicated that the public's fear of terrorism escalated at a time when key social and political attitudes shifted in favor of the Bush administration's plans for countering terrorism.

Considering the extant theories on the effects of perceived threat, it is tempting to identify the fear of terrorism as the driving force of history in the twenty-first century. Although such a perspective is plausible, it lacks appreciation for the antecedents of fear, as well as a more detailed understanding of the causal mechanisms behind this relationship. For this reason, in chapters 5 and 6, the focus will move from description to explanation, from the question of what changed after 9/11 to the issue of why it happened.

5

RADICAL ISLAM, LOOSE NUKES, AND OTHER REASONS TO FREAK OUT

Let's reminisce for a moment: After 9/11, we hugged each other, bonded, backed our leaders, and generally came together as a nation. We also identified and declared war against our enemy; bombed one country back to the Stone Age; invaded another country in search of a nasty stockpile of fictitious weapons; really scared a lot of people (not to mention making some of their lungs, ears, and intestines collapse); opened secret prisons; tortured people; dumped gazillions of dollars into national defense and homeland security; built more pointless fences on the Mexico border; treated Arabs, Muslims, and anyone who sort of looked like them very poorly; allowed the FBI and National Security Agency to delve into our private lives like never before; submitted to touchy-feely pat downs in public places; and, of course, waited and waited and waited in line at the airport. Although our resolute leaders drove this vehicle of change, we all went along for the ride.

In this chapter, my hope is to explain in greater detail how public concerns about terrorism propelled us along this path. The first item of business is to identify the origin of these fears. Why, in other words, is terrorism scary? One might begin by suggesting that Americans are worried about terrorist acts, and therefore abundantly determined to stop them, because they kill people. Though no doubt plausible, such a perspective masks much of what makes terrorism frightening. If the premise were true, wouldn't we wage wars against things that have in the past demonstrated a greater likelihood of killing us? Prioritizing the probability of death, we might, for instance, consider a war against bumblebees, slippery bathroom floors, automobiles, or swimming pools. We might forgo the purchase of duct tape for terror-proofing our homes and invest instead in headgear that prevents lightning bolts from splitting us in two. We might rethink our concerns about al Qaeda and turn our attention to riskier situations, such as crossing the street, chewing food, sunbathing, and standing on a ladder to clean the eave troughs. We would, without doubt, halt the construction of new high-rises, subdivisions, and day spas along the San Andreas Fault in California.

It is certainly possible that our perceptions of terrorism are unrealistic. As declared by political scientist John Mueller, our fears may indeed be "overblown."[1] However, given the lack of sound probabilistic data on the threat, spouting confidently about the absence of danger is just as knotty and potentially invalid as fear mongering. I suggest, for this reason, a somewhat different inquiry—an investigation into why some dangers, whether proven to be harmful or not, frighten us more than others.

What is it about the public discussion of terrorism that preoccupied us after 9/11? Why weren't we more concerned about heart disease, which kills roughly 600,000 people each year?[2] Why is al Qaeda a household name while few Americans have even heard of nephritis and septicemia? Combined, the latter illnesses killed roughly twenty-seven times more Americans in 2006 than terrorism did during its bloodiest year in the history of the United States.[3] To make sense of these questions, in this chapter I link the psychology of terrorism to the science of communication and reveal how certain characteristics of media messages (*news frames*) capture our imaginations and fuel our concerns.

Framing Terrorism

In addition to the post-9/11 flood of public opinion research discussed in chapters 2, 3, and 4, several scholars converged on the mass media and examined its effects on people's perceptions of terrorism.[4] Many of them speculated that heavy media coverage of the threat was to blame for our sustained worries about the danger, and yet little research has directly investigated the particular aspects of the news that may be responsible for these concerns. Moreover, most studies on this topic have conceptualized the threat of terrorism as a one-dimensional hazard—that is, a threat to which people consistently attach the same or similar meanings. As a result, we know much about the public's reactions to "*the* terrorist threat," or how "*the* war on terror" became the dominant frame used by politicians and journalists to discuss international security issues.

A careful examination of the media, however, shows that news coverage of terrorism consists of multiple storylines or ways of describing terrorism, including stories about the vulnerability of the nation's critical infrastructure (airports, seaports, the postal system, the food and water supply), the potential delivery systems of an attack (biological, chemical, nuclear, conventional), the possible strategies of the terrorists (urban versus rural targets), their political or religious motives and backgrounds (international radical Islam versus home-grown extremism), and whether certain acts of violence should be labeled "terrorism," "crime," "acts of war," or a "struggle for freedom."[5] We should care about these various portrayals of terrorism because some of them may be more potent than others. As shown in this chapter, some stories about the threat are relatively easy to ignore, while others seize our attention and generate support for new legislation. Put differently, in any given news story, the ideas and images of terrorism can be mixed like a cocktail that has greater or lesser effect on its consumer depending on its ingredients.

The Concept of News Frames

Some communication scholars refer to the different aspects of news stories as "frames," and to the choices made by writers, journalists, and commentators as "framing."[6] The framing of news is akin to the framing of a photograph or a painting. Just as an artist decides (consciously and unconsciously) what to include in a painting and how to include it, newsmakers are responsible for sculpting each word, phrase, and image that goes into a published or televised report.

The parallel between art and news is particularly useful when considering a situation in which two paintings (or stories) of the same subject produce different effects on audiences. Consider, for example, Leonardo da Vinci's "The Last Supper." In many ways, it was similar to the many depictions of the Last Supper that preceded it. Da Vinci's rendering, like theirs, followed the events chronicled in the Christian New Testament. One finds a dinner gathering of thirteen men in comfy robes sitting at a table flush with bread, wine, cups, assorted victuals (and, of course, Jesus breaking the bad news of betrayal). Although my eighth-grade art education has it limits, I feel comfortable suggesting that Leonardo's take on the Last Supper, while fundamentally similar to early works, diverged from its predecessors, and in so doing produced varying effects on audiences for centuries to come. For one thing, Leonardo was the first to give his heavenly subjects human expressions, identifiable gestures, looks of dismay and trepidation. Those with a penchant for biblical conspiracy theories might also suggest, among other things, that the distinctly feminine appearance of the apostle seated at the right hand of Jesus was Leonardo's way of telling us that Mary Magdalene was present at the Last Supper.

Each identifiable characteristic of a painting or a news article may be thought of as a "frame."[7] And each frame, controlling for its interaction with other frames, may have varied effects. News frames take many forms and appear in a variety of media and communication outlets. Scholars have conceptualized them as short phrases such as "the Cold War," single words such as "communism," images such as a photo of a crumbling Berlin Wall, or particular patterns or styles in which words, phrases, and images appear in news content. The primary frames of interest in this chapter include the terms "terrorism," "radical Islam," and "nuclear," which were commonly found in print and electronic media in the decade following 9/11. Any conjecture about why these terms were used or what meanings people attached to them should be filed as theoretical assertions.

Theories of Framing

In an effort to reveal why certain frames are important, scholars from a range of fields have examined the social construction of reality and the interpretive process through which the framing of various objects, people, and events becomes subjectively meaningful to audiences.[8] In the context of media studies and political communication, theories of framing attempt to explain either the conditions under which frames appear in media content, or the effects of these frames on a range of social outcomes, from changes in individual attitudes, beliefs, and behaviors to the formation and maintenance of social movements.[9]

Interest in the former objective—explaining the conditions under which frames appear in media content—has spawned investigations across the social sciences. In this line of research, for instance, one might begin by assuming that the framing of political legislation influences public attitudes toward it. Without testing the assumption, the researcher focuses instead on the conditions under which a given frame is used in the mass media or other sources of political communication. Such a study might find that Republicans are more likely to use the phrase "death tax" to describe the federal tax on assets of the deceased, while the Democrats prefer the phrase "estate tax."[10]

In the case of terrorism, sociologists, political scientists, and communication researchers have examined how frames are constructed and reinforced, and how coverage of this topic depends on the social, political, cultural, and organizational context of news production.[11] This body of research shows that the characteristics and availability of terrorism frames are shaped by an ongoing contest over meaning that engages a number of powerful actors in society. Similar battlegrounds have shaped the framing of a variety of controversial issues, from the abortion debate[12] to the French "riots" of 2005.[13]

While this line of research provides an essential piece of the framing-effects puzzle, it does not explain how news frames actually affect the attitudes, beliefs, and behaviors of individuals. Drawing mostly on the cognitive perspective, much of the empirical evidence for such effects comes from experimental studies that control for other factors and offer precise measurements of influence.[14] A classic study by Kahneman and Tversky, for instance, found that people's preferences for or against undergoing a medical procedure depended on how the potential outcomes were presented to them.[15] The subjects were more willing to consider a hypothetical surgery when told that "95 percent of patients live" as opposed to the statistically equivalent message, "5 percent of patients die." Using an experiment embedded in a large, representative survey, Hurwitz and Peffley found that the racially coded words "inner city" had an effect on people's attitudes toward funding prisons.[16] With their noted "rally experiment," Sniderman and Theriault demonstrated that slight variations in frames can even influence people's views when they hold strong attitudes in the opposite direction.[17] These studies suggest that the differences between two frames need not be extreme in order to elicit noticeable variations in people's perceptions of social problems.

One important critique of the framing literature suggests that audiences "tune out much, if not all, undesired content" and base their understanding of broad social issues not on the content of the news media, but on personal experiences in everyday life.[18] Rather than a fatal flaw, this point elucidates one of the conditions under which news frames may have more influence on public perceptions. As sociologist William Gamson and his colleagues suggested, a person's dependence on information from the media is "heavily influenced by the issue under discussion."[19] People's personal experiences probably do play the dominant role in the formation of some attitudes and emotions, especially those related to everyday life, such as unemployment, health care, and local political campaigns.

However, such experiences likely have less influence in the cases of remote, unfamiliar, or distant topics, such as foreign policy issues, international conflicts, and terrorism. Although many people were tragically exposed to the attacks on 9/11, the great majority of us experienced these events, and the subsequent public discussion of the terrorist threat, indirectly through the media. For this reason, the framing of the terrorist threat in the decade following 9/11 probably had an especially strong effect on public perceptions of the danger.

The Anatomy of a Scary News Frame

In order to investigate whether some news frames elevate public perceptions of terrorism more than others, I should also review and add a bit to our definition of "perceived threat." In the risk perception literature, perceived threat is commonly used as an umbrella term for three distinct, yet related, psychological responses to danger: dread, risk judgment, and worry.[20] The first two components fall in the category of cognitive responses. "Dread" refers to people's beliefs about the catastrophic potential of a terrorist attack, such as the number of deaths that would occur if a particular act of violence were carried out. "Risk judgments" are beliefs about the likelihood of an attack occurring over a specified period of time. The third component, "worry," refers to people's emotional reactions to the hazard.

In the context of a framing effects experiment, the separation of these three dimensions is necessary, because any given danger may evoke varying levels of each response. Someone might, for instance, believe that a nuclear terrorist strike would result in millions of deaths (high dread), but also believe that such an attack is very unlikely (low risk judgment) and therefore experience little fear of it (low worry). The three dimensions are also known to have differing effects on other social and political attitudes.[21]

The next task is to decide which frames to investigate, and hash out a theory that explains why these frames frighten us. As discussed, much has been written about the public discussion of terrorism; testing all the relevant frames, from food terrorism to cyber terrorism, would be impractical. In this chapter, the discussion will be limited to three frames that are particularly relevant to the ongoing debate and scholarly research on the relationship between terrorism, the media, politics, and society.

Terrorism Frame

The first frame I consider is the term "terrorism" itself. The use of this term in public discourse has generated a great deal of interest and contention among researchers, journalists, and politicians. Some regard it as a political tool, because the simple act of labeling a violent act as "terrorism" can prime people's concerns about the danger, shape their attributions of the behavior, as well as influence their assumptions about what should be done to stop it.[22] In the context of American media portrayals, the word "terrorism" may function as a peripheral cue that activates a schematic representation of a particular type of dangerous situation, as well as a correlated set of emotional and cognitive reactions to it.[23] By "schematic representation," I mean a preconceived set of ideas, which allow us to quickly (almost instantaneously, in fact) make sense of objects, people, events, and situations. The situation evoked by the terrorism frame is likely to differ from the schematic representations that are primed by alternative frames for violent acts, such as "crime," "insurgency," or "a struggle for freedom."

As a mental construct, the terrorism frame not only represents a qualitatively distinct form of danger, but one that has been repeatedly described in mass media as a *new* social problem.[24] According to risk perception research, a danger that is perceived as new may evoke greater levels of perceived threat than an old or familiar hazard, even when the new danger is statistically less likely to cause harm.[25] For instance, news portrayals of fatal car crashes may produce lower levels of risk judgment, dread, and worry than terrorism coverage, in part because the dangers of driving are perceived as more familiar and conventional, even though they are far more deadly (for instance, 42,116 Americans died in motor vehicle crashes in 2001, while fewer than 3,000 died in terrorist attacks).[26]

Radical Islamic Frame

Like "terrorism," the radical Islamic frame is thought to activate a schematic representation or stereotype, one associated with a religious category, in this case making that representation more likely to be used in a range of negative social perception judgments.[27] While the popular association between Islam and mass violence certainly predates 9/11, as seen in media coverage of events ranging from the Iranian hostage crisis in 1979–1981 to the bombing of the USS *Cole* in 2000, the link between these constructs became more prominent in people's minds as media coverage on this subject greatly increased after 9/11.[28] As discussed in chapter 4, in the years after 9/11 the belief that Islam encourages violence more than other religions was held by a large percentage of Americans.[29]

Interpreting the threat of terrorism using stereotypical notions of Islamic fundamentalist groups may lead some people to conclude that acts of "terrorism" have no logical basis, that the motives for such acts are irrational or otherworldly, that compromise is unattainable, and that the threat itself can therefore not be controlled.[30] As in the case of hazards perceived as new, threats perceived as hard to control evoke higher risk judgments.[31] Both new and uncontrolled hazards are also thought to engage people's emotions, which may affect the cognitive processing of these threats.[32]

The radical Islamic frame may be particularly influential because it goes beyond merely labeling acts of violence, as in the case of the terrorism frame. The frame has a "diagnostic" component—an explanation of why violent acts are carried out. In addition to identifying a social category (Islam), the frame suggests that terrorism is the product of an extreme motivation. Diagnostic frames are known to have greater influence on attitudes, beliefs, and behaviors than frames that merely name the problem.[33]

In testing the effects of the radical Islamic frame, rather than simply excluding any mention of it, as in the case of the terrorism frame, I opted for the more conservative procedure of comparing it with an alternative identity and motivation—namely, "American citizens who view their government as the enemy." While this comparison condition is also a diagnostic frame, the threat of "homegrown terrorists" has received far less attention in the media and may, therefore, be less familiar and accessible to the subjects in this study.

Nuclear Frame

The third frame I test draws on the straightforward assumption that people's reactions to the threat of terrorism depend in part on the perceived catastrophic potential of an attack.[34] As in the previous case, I compare a theoretically high-threat frame ("nuclear") with one that may be perceived as less innocuous ("conventional explosives"). It goes without saying that the nuclear frame will likely activate a mental representation that leads to higher levels of dread (beliefs about the number of deaths that would result from an attack) in comparison with the conventional explosives frame.

More intriguing is a related argument made by Cass Sunstein that the affective processes involved with imagining a nuclear catastrophe may produce "probability neglect" and thereby elevate people's perceptions of the likelihood of an attack occurring. Sunstein, an eminent legal scholar who has studied and written on all topics imaginable, became interested in why people often overestimate the chance of low-probability catastrophes, such as terrorism. When a danger evokes high levels of emotion in people, they tend to focus on the "badness of the outcome, rather than on the probability that the outcome will occur," which explains the common misjudgment of some very frightening, yet extremely low-risk, hazards.[35] It would seem, if the idea holds, that public perceptions of terrorism would rise not in accordance with the probability of an attack, but with the shivers up one's spine from the thought of it. While the experiment described here does not attempt to strictly test Sunstein's probability-neglect hypothesis, it may produce evidence that is at least suggestive of his claim.

The Experiment

In order to demonstrate whether news articles containing the frames *terrorism, radical Islamic,* and *nuclear* evoked higher levels of perceived threat (risk judgment, dread, worry) than articles without these terms, I conducted an experimental framing-effects study.[36] A composite article was created by combining two real stories from the Associated Press. The article offered details about a federal commission's report on security threats to American cities. Eight different versions of the article were composed in order to test the effects of each frame. Treatment 1 was thought to be least threatening, because it contained no high-threat frames (the term *terrorism* was never used, the sources referred to the threat of "explosives," as opposed to "nuclear weapons," and the most likely perpetrators were referred to as "homegrown militants," as opposed to "radical Islamic groups"). Treatments 2, 3, and 4 each contained one of the high-threat frames. Treatments 5, 6, and 7 contained two of these frames, and treatment 8 included all three of them.

The Subjects

A total of 176 subjects were recruited from a large Midwestern university to take part in the experiment. The subjects were similar to the general population in terms of race and gender, although the great majority was aged eighteen to twenty-two. Before reading the article, the subjects were asked two pretest risk judgment questions aimed at measuring their general beliefs about the likelihood of a terrorist attack occurring in the next twelve months. The subjects were then asked to read the article and answer a series of additional questions designed to measure dread, risk judgment, and worry, as well as their attitudes toward the Iraq War and the idea of trading civil liberties for security.

The Findings

The findings of the experiment supported the general assumption that our perceptions of the terrorist threat depend in part on how it is framed in newspapers and other forms of communication. While all of the treatments produced a significant increase in concern among the subjects, some of the frames therein produced more perceived threat than others. Starting with the terrorism frame, the data indicated that manipulating this term had no effect on worry, risk judgment, or dread. It appears that merely labeling acts of violence as "terrorism" does not elevate threat perceptions more than describing them without using the term. It is possible that any article about violent, organized groups will be contextualized by audiences as "terrorism," whether the term is used copiously or not at all. Future research should investigate the possible relationship between the context of stories about the threat of mass violence and the use of the terrorism frame. The frame may, for instance, have an effect when applied to a more ambiguous news item, such as a story about the danger of school shootings or the aggressive protest activities of radical environmental groups.

As expected, subjects who received the nuclear frame estimated the number of potential casualties (dread) as significantly higher than those who received the conventional explosives frame. The nuclear frame did not, however, have a significant main effect on risk judgment or worry. While the subjects' reactions to this frame contradicted expectations, the lack of any influence at all on risk judgment justifies a pause for reflection. The results showed that the subjects judged the likelihood of a nuclear strike against the United States as roughly equivalent to that of an attack utilizing conventional explosives. Given the far greater availability of the latter, not to mention the vast technological and material resources required for building a nuclear device, it would seem that the subjects neglected a logical way of establishing the risk of such attacks. While this study cannot speak directly to Sunstein's probability-neglect hypothesis, the subjects did seem to exhibit difficulty in assessing the emotionally engaging yet low-probability risk of a nuclear terrorist attack.[37]

The data demonstrated that the radical Islamic frame produced a significant effect on all three indicators of perceived threat. The subjects who read about potential attacks carried out by groups "motivated by Islamic extremism," as opposed to "American citizens who view their own government as the enemy," reported higher risk judgment, dread, and worry. As previously discussed, one explanation of the strong influence of this frame, as compared with the others, lies in its "diagnostic" component.[38] Whereas the nuclear and terrorism frames may have been perceived merely as labels, the radical Islamic frame was likely understood as an explanation of why violent acts are carried out. By focusing the subjects' attention on a mechanism that supposedly causes terrorism, the subjects perceived the violence as more likely to occur (risk judgment) and cause greater casualties (dread). It also led them to report higher levels of worry.

In addition to showing how framing can elevate perceived threat, the experiment also demonstrated how these heightened fears can produce greater support for two aspects of the war on terrorism (the use of military force and the Patriot Act). Worry was a significant predictor of these key social attitudes, even when controlling for the effects of the subjects' sex, race, political ideology, and age. Subjects who reported greater worries about terrorism were more willing to trade some civil liberties for added protection. The effect of worry was greater than that of political ideology, which is a known predictor of people's willingness to make the civil-liberties-for-security trade-off.[39] In the case of support for war, worry was still a significant predictor, but political ideology played a greater role in explaining these attitudes. Sex was also a significant variable in this model. Women showed less support for the Iraq War than men, confirming previous studies.[40]

Real-World Implications

Exploring the issue of why research findings are important to people's everyday lives, though often treated as an afterthought by social scientists, is an essential part of any empirical investigation.

The Anti-Islamic Stereotype

The findings of the experiment have a number of implications. The study suggests that in the decade following 9/11 many Americans relied on an anti-Islamic stereotype to understand the issue of terrorism. The word "Islam" seemed to activate a negative mental representation of a religious group that elevated people's fears more so than other ideological or motivational frames. Some critics may suggest that this finding is unremarkable, that neither our worries about Muslim terrorists nor the news media's obsession with them are unfounded, that fearing al Qaeda rather than homegrown villains simply reflects reality, and that the stereotype is, essentially, true and therefore a study that verifies its use is of no particular interest. Such an argument is problematic for at least two reasons.

First, the anti-Islamic stereotype may have encouraged faulty terrorism-risk assessments and distracted the public, news media, politicians, and law-enforcement officials from other potential sources of mass violence. The widely held assumption that multivictim murders are more likely to be committed by people from the Middle East with radical Islamic beliefs than by people with other extreme ideas is particularly dubious in light of the many heinous attacks carried out both before and after 9/11 by non–Muslim American citizens.

While writing this book, I talked to numerous friends, colleagues, and students about their perceptions of terrorism. On several occasions I asked entire classrooms of students to "name a terrorist." Osama bin Laden almost invariably received first mention. When prompted, most students also showed some familiarity with Ayman al-Zawahiri, Khalid Sheikh Mohammed, Ramzi Yousef, Mohamed Atta, "Shoe Bomber" Richard Reid, and the "Underwear Bomber," Umar Farouk Abdulmutallab. Next, I would inquire about whether these people belonged to the same group or social category. Without hesitation, almost everyone linked them to radical Islamic terrorism. Finally, I would ask the students whether they knew the names Bruce Ivins or Joe Stack. What about Jared Loughner, Kevin Harpham, Scott Roeder, Eric Rudolph, or George

Metesky? How about groups such as the Hutaree Christian sect? The over-whelming majority of my casual respondents was completely unfamiliar with these names or could not connect them to historical events.

In spite of their obscurity, all of these individuals and groups carried out noteworthy terrorist attacks, and none of them was motivated by radical Islam. According to the FBI and other prominent sources, microbiologist Bruce Ivins committed the 2001 anthrax attacks.[41] A computer software consultant, Joe Stack, executed a suicide strike in February 2010 when he slammed an airplane into an IRS building in Texas. In January 2011, Kevin Harpham, a white supremacist, allegedly planted a backpack bomb, which was classified by authorities as a "weapon of mass destruction," along a Martin Luther King Jr. parade route in Spokane, Washington.[42] Factory worker Scott Roeder shot and killed physician George Tiller in May 2009, becoming the latest among several antiabortion activists who have used deadly violence to spread fear in abortion clinics.[43] Moving back in history a bit, Eric Rudolph set off a bomb in Centennial Park at the 1996 Olympics in Atlanta, killing one person and injur-ing more than a hundred others (he was also behind three other bombings).[44] George Metesky terrorized New York City for sixteen years in the 1940s and 1950s, planting thirty bombs, nearly half of which exploded, in theaters, train terminals, libraries, the police station, and phone booths throughout the city.[45] In March 2010, members of the Hutaree Christian sect in Michigan were ar-rested on charges that they conspired to kill police officers and then bomb their funerals.[46]

Aside from being "terrorists," all of these individuals belong to the same social category. The connection between them, however, is almost always ne-glected. In fact, to my best knowledge, no scholar or commentator has ever linked these people to the same group—white males. On the contrary, had they all been Muslims, the link would have been obvious. Had they all been women, the news media would have surely introduced gender as a framework for un-derstanding these acts. Had they all been African Americans, immigrants, athe-ists, or communists, the categorization of these individuals would have been irresistible and for many Americans beyond reproach.

But the fact is, they were all white men, and white men in the United States suffer from few negative stereotypes. Whiteness and gender rarely play roles in media representations of boys behaving badly. The misdeeds of white men can certainly be found in the news, but most receivers of these messages do not have well-formed cognitive frameworks with which to broadly categorize these people in a negative light. For this reason, when white guys commit terrorist acts, the events are less memorable, and the categories of race, ethnicity, and ideology rarely materialize. Put differently, stereotypes not only falsely shape how we see the world, but also how we *don't* see it. If it seems absurd to suggest that law-enforcement officials should subject white men to racial profiling, or that politicians should hold public hearings on the radicalization of white males, it is equally ridiculous to demonize one of the most popular religions in the world and publicize the threat of terrorism using religious, ethnic, or national categories.

A second and more immediate reason to be concerned about the anti-Islamic stereotype involves the safety and well-being of Muslims and Arabs living in the United States. As previously discussed, some non-Muslims have committed acts of violence and intimidation against these minority groups,[47] while many others have openly admitted to having negative attitudes toward them.[48] The experiment confirmed the concerns of scholars, activists, and law-enforcement officials who have stressed the need for a concerted public effort to promote religious tolerance and protect ethnic minorities. It showed, alarmingly, that an inaccurate, negative stereotype linking Islam to large-scale violence was being used by a group of subjects (college students with liberal arts backgrounds) who were generally known for being more open-minded and tolerant toward minorities than the general population.

Selling War and Aggressive Law Enforcement

One of the main goals of this book is to show how public officials, if so inclined, can use the mass media to propagate the fear of terrorism, and thereby generate support for their policies and positions. Chapters 2, 3, and 4 demonstrated how the perceived threat of terrorism was *correlated* with a number of other important attitudes and behaviors (pro-social tendencies, rally effects, and authoritarian tendencies), but did not make a case for *causation*. Because of the nature of controlled experiments, the findings revealed in this chapter begin to make such a case. The experiment showed that the subjects' fears could be manipulated by merely including or excluding certain words and phrases, and that fear itself shaped the way they assessed the war on terrorism.

The data corresponding to the nuclear frame is particularly relevant to the political discourse on the Iraq War. Within a year of 9/11, the Bush administration began justifying its call for a preemptive strike against Iraq by regularly linking radical Islamic terrorism to both the Iraqi government and its possession of weapons of mass destruction.[49] A number of media scholars showed how the "triple threat" (the dictatorship of Saddam Hussein, his links to al Qaeda, and access to nuclear and chemical weapons) became ingrained in news coverage in the year prior to the war.[50] (As it turned out, some news organizations would later criticize their own coverage and apologize for printing flawed intelligence and relying too heavily on questionable sources.)[51]

Given its supposed links to terrorist organizations, the potentially severe consequences of a "nuclear Iraq" were thought to elevate the threat perceptions of many Americans and thereby convince them that a preemptive military strike against Iraq was warranted. The experiment described above provided an empirical basis for this speculation and showed that manipulating the type of danger (nuclear versus conventional) and the motive behind it (radical Islam versus homegrown extremists) did indeed elevate the subjects' level of perceived threat, which in turn increased their support for war.

Fear as an (Effective) Affective Ideology

Because of the power of perceived threat in harnessing public opinion, it may be worthwhile to expand conventional thinking on this concept. More than a temporary response to an isolated danger, I suggest that the perceived threat of terrorism is similar, in some ways, to an ideology or belief system. Like an ideology, the perceived threat of terrorism has remained stable over time. As emphasized here and in the previous chapters, these concerns exhibited both "consistency" (correlations with other attitudes and beliefs) and "instrumentality" (behavioral effects)—two key aspects of ideologies according to a standard definition.[52] The perceived threat of terrorism, like an ideology, also has the potential to polarize the population. While many Americans were "very concerned" about the threat, many others were "not at all concerned," thereby creating a possible divergence between the two segments on a range of policy issues.

Pushing this argument further, the perceived threat of terrorism may have an even more powerful effect than conventional ideological dimensions such as the liberal-conservative spectrum. For one thing, as political scientist Philip Converse famously asserted, the development of complex ideological frameworks requires an understanding of complicated issues and, more important, a willingness to spend the time and effort that is necessary for attaining this knowledge.[53] An appreciation of the terrorist threat, in contrast, can be reached with far less cognitive exercise, and its logical connections to other social issues is, in most cases, straightforward. The terrorist threat may function as an easy-to-use, multifunctional tool for differentiating and evaluating domestic and international policies and political leaders. A sort of cotton-candy ideology, it is widely available to the public, affordable, attractive, stimulating, and often distributed in the context of entertainment, from Hollywood movies to sensationalized TV news programs.

Perceptions of imminent danger are rarely thought of as reassuring, but perhaps, in certain ways, they do give us comfort. Imagine, for a moment, that al Qaeda does not exist, that the Osama bin Laden you saw in those cave photos was actually a Muppet, that he was neither killed nor buried at sea, that the international terrorist network is nothing more than a handful of windbags on Facebook, that there is truly and utterly nothing for us to worry about. If this were even partially true, much of our current foreign and domestic policy framework would cease to make sense. If the risk of terrorism was widely questioned by the public, there would be nothing to justify the most important American policies of the twenty-first century. Without the perceived threat of terrorism, we would be adrift, a rudderless nation, a weightless object floating in political space.

Now imagine that thousands of rabid Islamic terrorists do indeed exist and that they will stop at nothing to kill us all. Aside from the fear it evokes (and because of it), such a perception mitigates, to some extent, our worldly concerns. It puts an end to our moral handwringing, apprehensive prognostications, cross-cultural research, and complicated foreign policy considerations. The fear of terrorism cuts through the confusion, answers those nagging questions about our past and future, about the morality of war, about the numerous changes in foreign and domestic policy, about our humanity. Fear makes the onerous task of sincere cognition unnecessary. Here perhaps is what made the perceived threat of terrorism so powerful in the years after 9/11. As the war on terrorism expanded and American society changed, the act of embracing the fear of terrorism was, in a way, convenient.

It is also worth noting that, unlike conventional ideological dimensions, the perceived threat of terrorism comprises both a cognitive and an emotional component. The idea that emotions play a role in people's judgments and decision making represents a relatively new trend in the social sciences. Researchers are now paying greater attention to the influence of emotions on the way people process and store information, evaluate their environments, and make decisions.[54] From this perspective, the threat of terrorism might be seen as an affective ideology that directs public thinking on a range of political and social problems. Such an organizing force would be shaped more by the intensity of our emotions than by new information, empirical justifications, expert assessments, or "central-route" processing. Emotional reactions to terrorism can be primed by news and images, political rhetoric, and any number of related cultural artifacts and social interactions. A heavy dose of these reminders may act like an emotional booster shot that not only reinforces the perceived threat of terrorism, but also its ideological links to other issues. Given the vast policy implications discussed in chapter 1, the role of fear in the development, integration, and maintenance of ideological formations is worthy of further research.

Conclusion

Terrorism is a multidimensional hazard that evokes a range of thoughts and feelings, depending upon which of its elements are made accessible in communicating texts. While the theoretical basis of this finding is not new, no other empirical study, to the best of my knowledge, has substantiated this perspective in the case of terrorism. The experiment showed that two frames in particular—*radical Islam* and *nuclear*—can elevate public perceptions of the terrorist threat, which, in turn, have a powerful influence on attitudes toward war and civil liberties. In the case of war, it was even more potent than the traditional liberal-conservative ideological framework. Though further research is needed, the perceived threat of terrorism seems to be functioning like a broad mental construct, an organizing force that helps us quickly make sense of the world.

These findings have limitations, of course. The first and most obvious issue involves the representativeness of the subjects—a concern that inevitably arises when student samples are used in research. In such cases, a strong argument for external validity can never be made, especially when it comes to explaining the psychology of terrorism in other countries or diverse social contexts. It goes without saying, for instance, that the radical Islamic frame would not have the same effect on students living in Cairo, Egypt, or even Toronto,

Canada. These findings can only be generalized to the wider student body at the university where the study was conducted or at best to the population of students at similar universities across the United States.

A more profound limitation of the study is its inability to explain the social conditions under which real media messages about terrorism are designed and circulated among the public. All experimental findings are only interesting if they are relevant to, if not precise approximations of, real life. The discovery that certain news frames scare us doesn't really matter unless people are actually coming into contact with such messages.

To make these findings meaningful, I'll need to move from the psychology of terrorism to the sociology of media, an analysis of American political culture and capitalism, a consideration of power relations in society, and the structure of media organizations. In pursuit of these aims, the remaining three chapters deemphasize the inner lives of individuals and focus instead on the national and international politics of fear.

6

THE FEAR FACTORY UNDER THREE PRESIDENTS

I'm afraid it's not going to end well. In fact, it may not end at all. Chances are we'll be fighting the war on terrorism, if by another name, for years to come. There are at least three reasons for making such a prediction. First, simply put, terrorism works. It has proven to be one of the most effective political tools of the twenty-first century. In an atomized society with hyper-individualism and endless distractions, collective deliberation is difficult to achieve. But when things explode, people pay attention. In fact, even when we merely talk about things exploding, people take notice. Annihilation has a way of bringing us together, placing us on the same ideological page, and focusing our attention on avoiding the impending harm. A common ground suddenly appears—a mutual jumping off point from which social mobilization becomes possible.

A second reason for the staying power of the war on terrorism can be found in its flexibility as an instrument of persuasion. While a great deal of journalistic and scholarly effort has revealed how the Bush administration wielded this tool after 9/11, its maneuvers represent only one chapter in a much longer story. The fear of terrorism has been used to generate support for a variety of policies and special interests. In the decade following 9/11, it played out in controversies stemming from numerous social issues, including torture, prisoner rights, civil liberties, and gun control; immigration reform, border security, and homeland security funding; the safety of our critical infrastructure and the use of nuclear energy; oil drilling in the Arctic National Wildlife Refuge and natural gas extraction across the United States; the taxing of cigarette companies; national defense spending, missile defense systems, and chemical, biological, and nuclear warfare; and numerous foreign policy concerns involving the Middle East, Central Asia, Mexico, Russia, China, and North Korea. At times, partisans evoked the same threat of terrorism to justify contradictory positions. For instance, during the 2004 presidential campaign, the Republicans promised us safety from terror so long as we stayed the course in Iraq, while the Democrats told us that we were actually less safe, because Iraq was a dangerous diversion from the real threat posed by al Qaeda in Afghanistan.

A third reason to expect terrorism to remain high on the nation's list of problems lies in its relevance to the history and dominant culture of American society. The "war on terrorism" discourse was certainly new in some respects, but it tapped into a preexisting cultural script—a way of seeing the world that formed over decades, not months or years. If there is one thing that left-leaning historians do not embellish, it is the extent to which the United States has been involved in active military conflicts. In fact, there is scarcely a moment of peace to be found in American history. Regardless of what originally caused these wars, they have promoted a set of ideas, outlooks, and behaviors that, in turn, increased the ease and likelihood of war in the future. For this reason, there was no need for the Bush administration to invent a new ideology on 9/11. The norms and values that cultivated support for aggressive foreign policies were already in place, and the news media willingly propagated the Bush administration's war on terrorism.

As a result, our country's swift and dramatic military response came as a surprise to precisely no one. Like the actors in a well-rehearsed play, Americans knew their lines ("evil," "freedom," "let's roll"), where to stand (*with us*), the lighting and set coordination (bombs abroad, fences at home), the musical arrangement ("U.S.A., U.S.A."), and the expected moods and emotional overtones of each scene (sorrow, innocence, resolve). It wasn't long before the theaters of war in Afghanistan and Iraq seemed normal, expected, and reasonable.

As President Obama took office in January 2009, a number of commentators believed that the script would be rewritten, that the politics of fear, as constructed by the previous administration, would be no more, that the incoming president would create a new paradigm for understanding the threat of terrorism and what to do about it. In this chapter, I investigate the cultural and social structural foundations of America's conflict with violent extremists in hopes of determining whether such a transformation actually took place.

The War on Terrorism as a Framing Nexus

While chapter 5 examined the effects of frames on perceptions of terrorism and attitudes toward the war in Iraq and the Patriot Act, this chapter explains the conditions under which certain frames are assembled and delivered in media content. To this end, I should begin by defining the concept of a *framing nexus*. A "nexus," as its general definition specifies, is a connection or link between objects. Cellular biologists define a nexus as the fusion of the plasma membranes of two or more adjacent cells.[1] Nexuses permit chemical or electrical communication to pass between cells, enabling the organization and operation of complex biological functions. In cardiac muscles, for instance, nexuses allow the muscles of the heart to contract in tandem. In a similar fashion, a framing nexus involves the fusion of two or more news frames in a given newspaper article, television show, or political speech.

The persuasive power of any news message lies partially in the logical, rhetorical fusions that join and organize news frames in communicative packages.[2] For instance, the news frame "terrorism" carries significance for many people on its own, but as demonstrated in chapter 5, a framing nexus connecting Islam to terrorism is far more powerful. Although I did not test these experimentally, the frames "threat level Orange," "weapons of mass destruction," "Saddam Hussein," and "Iraq" may also be joined to terrorism with a similar result. This particular framing nexus was circulated by the Bush administration not long after 9/11 as it began justifying its call for a preemptive military strike against Iraq.[3]

A framing nexus is similar to what Rhys Williams and others refer to as the "dominant symbolic repertoire."[4] They define this concept as the "enduring norms, beliefs, language, visual images, narrations, and collective identities circulating widely among the general public" and suggest that ruling elites are the source of these institutionally privileged ideas and the main benefactors of the political legitimacy they bestow.[5] Although I find their concept of a "repertoire" quite useful, I suggest that framing research requires a clear separation between its conceptual and theoretical components. A framing nexus is merely a co-occurrence of carefully identified words, phrases, or images that have been deemed worthy of analysis by researchers. Three related issues—to what extent framing nexuses exist in the mass media, why they exist as they do, and whether they influence human consciousness—represent a challenging set of empirical questions to which there may not be a straightforward set of an-swers. As addressed in the next sections, framing nexuses may indeed be used pervasively by ruling elites to curb dissent and legitimize their positions, but they also may be used by "frame challengers" to defy the dominant symbolic repertoire.[6]

Pluralism or Hegemony?

The objective of this chapter stems from a classic question in the social sci-ences, and one that has attracted a great deal of attention from scholars in the decade following 9/11. Do the American news media exercise their freedom to question and contest the dominant frames used by political and economic elites? The various answers to this question fall along a continuum. On one side, the *pluralist model* assumes that power is disseminated among diverse groups in a free society, and that a range of social actors, holding mutually ex-clusive goals, are allowed access to the media, resulting in a plurality of views in the various media outlets. Approaching the Jeffersonian ideal, the news me-dia represent a storehouse of diverse ideas, an instrument of enlightenment, and a tool for establishing government accountability.

On other side, advocates of the *media hegemony* thesis suggest that ruling elites use their disproportionate access to media outlets in order to gain consent from the public and reinforce the established social and political order.[7] Public support for elite positions is achieved in one of two ways: by excluding and delegitimizing dissenting voices, or through persuasion.[8] As an example of the first type of hegemony, Erika King and Mary deYoung showed how a noted university professor's negative critique of the Bush administration's "war on terror" was excluded from mainstream thinking and delegitimized through a systematic, mass-mediated process that derided the professor both as a person and a scholar.[9] In this case, power holders attempted to establish and perpetu-ate the dominant symbolic repertoire, whether persuasive in any particular way or not, through a one-sided public discourse—"more of a monologue than a dialogue," as Marc Steinberg put it.[10] Seen from this perspective, the media hegemony thesis suggests that the elite's control of media content functions like a sort of wall or gate that holds back challengers and punishes any dissent-ing voice that happens to slip through the cracks.

Consent can also be gained through enticement and persuasion, through a repertoire that is flexible, interchangeable, and alluring, through a set of framing nexuses that tap into preexisting cultural scripts and provoke strong, socially acceptable thoughts and emotions.[11] When a nation is attacked, the institutionalized norms for its citizens are to express pride in one's country, while displaying outrage against the enemy. As suggested by Maney, Woehrle, and Coy, ruling elites can utilize these "emotional opportunities" as they create and disseminate certain frames that justify their status, authority, and social position.[12] In the case of the war on terrorism, one rather powerful emotional opportunity was fear or perceived threat.[13] As demonstrated in chapter 5, the terrorist threat was a potent cognitive and emotional cue that encouraged compliance with President Bush's foreign and domestic policy prescriptions.

With the goal of bridging the sociological and psychological literatures, a fully theorized media hegemony thesis should draw on theories involving the power of ruling elites to exclude and delegitimize dissenting voices,[14] as well as on the social-psychological research discussed in previous chapters, which sheds light on the psychological mechanisms through which persuasive characteristics of news content are surmised to operate. Public perceptions of the terrorist threat, when elevated by the consumption of frightening terrorism news frames, may indeed generate public support for a range of public policies associated with homeland security, civil liberties, immigration, the treatment of Arab and Muslim Americans, harsh antiterrorism tactics, and military actions in foreign lands. The persistent deployment of high-threat frames may also reinforce an ideological platform for understanding the source of the threat (radical Islamic ideology), the origin of the adversary or out-group (the Middle East), and the overall character of the conflict (a *war* against terrorism). The strengthening of this platform, in turn, would perpetuate the status quo and help elites stay in power.

As a final clarification of the media hegemony thesis, it is important to note that news frames cannot affect audiences unless they are made available to the public. Although this point may seem self-evident, most media hegemony studies have focused on clarifying the dominant symbolic repertoire with qualitative forms of discourse analysis that do not attend to the quantitative issues of salience and availability. This chapter attempts to articulate both the qualities of the dominant repertoire and the extent to which it can be found in the opinion-leading press over the course of three presidential administrations (of Bill Clinton, George W. Bush, and Barack Obama).

Five Dimensions of Threat

In chapter 5, I identified some of the news frames that elevate people's worries and produce support for the dominant symbolic repertoire. The job now is to determine the conditions under which these frightening frames appear in media. To this end, drawing in part on the experimental findings, I have classified the range of potentially frightening frames and aspects of media content into five dimensions: *dynamics, magnitude, dread, salience,* and *balance.*

News frames from the first dimension—dynamics—take many forms but share a common emphasis on the elevated nature of the danger. Inspired by a range of events, the threat of terrorism is often framed as being "new," "elevated," "increased," or suddenly worthy of a public "warning." As mentioned, a danger that is perceived as new may evoke greater levels of perceived threat than an old or familiar hazard, even when the new one is statistically less likely to cause harm.[15]

A similar dimension is magnitude. Without giving statistical estimates, voices in the press commonly describe the terrorist threat as being "high," "serious," "major," "frightening," "potentially devastating," or something of great concern. My interest in accounting for frames of this sort is straightforward. These modifiers represent the most widespread communicative technique for making sense of the risk.

The third dimension—dread—comprises frames that describe particularly dire or uncontrollable scenarios. As shown in the previous chapter, hazards that could harm many people, cause catastrophic or gruesome damage, or have lasting effects on society or the environment are known to inflate risk perceptions.[16] This category includes news frames invoking high-impact weaponry such as "nuclear" and "chemical" weapons, "biological" agents, or "weapons of mass destruction."

The fourth dimension accounts for the salience of terrorism as a news topic. The salience or "availability" of a threat, whether a terrorist strike or a shark attack, is known to increase public perceptions of its likelihood of materializing.[17] When people lack information about a given danger, they assess its likelihood of causing harm in part by whether an example of the danger comes easily to mind.[18] In this way, news organizations that publish numerous articles about terrorism may increase public threat perceptions not only by describing the danger as something "new," "serious," or "nuclear," but also by repeatedly invoking the news frame "terrorism" itself. The salience dimension may be conceptualized as the number of published articles over a given time period that contain at least one reference to terrorism, or as the number of references to terrorism in a single article.

Balance, the fifth dimension and one of the basic precepts of "good journalism," refers to the practice of covering "both sides" of important social issues.[19] There are at least two reasons to assume that balanced framing of the terrorist threat would diminish people's concerns. First, balanced accounts, by definition, directly scrutinize some aspect of the risk itself. A message containing counterframes or contrasting information about terrorism would likely decrease the target's perceived susceptibility. This assumption is consistent with the literature on appeals to fear, or "fear appeals." A study by Kim Witte and Mike Allen, for instance, demonstrated that strong fear appeals (unbalanced messages) produced higher levels of perceived susceptibility than low or weak fear appeals (balanced messages).[20] Second, research also shows that people desire a sense of control over their lives when facing potential danger.[21] A balanced account—that is, a message that supplies a rationale for questioning the threat of terrorism—may help people rationalize their low levels of perceived susceptibility and their high levels of perceived control. An unbalanced portrayal, on the other hand, would likely increase public perceptions of the danger.

Together, the five dimensions—dynamics, magnitude, dread, salience, and balance—represent a useful new tool for studying mass-mediated accounts of the terrorist threat. The framework serves as a guide for evaluating the level of perceived threat that is likely to be stimulated in the audiences of any type of written news items, speech, or text. As a concrete example of how these frames have been used in political communication, consider Vice President Dick Cheney's description of the terrorist threat during a 2004 town hall meeting at a Cabela's sporting goods store in Minnesota:

> Remember those 20,000 terrorists who went through those training camps in Afghanistan, in the late '90s, they then set up cells in about 60 different countries around the world, including here in the U.S. They're doing everything they can to find ways to strike us. And they are actively seeking, trying to get their hands on deadlier weapons than anything they've ever used before—specifically chemical, biological agent, or even a nuclear

weapon, if they can. And you can imagine what would happen if we had an al Qaeda cell loose in the middle of one of our own cities with a nuclear weapon. The devastation that that would bring down on hundreds of thousands, maybe millions of Americans, obviously is something that you don't want to think about.[22]

Mr. Cheney's depiction of "terrorists" "actively seeking" "nuclear weapons" to produce "devastation" evokes the dimensions of salience, dynamics, dread, and magnitude, respectively. The speech also contained no counter-frames or critical thinking about the danger, which applies to the fifth dimension, *no* balance.

Predictors of High-Threat Framing

Now that I have described some of the framing devices that are likely to elevate concerns about terrorism, the next task is to consider the factors that might predict the use of these frames in the opinion-leading press.

Government Sources

Although terrorism was an important issue before the attacks, after 9/11 it became one of the most salient topics in the world. As suggested by Marta Lagos, an international public opinion expert, everyone, regardless of where they lived or what language they spoke, had an opinion about 9/11.[23] A wide range of journalists, politicians, religious leaders, experts, and ordinary people declared their positions, exchanged views, interacted, shared this moment, and thereby gave meaning to 9/11 and the ensuing developments. The "war on terrorism" discourse was constructed by counterterrorism experts discussing the operational capacities of al Qaeda on CNN, by scholars riffing international relations on *Charlie Rose,* by evangelical pastors spouting invectives on *60 Minutes,* by politicians on stage, by letter writers in local newspapers, by lawyers in courtrooms, by teachers in class, by mothers and fathers and friends.

Almost all Americans, in one way or another, participated in the creation, diffusion, and critique of the war on terrorism. However, an important question remains as to whether ruling elites shaped and controlled this conversation. To what extent did the dominant symbolic repertoire serve as a guideline for the collective understanding of these events? Drawing on the pluralist model of the press, one might answer "not much," and predict instead that the discourse on terrorism consisted of numerous dissenting voices and a range of opinions on the nature of the threat and the appropriate response. Theorizing from the media hegemony standpoint, however, one would suggest that government officials used their disproportionate access to the media to dominate the discussion, propagate concerns about terrorism, and thereby justify their aggressive policies and viewpoints.

In a systematic analysis of the mainstream press, I will begin addressing these divergent assumptions by answering two key questions. First, in articles about terrorism, were journalists more likely to cite government officials than any other sources of information? And second, did newspaper articles that relied predominately on government sources contain more high-threat terrorism frames than articles in which nongovernment sources prevailed? While previous studies have shown that journalists follow an organizational routine that leads to the heavy use of government sources on national security stories,[24] there has been little investigation into whether government officials systematically offer more frightening terrorism framing than nongovernment sources.

Calls for War and the USA PATRIOT Act

As discussed in chapter 5, two of the key elements of the war on terrorism involved the use of military force and the adoption of security measures that diminished civil liberties.[25] If, as suggested by the media hegemony thesis, ruling elites justified and pushed for these policies by injecting fear into the public discourse, my analysis of the press should also reveal a notable co-occurrence in articles (a framing nexus) between high-threat terrorism frames and arguments in favor of military campaigns and the USA PATRIOT Act. Given the prominence of these topics in other parts of the book, I will save further comments for the conclusion of this chapter.

Islam

Where did Muslims fit in the terrorism discourse? Judging from President Bush's most famous statements on the subject, one might expect to find a wave of religious tolerance in post-9/11 political culture. Not long after the attacks, the president declared that Islam was "a religion of peace," clearly differentiating Muslims from the "evil" terrorists, and he regularly rejected the idea that the "war on terror" was against Arabs or Muslims. During a visit to the Islamic

Center of Washington, D.C., on September 17, 2001, President Bush said that Muslims all across the world had been just as outraged by the attacks as non-Muslims, that "acts of violence against innocents violate the fundamental tenets of the Islamic faith," that Islam brings "comfort and solace and peace" to billions of people, and that anyone who harasses, intimidates, or harms Muslims represents "the worst of humankind, and should be ashamed of that kind of behavior."[26]

Although these genuinely supportive statements should not be ignored, other aspects of the war on terrorism discourse contradicted them. In his address to a joint session of Congress on September 20, 2001, President Bush stated that the terrorists practiced "a fringe form of Islamic extremism," and linked them to a broader network of terrorist organizations, including "Egyptian Islamic Jihad and the Islamic Movement of Uzbekistan."[27] As time went on, the emphasis on Islam, though never evoked without a reference to extremism, became a consistent theme in President Bush's public statements. Meanwhile, other members of the Bush administration were far less sensitive to the image of Muslims. Vice President Dick Cheney and Secretary of Defense Donald Rumsfeld showed no restraint in associating radical Islam with the most frightening acts of violence imaginable. During an interview with syndicated columnist Cal Thomas, John Ashcroft, U.S. Attorney General under Bush, was quoted as saying, "Islam is a religion in which God requires you to send your son to die for him. Christianity is a faith in which God sends his son to die for you."[28]

The views of other elites associated with the president were no less controversial. As one example, in August 2003, President Bush appointed Middle East scholar Daniel Pipes to the board of directors of the U.S. Institute of Peace, a government-funded think tank that had seventy staff and fifteen board members.[29] The appointment of Pipes—pushed through while Congress was out of session—upset Muslim organizations and other groups that regarded his views as anti-Muslim. A report by the American-Arab Anti-Discrimination Committee stated that "Daniel Pipes had made a career out of attacking the Arab-American and Muslim communities."[30] His commentary, which increased in popularity after 9/11, often demonstrated a common anti-Muslim script—an argument that generally warns against blaming Muslims for 9/11 while at once positing the most ridiculous, anti-Islamic generalizations:

The Muslim population is not like any other, for it harbors a substantial body—one many times larger than the agents of Osama bin Laden—who have worrisome aspirations for the United States. Although not responsible for the atrocities in September, these people share important goals with the suicide hijackers: Both despise the United States and ultimately wish to transform it into a Muslim country.[31]

Anti-Muslim sentiment flourished across American politics, culture, and media in the first post-9/11 decade.[32] A number of elites trumpeted their religious bias in highly publicized actions and statements. Some leaders associated Muslims with the villains of 9/11 in the summer of 2010 as a controversy arose over the proposed construction of an Islamic center two blocks away from Ground Zero in New York City. Prominent Republicans and even some Democrats objected to the new building, politicized the issue, and pushed it into the media spotlight. Newt Gingrich, a former Speaker of the House and a 2012 presidential candidate, put it this way: "Nazis don't have the right to put up a sign next to the Holocaust Museum in Washington. We would never accept the Japanese putting up a site next to Pearl Harbor. There's no reason for us to accept a mosque next to the World Trade Center."[33]

In March 2011, Representative Peter King, the Republican chairman of the House Committee on Homeland Security, began a series of congressional hearings on Islamic radicalism in the United States. In justifying the hearings, he told the Associated Press, "There is a real threat to the country from the Muslim community, and the only way to get to the bottom of it is to investigate what is happening."[34] An unapologetic Mr. King went on to make several statements attesting to the seriousness of the radicalization problem, linking it to al Qaeda, and suggesting, against evidence to the contrary, that the Muslim community has not cooperated with law-enforcement officials in terrorism investigations. Roughly ten years out from 9/11, King's provocative claims and the institutionalized religious bias of the congressional hearings he led demonstrated how the "war on terrorism" discourse created and sustained fear and bigotry in mainstream politics.

Hostility toward Muslims took many forms as media commentators discussed the hearings and other related cases, such as the Florida pastor who burned a Koran in 2011. On the Fox News channel, Bill O'Reilly made a thinly veiled comparison between the Koran and Hitler's *Mein Kampf*.[35] As reported on CNN, Tom Tancredo, a 2008 presidential hopeful and Republican congressman from Colorado, suggested that the best way to deter terrorism was to threaten to bomb Mecca and other Muslim holy sites.[36]

Washington Post columnist Richard Cohen chided the politically correct news media and suggested that refusing to link terrorism to Islam and Arabs was idiotic: "We have become driveling idiots on matters of race and ethnicity," he wrote. "One hundred percent of the terrorists involved in the Sept. 11 mass murder were Arabs. Their accomplices, if any, were probably Arabs, too—at least Muslims. Ethnicity and religion are the very basis of their movement." To ignore these facts, he asserted, was simply ridiculous. Martin Peretz, the editor of the *New Republic,* criticized Muslims for not raising their voices against the murder and violence in Islamic lands. "Frankly," he wrote, "Muslim life is cheap, most notably to Muslims." Peretz also noted the potential danger posed by radicalized Muslim Americans and argued that Muslims do not deserve the same constitutional privileges as other citizens: "So, yes, I wonder whether I need honor these people and pretend that they are worthy of the privileges of the First Amendment which I have in my gut the sense that they will abuse."[37]

Although these high-profile examples reveal some of the qualities of the anti-Islamic discourse, the study described below will systematically measure the extent to which these ideas were available across the mainstream press. In particular, I will address two questions: How often is Islam identified as the motivation behind terrorism? Are high-threat terrorism frames more common in articles containing the Islamic frame than in articles that do not contain this frame?

Three Periods, Three Presidents

My final set of assumptions involves the historical consistency of the relationships discussed above. The aim is to consider whether the discourse on terrorism changed during the administrations of Clinton, Bush, and Obama. Did government sources consistently dominate the public conversation of terrorism in all three periods? How long have the nexuses between high-threat terrorism framing and calls for military action and aggressive law enforcement been around? Did the nexus between Islam and terrorism exist in the mainstream press before, during, and after the Bush administration?

Although many commentators have suggested that the Bush administration transformed the discourse on terrorism, there has been little empirical investigation into the validity of these claims. Moreover, there are reasons to suggest the opposite is true. All three administrations framed the violent acts of extremists as "terrorism." Each of them utilized military force in response to it, including the Clinton administration's 1998 cruise-missile strikes on supposed sources of international terrorism in Sudan and Afghanistan, the Bush administration's lengthy war on terrorism, and the Obama administration's increase in troop strength in Afghanistan and its continued counterterrorist activities in Pakistan. Based on official White House statements, there are grounds to suppose that all three presidents launched these efforts from a similar ideological platform, one that evoked Islam, catastrophic threats to national security, and calls for a military response.

Drawing on the media hegemony thesis, it seems plausible that the dominant symbolic repertoire was as stable as the enduring structural and cultural foundations that supported it. While the nexus between high-threat terrorism frames and calls for war had special resonance in the immediate aftermath of 9/11, it rested on a cultural framework that has been propagated by ruling elites and used by citizens throughout much of American history. Many elements of the terrorism discourse is indeed reminiscent of the Cold War, a story that also brought together high-threat frames (nuclear war), frames denoting the origin and idealistic motives of the enemies (communism), and a host of policy prescriptions (upward-spiraling defense budgets and military incursions). Similar to the Cold War narrative, the current framing nexus connected with the traditional belief that the state is responsible for protecting its citizens and citizens are obliged to support the state in times of war.

However, before moving forward with the *stable hegemony* thesis, the possible differences between news coverage in the Bush and Obama eras deserve a special note. As mentioned in chapter 1, many of President Obama's actions during his first years in office signaled a break with the Bush administration.[38] He openly declared that the fear of terrorism would no longer be used as a locus for controlling government policies, offered a more nuanced set of conjectures about Islamic extremism, refused to fully adopt the phrase "war on terror," regularly professed his support for protecting civil liberties, and advocated a more transparent and thoughtful discussion on the problem of terrorism and other terrorism-related issues. In summer 2010, Obama declared an end to the combat mission in Iraq and drew down troop strength to 49,700.[39] He also reduced overall spending on national defense and agreed to withdraw U.S. troops from Afghanistan and turn over full responsibility for the security mission to Afghan forces by the end of 2014.[40]

But then, not all of the administration's signals pointed to a new presidential stance on terrorism. A number of Bush-era policies, such as the surveillance program, the Patriot Act, and the use of military force, remained intact during Obama's first years in office.[41] Several experts called attention to the continuity between the Bush and Obama administrations' responses to the problem. Michael Hayden, the last CIA director under Bush, suggested, "There is a continuum from the Bush administration, particularly as it changed in the second administration as circumstances changed, and the Obama administration."[42] Editorials in the *New York Times* also pointed to similarities between the two administrations, suggesting that, like its predecessor, the Obama administration's counterterrorism strategy sometimes transgressed international law and abused the congressional mandate to go after only those groups that carried out 9/11.[43]

Even the way President Obama talked about terrorism did not always stray from the language of his predecessor. As an example, consider his statements during a 2008 presidential campaign rally in Iowa. Declaring what seemed like a new position on terrorism and a decisive break from the Bush administration, Obama said, "We have been operating under a politics of fear: fear of terrorists, fear of immigrants, fear of people of different religious beliefs, fears of gays that they might get married and that somehow that would affect us. We have to break that fever of fear." Within nearly the same breath, however, Obama continued his thought in this way:

> It's absolutely true there are 30,000, 40,000 hard-core jihadists who would be happy to strap on a bomb right now, walk in here and blow us all up. You can't negotiate with those folks. All we can do is capture them, kill them, imprison them. And that is one of my pre-eminent jobs as president of the United States. Keep nuclear weapons out of their hands.[44]

The fact that a candidate whose slogan was "Got Hope?" still ended up evoking such frightening images of death and destruction illustrates the difficulty

of straying from the dominant symbolic repertoire. Given these conflicting accounts, the comparison between the Bush and Obama periods may provide
especially interesting insight on the media hegemony thesis. The empirical
results will show whether the dominant framework—as it pertains to terrorism, national security, war, Islam, and civil liberties—is a stable ideological
formation that reflects the spirit of the media hegemony thesis, or one that is
ephemeral, pluralistic, and responsive to changes in the presidency.

The Study and its Findings

The aim of this study is to investigate the questions and assumptions outlined
above by analyzing a large sample of published materials that represent elite
political culture in the United States.[45] Drawing on previous studies, I chose the
New York Times and *Washington Post* as acceptable proxies of the "elite" or
"opinion-leading" press.[46] These newspapers are known for playing key roles
in national decision making.[47] Studies have also shown that these outlets are
ideologically left-of-center, which makes them more likely to question the status quo and refute the dominant symbolic repertoire.[48] In effect, the choice of
these newspapers may make it more difficult to find empirical support for the
media hegemony thesis. Put differently, the newspapers represent a cautious,
purposive sample that will allow for tentative assumptions to be drawn about a
larger number of similar media outlets and particularly those known to be more
conservative.[49]

A random sample of articles related to terrorism was taken from the *New
York Times* and *Washington Post* between September 11, 1997, and September
11, 2005. This time period overlaps with both the Clinton and Bush administrations and targets the same number of years from the pre-9/11 and post-9/11
periods; I also sampled articles published between January 20, 2009, and January 20, 2010, the first year of the Obama administration.[50] The five abstract
dimensions of terrorism threat in newspaper articles were measured using a
total of eight components. By combining these components in a single index,
each article was rated on a scale between 0.1 and 8.0 (the higher the rating, the
greater the terrorism threat).[51]

A total of 752 articles was analyzed, 161 articles appearing during the
Clinton administration, 391 during Bush, and 200 under Obama. Roughly the
same number of articles was sampled from the *New York Times* (48 percent) as

Washington Post (52 percent). Government officials were the most prevalent sources in 48 percent of the articles; nongovernment sources were dominant in 52 percent of the articles. Nearly one in four articles (23 percent) associated the threat of terrorism with Islam; 18 percent of articles indicated a predominantly favorable stance toward the use of military force as a response to terrorism; 6 percent of articles supported the Patriot Act or similar security measures that diminish civil liberties or human rights.

Moving to the five dimensions of terrorism threat, 41 percent of articles framed the danger as something new or increasing (dynamics); 44 percent referred to it as high or serious (magnitude); 27 percent mentioned some form of nuclear, chemical, or biological attack (dread); 7 percent talked about suicide bombers (dread); 39 percent of articles were considered "on topic," that is, more than 50 percent of the paragraphs were relevant to the threat of terrorism (salience); and 64 percent of articles did not question or balance claims about the threat (no balance). The mean number of references to the term "terrorism" per article was 4.2 (salience); the mean coder rating, which ranged from 0.0 to 1.0, was 0.36. I combined these attributes in the terrorism-threat index. Based on this index, the mean terrorism threat level in articles was 3.0.

As expected, portrayals of the terrorist threat were commonly used as justifications for war and deeply interwoven in the framing of military interventions in foreign lands. This relationship was seen under all three presidents. Articles that made a case for a military response to terrorism tended to contain significantly higher levels of terrorism threat than articles that did not. The same association was found between terror threat and the proposed need for enhanced homeland security measures, such as the USA PATRIOT Act, which effectively degraded some of the freedoms and civil liberties enjoyed by Americans.

Supporting the findings of Bennett and others, the articles in this study relied heavily on government sources when describing the threat.[52] Roughly half the articles included more government sources than nongovernment sources. Meanwhile, when these officials described the danger, they were significantly more likely than nongovernment sources to use ominous terms and high-threat framing. Again, this relationship was found during all three periods (Clinton, Bush, and Obama).

Islam was another important issue that consistently emerged in the sample. In fact, every fourth article in the sample associated Islam in one way or another with the threat. Under all three presidents, articles that mentioned Islam contained significantly higher levels of terrorism threat than articles that did not.

Conclusion

I should begin by pointing out that the discourse on terrorism did not always match my expectations. Many news articles did not correspond to the media hegemony thesis, nor even reflect an organized repertoire of framing devices. Some journalists and commentators questioned the terrorist threat and refuted the dominant symbolic repertoire's emphasis on perpetrating war, trading civil liberties for security, and pointing a finger at Muslims. Even the articles that matched my assumptions may have been interpreted by people in unexpected ways. As argued by other scholars, any two readers may assign multiple, incongruent, politically divisive meanings to the same news story.[53] Furthermore, no framing nexus, however pristine or consistent, can affect an audience unless it is made widely available and repeated often. Though well intact during all three presidential administrations, the repertoire in question was much more salient during the Bush administration than under Clinton and Obama. In other words, the cultural script stayed the same, but was recited to the public less frequently under the Democratic administrations.

With these limitations in mind, I suggest, nevertheless, that a parsimonious model is vital for identifying general trends in mass media and political culture. Over the course of three different presidential administrations, representations of terrorism in the opinion-leading press followed an observable pattern. Evidence from the study showed that the news about terrorism contained significantly higher levels of threat under four distinct conditions: (1) when government sources were dominant, (2) when a military response to terrorism was supported, (3) when liberties reductions were advocated, and (4) when Islam was associated with the danger. Again, these results were found not only in articles published during the Bush administration—the high-water mark of the "war on terror"—but also prior to the events of 9/11 under Clinton and later during the first year of Obama's presidency.

These findings shed new light on the conclusions of chapter 5. Using an experiment in the previous chapter, I showed how certain news frames elevated worries about terrorism, and how these concerns increased support for war and the civil-liberties-for-security trade-off. My aim was to identify one of the psychological formulas that could be used to produce mass-mediated fear. In this chapter, I turned to the real-world process of news production and revealed the conditions under which such a formula appeared in the mainstream news media. I found that national security policies probably gained support from the public not only by virtue of exclusionary mechanisms that limited dissent, but also through a constantly reasserted set of definitions that evoked fear, encouraged compliance with authority, and thereby reaffirmed the status quo.

Elites have been writing and rewriting this script for decades. During the Cold War, the Soviets were framed as idealists, as ideologues who were fervently engaged in the task of spreading communism throughout the world. Driven to create a communist paradise, the godless "reds" would stop at nothing to drain American bank accounts and send Christianity to the dustbin of history. Pragmatism, nationalism, and the pursuit of economic domination were absent from the discourse on the Soviet Union. The idealist image of the USSR, which dominated American public opinion at mid-century, ignored the material and geopolitical interests of the Soviets and thereby overlooked the many similarities between "us" and "them."

Decades later, nearing the ten-year anniversary of 9/11, the idealist image of our *new* enemy still inspired the imaginations of most Americans. The terrorists, as described in countless news articles (and not only by obnoxious pundits), were driven by a radical Islamic ideology, one that was diametrically opposed to the American way of life. We were engaged in a clash of civilizations, not a conflict of interests. The dominant paradigm suggested that the religious character of terrorism was indisputable, that culture mattered most in international conflicts, and that appreciating this fact was crucial to the proper formulation of U.S. foreign policy.[54]

Many Americans not only perceived terrorism as a serious threat, but also saw few real alternatives to the government's aggressive efforts to combat it. Confronted by an uncompromising, idealistic enemy with the power and intent to carry out heinous acts against innocent civilians, what other choice did a citizen have but to put forward equally powerful leaders to quell the danger? The dominant symbolic repertoire not only urged us to support a particular course of action, but also to see it as the only path forward.

7

GLOBAL RESPONSES
TO TERROR

It's not usually advisable to begin an argument with a flawed assumption, but let's start with one anyway: All people share a roughly equivalent attitude toward the prospect of dying. In spite of our disputes over the metric system, the proper way to make coffee, and the meaning of hand gestures, people from around the globe agree about one thing. Death is a destination they'd like to avoid. The end of life often hurts, sometimes really bad. It separates us from the things we love—friends, family members, flat-screen televisions. And no matter how strong our faith, death presents us with a range of unsettling questions about what happens *after*.

Because the fear of death is universal, people respond, whenever they find themselves in such a state, in predictable ways. One of the big proponents of this idea is Ernest Becker, a cultural anthropologist who wrote convincingly and without devotion to any one social scientific field about the fear of death and how it influences human behavior.[1] "The idea of death," he wrote, "the fear of it, haunts the human animal like nothing else; it is the mainspring of human activity—activity designed largely to avoid the fatality of death, to overcome it by denying in some way that it is the final destiny for man."[2] Applying Becker's thinking to the subject at hand, we might draw a relatively simple conclusion about how individuals and groups react to the threat of being killed by terrorists. Terrorism taps into our universal fear of death, triggering a standard set of defense mechanisms, and thereby leads whole societies down the destructive path described in chapter 1.[3]

However, even if we could embrace this simplistic understanding of how people react to the terrorist threat, we still wouldn't understand the conditions under which people come to feel threatened in the first place. To fear for your life, you must first be aware that your life is in jeopardy. The conditions that produce such awareness depend, without doubt, on social circumstances, not universal or natural ones. We know, for instance, that worries about terrorism were not equally distributed across the diverse regions of the United States. New Yorkers tended to be more concerned about terrorists than people living one hundred miles outside the city.[4] In fact, one study found that people living in the heart of urban areas in Michigan reported higher levels of fear than those living just five miles away from the center of these cities, and that those living around the five-mile mark were more worried about terrorism than those living outside a fifteen-mile zone.[5]

If levels of perceived threat varied within the United States, the differences were even greater between countries. The first goal of this chapter is to explore the diverse reactions to terrorism around the world, with a focus on the global response to 9/11. Examining these reactions will provide context for a better understanding of the American response. It will demonstrate that much of what Americans took for granted about 9/11 (the identity of the perpetrators, the extent to which the victims were innocent, and what to do about the attacks) was not accepted by many people in other nations.

A second (far trickier) objective is to identify patterns in the global responses to 9/11 and explain why some countries reacted in ways similar to those of the United States, while others most certainly did not. There is, I argue, a close relationship between foreign perceptions of international terrorism on the one hand and views of the United States on the other. The horrifying video footage and news reports that spread across the globe on 9/11 were certainly evocative in their own right, but people's perceptions of these images and their understandings of what to do about violent extremism were shaped by their preestablished worldviews, their attitudes toward the symbolic target of the attacks, their thoughts about the victims and perpetrators, as well as the broader social context in which they lived.

The "Common Enemy" Rationale

In his book *Why the Allies Won,* British historian Richard Overy contended that the Allies were victorious in the Second World War in part because they were drawn together by a particularly ambitious and perilous enemy. As Overy put it,

"Hitler's ambition to impose his will on others did perhaps more than anything to ensure that his enemies' will to win burned brighter still."[6] Along a similar line, Winston Churchill famously quipped, "If Hitler invaded hell I would make at least a favorable reference to the devil in the House of Commons." Throughout history, as many scholars have argued, the accord found between nations has solidified and dissolved with the wax and wane of common threats. The threat posed by the Central Powers during World War I (1914–1919) and the Axis Powers during World War II (1939–1945) generated a mutual understanding, group identification, a spirit of cooperation, and positive interaction between Britain, Russia, France, and the United States.[7]

Even the most uncomfortable WWII alliances warmed as a result of the rising menace of Germany. When the United States joined the war front, for instance, its image in the Soviet Union improved. American movies were played in Soviet theaters and the Soviet press regularly quoted American radio and other news sources. In his analysis of the Soviet media, Jeffrey Brooks explains that during the war the British and American allies had been a real presence in the Soviet press, and that the editors who printed such coverage allowed foreigners a legitimacy and authority that contrasted with the xenophobia of the 1930s.[8]

For five decades after WWII, while hostility toward the United States was on the uptake in the Soviet Union, the Western European capitals remained benign, if not favorable, in their attitudes toward America. According to a study on national stereotypes conducted in 1948–1949, the four adjectives most frequently used by the French, British, Australians, West Germans, Italians, Dutch, and Norwegians to describe Americans were "progressive, generous, practical, and hardworking." In contrast, the four adjectives used most frequently to describe Russians were "domineering, backward, cruel, and hardworking." These stereotypes, as the authors suggested, were partially caused by threats of war and territorial insecurity.[9]

Sketching the historical context of twenty-first-century anti-Americanism, a number of contemporary scholars and commentators have discussed the generally positive views of the United States during WWII and even later during the Cold War. As political analyst Fareed Zakaria suggested, despite the fact that 1968 was a "bad" year for America's image abroad in light of the developments in Vietnam, it was also the year of the Soviet invasion of Czechoslovakia. During the Cold War, the Europeans' critical views of America were always balanced by the wariness of the Soviet and communist threats.[10]

Focusing on large social and ethnic groups or entire nations, social scientists, political scientists in particular, have applied the common-enemy rationale to the study of international relations, negotiations, conflict resolution, and the development of prejudice, patriotism, and nationalism. Mass media and communication scholars have also drawn on these theories to describe a broad range of social processes, from media effects[11] to the relational ties in global telecommunications networks.[12]

Sociologists are also quite interested in how groups and entire nations may be influenced by mutual perceptions of threat from a third party. Simmel and Coser, as discussed earlier, talked about how conflicts create associations and coalitions, sometimes even binding reluctant allies in a common pursuit.[13] The underlying logic here can be detected in any number of creative works, from Ibsen's classic play *An Enemy of the People* to Ron Howard's comic film, *Gung Ho*.

Moving the analysis from nations and large groups to individuals, we might also consider the gestalt movement in psychology. Essential to this tradition is the notion that our perceptions of any one object, person, or event are affected by our perceptions of other elements of the environment in which the event occurs or the object is situated.[14] This view precludes a universal reaction to anything, given the fact that all things appear to us within diverse environments and circumstances. Even actions that are widely perceived in a negative light, such as robbery, adultery, and murder, do not exist as singular, absolute ideas in our minds. Rather, they exist as a set of thoughts and feelings that are intertwined with our perceptions of the situation surrounding the act, its perpetrator, and the victim. In the same vein, our reaction to an act of international terrorism depends greatly on how we identify with the target of the attack, as well as the perceived national, cultural, and personal characteristics of the perpetrators.

Following the gestalt tradition, Fritz Heider and other cognitive theorists suggested that people do more than simply react to external stimuli; they actively interpret their environments in a way that provides them with "balance" between their attitudes.[15] Important for the purpose of prediction is the contention that a balanced structure, or "triad," tends to remain balanced, while imbalanced triads naturally move toward a state of internal congruence.[16] A woman with a negative attitude toward the act of smoking cigarettes, for instance, experiences an imbalanced cognitive state if her lover favors cigarettes and actively uses them. The result often includes a series of adverse events (unpleasant facial expressions, hand gestures, snide comments, open arguments, irreverently blown smoke, and perhaps the clandestine destruction of the offending tobacco product) followed by a balancing of attitudes along one of three paths: the woman becomes more tolerant of smoking, the smoker becomes less intent on lighting up, or the two of them maintain their initial attitudes and go their separate ways.

One of the problems with this classic version of balance theory is that it treats people's attitudes as simply positive or negative and disregards the magnitude of these feelings. Responding to this limitation, Theodore Newcomb proposed a model that takes the intensity of attitudes into account.[17] Newcomb hypothesized that the psychic tension produced by an imbalanced relationship (and the need for resolving this tension) increases as the extremity of the attitudes involved increases. The imbalanced triad involving our smoker, nonsmoker, and the act of smoking is really not a problem unless the respective attitudes are held strongly, in which case the sparks (excuse the pun) are more likely to fly.

Applying balance theory to the issue of terrorism, it might be argued that a person's negative attitude or fear of the group that carried out 9/11 is "balanced" when coupled with a positive attitude toward the United States. The theory, given the way Newcomb couched it in particular, also suggests that fluctuations in the perceived danger of international terrorism may result in attitude change toward the United States. Facing what seemed like a new and especially sizable threat from al Qaeda, citizens across the world, even those who had once held critical views of the United States, would now, presumably, respond with an outpouring of support and good tidings toward the American people and their government.

This take on the common-enemy rationale is what supposedly held the Allies together during World War II and perpetuated mutual support and friendly relations between the United States and Western Europe during the Cold War. Likewise, when the Soviet threat dissolved in 1991 and the common enemy rationale lost some of its *rationale,* relations between the United States and

Western Europe soured. The question for this chapter is, did the threat of international terrorism perform the same role? Did al Qaeda, or the international terrorist network, reestablish the old bonds between states and reconfirm the ancient dictum, "My enemy's enemy is my friend"?

Before moving to an empirical analysis that sheds light on this question, the application of balance theory to this topic deserves a final clarification. So far it has been assumed that al Qaeda would play the role of the common enemy—the mutually perceived threat that would help the United States build positive relations with other countries. Using the logic of balance theory, however, one may find that the opposite may also be true. International perceptions of al Qaeda, or the terrorist threat in general, may depend on how foreigners perceive the United States, its culture and history, its current place in the world, and its effect on their own countries. Put differently, while the vicious atrocities of al Qaeda may have helped the United States make friends in the wake of 9/11, the harsh, militaristic policies of the United States may have helped al Qaeda do the same (or at least it may have created a reluctance among foreign countries to support the aggressive U.S. plans for countering terrorism).

Global Opinion of Terrorism and the United States after 9/11

With these theoretical and historical considerations in mind, let's begin by examining international public opinion of the United States after 9/11. In the immediate aftermath of the attacks, almost all countries embraced ours and showed their support for our people in our time of sorrow and crisis. American embassies around the globe were inundated with well wishers, makeshift memorials, and candlelight vigils. Heartening symbolic gestures were on display in all the major world capitals. As one example, the "Star-Spangled Banner" was played outside Buckingham Palace during the changing of the guard, as thousands of Londoners expressed their sympathy and solidarity by shedding tears and waving American flags.[18] Foreign authors, editors, and intellectuals often used the collective "we" in their commentary on the event, indicating their identification with the United States and its people. On September 12, for instance, the French newspaper *Le Monde,* not exactly a lover-of-all-things-American, ran the famous headline, "We are all Americans now."[19]

International aid poured in from almost everywhere, while a chorus of foreign dignitaries denounced the attackers, praised the United States, and offered their support for the inevitable response. For the first time ever, NATO invoked Article Five, which declares that "an armed attack" against any one member "shall be considered an attack against them all."[20] The post-9/11 statements of British prime minister Tony Blair, among others, could hardly be distinguished from those of President Bush. "This mass terrorism is the new evil in our world today," he declared. "It is perpetrated by fanatics who are utterly indifferent to the sanctity of human life and we, the democracies of this world, are going to have to come together to fight it together."[21] From a review of similar statements made by top international leaders, much of the world stood firmly by the United States.

The common-enemy rationale seemed to fare well in explaining the initial response to 9/11 in several countries. The moral outrage and mutually perceived threat seemed to generate sympathy and support for the country, as well as for the cultural vantage point through which most Americans understood the attacks and what to do about them. In the months and years following 9/11, however, the logic of balance theory still held, but it seemed now to function in the opposite direction. Much of the international community watched with trepidation as the United States readied its war plans and aimed for Afghanistan. American officials largely ignored, sometimes rudely, the offers of support from NATO members and other foreign countries. Rather than capitalizing on a rare opportunity for genuine international cooperation, the Bush administration embraced a brash stance in foreign affairs. As a result, many of America's would-be allies felt alienated and eventually came to see the United States itself as a threat to global stability, which took a toll on their support for the war on terrorism.

By the end of 2002, the possibility that the Bush administration would use military force against Iraq became a subject of deep concern in many countries. Around the same time, America's image in almost all regions of the world declined. According to a survey conducted by the Pew Research Center, the number of Europeans who rated the United States "favorably" decreased significantly between summer 2002 and spring 2004. In France, America's favorability rating dropped during this period from 63 percent to 37 percent; in Germany, from 61 percent to 38 percent; in Russia, from 61 percent to 47 percent; and in Great Britain, from 75 percent to 58 percent.[22] The plight of America's image in Muslim nations was even worse. (These Pew findings were corroborated by Gallup International's "Voice of the People Survey.")[23]

While attitudes toward the United States in Europe, the Middle East, and Asia showed some signs of improvement by 2005, America's favorability rating remained quite low in most regions of the world, particularly when compared with the ratings of other countries. China, for instance, was rated more favorably in 2005 than the United States in most of the European nations surveyed.[24]

It was not until the end of the decade, when Barack Obama emerged in the political spotlight, that opinions of the United States thawed and began to blossom once more. In 2009, the year President Obama took office, the U.S. favorability rating in Europe improved dramatically. Yo-yoing up from the Bush era's low-water mark of 2007, the percentage of French who reported favorable attitudes toward the United States increased by 36 percent (in Germany, by 34 percent; in Spain, by 35 percent; and in Britain, by 18 percent). Similar increases were seen in other countries, such as India, Indonesia, South Korea, Argentina, Mexico, and even some Middle Eastern countries, including Jordan and Lebanon (though most Muslim countries continued to hold negative attitudes toward the United States).[25]

Along with the vast improvements in America's image abroad in 2009, there were also increases in negative attitudes toward international terrorism and more willingness to use American strategies to fight terrorist groups. Confirming the logic of balance theory, the populations of several countries now showed greater support for "U.S.-led efforts to fight terrorism" than they had during the Bush era. Between 2007 and 2009, the increase in the percentage of the British who supported America's war on terrorism, if broadly defined, was 26 percent (there was a 31 percent increase in support in France, 38 percent in Spain, 26 percent in Germany, 24 percent in China, 33 percent in India, 27 percent in Indonesia, 11 percent in Pakistan, 13 percent in South Korea, and 25 percent in Mexico).[26] One year later, however, America's image in the world began to slip a bit, creating new concerns that the "Obama effect" on foreign opinion of the United States would gradually dissipate and take with it the new enthusiasm for the American-style fight against terrorism.

An International Study of the News

A correlation between foreign concerns about terrorism and attitudes toward the United States was also discovered in international press coverage of 9/11.

Working with a seventeen-member research team not long after the attacks, I was involved in a project aimed at analyzing press representations of 9/11 in the ten largest newspapers in seven countries (China, Colombia, Egypt, Germany, India, Lithuania, and Russia).[27] A total sample of 2,369 published articles was drawn from three brief periods in the first months following the attacks (September 12–15, October 8–11, and December 10–21, 2001).[28] Seventeen people were involved in the project as "coders." Each of them was a native speaker of the languages they analyzed and proficient in English. Dual coders were used to measure the reliability of our analysis, and the results were found to be satisfactory.[29] Press coverage on a total of ten major issues related to 9/11 was examined in each country. These issues were identified as the most popular international news items based on a pilot study of more than two hundred articles from around the globe. Three of these issues tapped into the mainstream press's portrayal of the 9/11 attackers, while two other issues measured press evaluations of the United States.[30]

Under statistical procedures, the five issues were combined and indexed as two variables: "condemns 9/11 terrorists" and "supports the United States."[31] The aim here, as discussed, was to look for a correlation between the two variables. The more a country condemned 9/11, the more they were expected to support the United States, and vice versa. This objective led to a rather difficult question. How could one distinguish between "favorable" and "unfavorable" assessments of the United States and the 9/11 terrorists? To solve the problem, we used forty-six public statements made by President George W. Bush as a reference point.[32] "Agreement" with the official U.S. position entailed the following: (1) clearly negative terms, such as "horrible," "terrible," "evil," or "a killing of innocent people," used to describe 9/11; (2) Osama bin Laden, al Qaeda, or Islamic fundamentalists named as the prime suspect; (3) support for a U.S.-led military response to 9/11; and (4) a favorable description of the United States, using terms such as "freedom-loving," "democratic," "compassionate," "brave," or "determined." As for the fifth issue, the first two answers in the scale ("completely" and "mostly" favorable toward the United States) were used to measure the level of agreement with the official position.

The Findings

The results by individual country revealed significant differences among the press responses in the seven project countries. In terms of foreign views of

America and the perpetrators of 9/11, a clear trend in the data positioned the German press on the favorable end of the spectrum and the Egyptian press on the unfavorable end. More interesting, perhaps, is the fact that even the countries that identified most with the United States and its take on terrorism often invoked ideological and analytical viewpoints that contradicted, sometimes vividly, the conventional wisdom and dominant symbolic repertoire used by the vast majority of Americans.

Describing 9/11

Although there was some variability in the responses between nations on this issue, most of the foreign press coverage unambiguously condemned the 9/11 attacks. In Germany, Lithuania, China, and Russia, three-quarters or more of the articles and quotes in the samples used decidedly negative terms to characterize what happened on 9/11. Signs of shock and disbelief as well as emotionally charged comments referring to the attacks as "cruel," "terrible," "murderous," "insane," or "evil" were far more common than neutral or positive terms such as "intelligent," "well organized," or "courageous." As the German politician Ursula Kelders (2001) said, "This is so terrible. I am speechless. The situation is like a horror movie."[33]

Only a small proportion of comments offered a justification for the acts, and most of these were found in newspapers with sharp ideological leanings, such as the ultranationalist *Zavtra* in Russia. At the same time, media elites in Egypt and to some extent India were less likely than the others to use negative or very negative comments (only 54 percent and 67 percent, respectively, used terms of total condemnation). In an open letter published in the Egyptian newspaper *Afaq Arabia,* Ahmad Almajhop wrote, "Osama, you are a hero! You are a man who has all the characteristics that men need."[34] This type of commentary, however, was extremely rare in the overall sample. Taken as a whole, international opinion was closest to the American perspective on this issue.

Prime Suspects

Americans were almost completely in agreement with their government's focus on Osama bin Laden as the chief organizer of 9/11. Within a week of the attacks, more than eight out of ten Americans said that it was very important to capture or kill bin Laden, while an even greater share said that the military should be used to attack Afghanistan if that country does not turn him over to the United States.[35]

World opinion, however, strayed to some extent from the American stance on this issue. Some foreign authors pointed out that the United States had several enemies besides Osama bin Laden who might have carried out the attacks. They voiced guesses such as Iran, China, Saudi Arabia, or even shadowy military specialists with ties to the United States, Israel, or a Masonic plot. Others aimed their speculation at homegrown terrorists, noting that an American citizen, Timothy McVeigh, had executed the last major attack on U.S. soil. In the Russian weekly *Argumenty i Fakty,* Leonid Shebarshin, a former high official in the KGB, commented early on that a new, non-Islamic organization had carried out the attacks, and followed this general speculation with conspiratorial details involving the American Special Forces.[36]

While Osama bin Laden was only explicitly mentioned as a prime suspect by a majority of media elites in Germany, agreement with the dominant American position was greater if we combined specific bin Laden mentions with any reference to Islamic fundamentalists or Muslim radicals. In this case, we found that Germany, Lithuania, and India mostly shared the American view of the perpetrators, while Colombia, Russia, China, and especially Egypt demonstrated greater skepticism.

War

The percentage of foreign commentators who endorsed the idea of using military force in response to the attacks—no doubt part of the dominant cultural framework in the United States[37]—dropped off considerably in comparison with the previous two issues. Germany was the leading supporter of such actions, though even here the level of clear endorsement was limited (30 percent).

In China, where colorful ideological opinions are rare in the mainstream press, many commentators still warned that the American military effort would destabilize security across the world and upset global financial markets. Numerous Russian authors, with far stronger polemics than the Chinese, described the military response as a power grab, an effort to advance U.S. economic and geopolitical interests across Central Asia and the Middle East. "This is a war for control of resources," declared Leonid Ivashov in *Nezavisimaya Gazeta.* "The U.S. is using the tragedy to realize its dream—world hegemony."[38] Clearly at odds with the American view, not a single article in the Egyptian press supported a U.S.-led military response to 9/11. By and large, media elites across the world were far less likely than Americans to support the call to war and far more likely to suggest that restraint should be exercised, that hasty actions would claim innocent lives, that the conflict should be resolved by the United Nations, that international law should be upheld, and that unilateral military actions should be avoided.

Seeing America

Even as the United States faced the world as a victim, many international authors described the country in unfavorable terms. Some of the popular words and phrases used in the Egyptian press included "religiously prejudiced," "unfair or unjust," and "arrogant." Russian respondents penned terms such as "vulnerable," "arrogant," and "warlike," while the Indian press emphasized America's indifference to the problem of terrorism prior to 9/11. The Colombian and Chinese press were somewhat less critical of the country. Positive comments about the U.S. economy as well as the term "compassionate" ranked among the five most salient images in the mainland Chinese press. "Compassionate" also made the top-five list in Germany, along with "healthy democracy." Popular terms in the Lithuanian press included "brave," "freedom loving," and "determined." Taking into account the hundreds of statements in the Lithuanian and German press, 78 percent of descriptions of the United States in both countries were favorable. On the other end of the spectrum, this indicator dropped to 20 percent in Russia and 25 percent in Egypt.

Similar findings were seen in the coders' general evaluations of the press materials. The coders judged 77 percent of the German authors as "completely" or "mostly" favorable toward the United States. In Egypt this indicator dropped to 16 percent, demonstrating once again the divergence between the German and Egyptian cases.

Condemning Terrorism and Embracing America

As shown in the previous sections, opinions on the study's five issues varied considerably across the seven project countries and certainly deviated from the dominant frames found in the American media and political establishment. There was, however, a rather clear pattern in these press materials. The data demonstrated a substantial correlation between a country's rejection of terrorism and its support for the United States. The more a country's press condemned 9/11, identified Osama bin Laden as the perpetrator, and supported the idea of a military response, the more likely it was to describe the United States in a favorable light. Put differently, the correlation between our two consolidated variables ("condemns 9/11 terrorists" and "supports the United States") stood at 0.41, a moderately strong statistical relationship according to academic standards (an equivalent correlation, for instance, has been found between adult levels of education and income).[39]

Conclusion

Americans do not hold a monopoly on the meaning of 9/11 or the terrorist threat. While the range of reactions to terrorism in the United States adhered to a rather narrow set of ideas (and did so before, during, and after the Bush era), views from abroad were far more diverse. The range of these views underscores the need for understanding the varied social, historical, political, and cultural circumstances across the globe. At the same time, the kaleidoscope of international perceptions of terrorism still appeared in predictable patterns. In the case of the 9/11 attacks and for years thereafter, perceptions of terrorism were closely aligned with perceptions of the United States. On the whole, those countries that demonstrated the most concern about Osama bin Laden and Islamic fundamentalists and the most willingness to confront them with military force also tended to show the most support for the United States.

There are two different ways to digest these findings. On one hand, the data suggest that the horrifying actions of 9/11 unified fearful nations and produced mutually positive interactions and attitudes between them. While likely accurate in the immediate aftermath of 9/11, the inverse of this thinking better characterizes later periods. A diminishing level of identification with the United States and growing disappointment in its policies led to lesser condemnation of international terrorism and weaker support for U.S. counterterrorism efforts. In the months and years following 9/11, the United States responded with overwhelming force against those it identified as terrorists. The strong military response, according to several scholars, was one cause of the decline in the U.S. favorability rating in many nations. Later, with the rise of President

Obama and a new sense of hope sweeping the globe, America's image in the world blossomed and support for the U.S. war on terrorism was regained.

It seems wise to take both interpretations to heart. Any effort to establish allies in the fight against radical extremism should be advanced not only by convincing other nations that international terrorism is a serious problem (if such a case can be made), but also by taking steps to improve America's image in the world, demonstrating the generosity and wisdom of its foreign policies, and highlighting the tolerance, hard work, scientific aptitude, and creativity of its people. Looking back at history from this view, one can explain the favorable foreign attitudes toward the United States after World War II and during the Cold War by both the uniting force of the Soviet threat, as well as positive factors such as the role of the United States in the formation of the United Nations and the North Atlantic Treaty Organization, and its contribution of vast amounts of financial aid to foreign countries under the Bretton Woods system and the Marshall Plan. In the future, our international alliances in the struggle against violent extremists will no doubt depend on a mutually perceived threat. But they will also demand a more hopeful common ground upon which a safer, more stable future can be established.

8

DEMOCRACY
ON THE FRITZ

One of the hopes of a democratic nation is the belief that the country's institutionalized freedoms are actually used by its citizens, and that such practices produce a multitude of unique voices, competing views, styles of leadership, and new ideas for solving society's major problems. Free political competition and the marketplace of ideas, as the story goes, safeguard us from dogmatism and one-sided thinking and lead us to innovation and change. Faced with crises and disasters, a nation's democratic institutions buoy it against the rising tide of authoritarianism, and protect its cherished freedoms when support is needed most.

Drawing on this conventional wisdom, it seems likely that the public discussion of international terrorism and how to respond to it is generally more lively and wide-ranging in strong democracies than in weak ones. If we compared the news coverage of 9/11 across nations, for instance, we should find that countries with well-established democracies were better equipped to handle the "authoritarian turn" discussed in chapter 4, and more likely to scrutinize the dominant symbolic repertoire described in chapter 6 than nations with nascent, struggling, or nonexistent democratic institutions.

The aim of this chapter, which may seem obvious by now, is to put these assumptions to the test. I'll consider whether the moving parts of democracy actually move in times of fear and crisis. Focusing on one of democracy's key parts (the press), I'll examine the level of "press pluralism" in the same seven countries discussed in the previous chapter (China, Colombia, Egypt, Germany, India, Lithuania, and Russia) and find out which of them produced the richest and least-inhibited public debate on one of the twenty-first century's most complicated and controversial issues.

Democracy and the Press

Social scientists have long been interested in how the political and economic forces in society influence the quality of mass media content.[1] According to a classic perspective offered by Siebert and his colleagues, media content is ultimately determined by where the given country falls on a political continuum. On one side we find a centralized authoritarian society ("authoritarian model") and, on the other, a free libertarian one ("libertarian model"). Countries closer to the libertarian model, if the theory holds, exhibit greater levels of press pluralism than those nearer to the authoritarian model.[2] Although a detailed discussion on this topic follows, "press pluralism" can be defined tentatively as media content that contains a wide array of opposing viewpoints.

In the half-century since the publication of *Four Theories,* media scholars have criticized this work from all directions. Some see it as nothing more than a Cold War artifact, a one-sided perspective fit only for Cold Warriors, an international media theory based on the ideologized models that existed in the United States at mid-century. In spite of its rhetorical and normative character, however, *Four Theories* remains influential as a broad framework for understanding the differences between media systems around the world.[3]

In fact, it is difficult to find a cross-national comparative analysis of media that does not exhibit some similarities to Siebert's classic model. For instance, by opposing the "dominance model" to the "pluralist model," Denis McQuail, a luminary of communication theory, offers a similar dichotomy for comparing media systems.[4] In the dominance model, the media is controlled by a small group of powerful individuals, and media content is "selective and decided from 'above.'"[5] In contrast, the pluralist model assumes that power is disseminated among diverse groups in a free society. People who hold mutually exclusive goals are allowed access to the media, resulting in a plurality of views in the various media outlets. Drawing on the normative logic of Siebert and company, the pluralist model has been associated with the free-market democracies of the West, while the dominance model has been linked to authoritarian nations such as Russia and China.[6]

Interest in the relationship between democracy and media pluralism increased in the late 1990s during the political upheavals in communist countries. Many authors suggested that the citizens in the democratizing nations of Central and Eastern Europe gained unprecedented access to new media outlets and increasingly diverse views of the world. Millard, for instance, discussed how this process took place in Poland, where a free media—"a characteristic of the democratization process"—ensured a diversity of viewpoints in the press.[7] Similar studies have considered the relationship between democratic transformation and various elements of media quality and performance in Russia,[8] particularly Tartarstan Republic,[9] as well as in Hungary,[10] Romania,[11] Chile,[12] Taiwan,[13] and other countries.[14]

Many of these studies demonstrate that the relationship between democracy and press pluralism is both positive and reciprocal. In other words, while the laws and principles of democracy are thought to be essential for free and diverse voices to emerge in the mass media, these same voices also protect and improve the conditions for democracy. A free press facilitates the flow of information about public events to citizens, exposes politicians and governments to public scrutiny, elucidates choices during elections, and urges people to participate in the political process.[15] And it does so in good times as well as bad.

In Jennifer Merolla and Elizabeth Zechmeister's *Democracy at Risk,* the idea that democracy is vital in times of crisis is given a brief, though professional, examination.[16] As made partially evident by their title, the authors' primary aim is to reveal the potentially damaging consequences of a thoroughly frightened citizenry. Using experimental measures employed in the United States and Mexico, Merolla and Zechmeister suggest that reactions to the terrorist threat are remarkably similar in the two countries (and perhaps elsewhere), and in both cases they are harmful to the institutions and spirit of democracy. The authors temper and refine these generalizations with a section near the end of the book called the Importance of Country Context. This discussion, for the most part, falls in line with the conventional wisdom discussed above. Democracy, they suggest, is our best and perhaps only hope of countering the authoritarian tendencies brought on by a fearful populace. As they put it, "the strength of a democracy plays an important role in mitigating the otherwise potentially damaging effects a terrorist threat has on democratic values and institutions."[17] They argue that a voice of reason, a voice of tolerance, a voice promoting civil liberties, a voice declaring the need for critical thinking and multiple viewpoints is more likely to emerge in the media and public discourse in democratic nations than in less democratic ones. Again, in their words: "We would expect such voices to be stronger where democracy is more deeply rooted and where, as a consequence, the media provides a venue for contrasting opinions and special interest groups promoting civil liberties and other democratic values and practices operate freely."[18]

Limits of Democracy

Although much has been written in support of the perspective described above, some social scientists have challenged the idea that the development of free-market democracy necessarily results in diverse and competing views in the mass media. In the next sections, I briefly discuss four closely related factors that may limit the level of press pluralism and other aspects of media quality: ideology, advertisers, ownership, and organizational structure.

Ideology

Whether media are controlled by state institutions or private firms, for critical scholars "media content is seen as both expressing and furthering the power of elites or propertied classes."[19] Theorists from this tradition argue that the scope of political and social debate in any society usually comprises an innocuous set of views, none of which question the prevailing ideology established by the powerful elites.[20] Drawing on this argument in chapter 6, I demonstrated how the dominant symbolic repertoire—a package of news frames that denoted what terrorism is and what should be done about it—remained intact over the course of three diverse presidential administrations (Clinton, Bush, and Obama). Our way of seeing terrorism, in other words, has a stable cultural and ideological foundation, which discourages thinking that strays far from the official viewpoint.

Extending this thinking to the realm of international news, it is especially likely that ideological forces played an important role in the creation of international coverage of 9/11. Much of the debate over these events and the surrounding issues fell along ideological lines, often pitting the interests and values of Western countries against those of the Arab and Islamic world. If a country's press coverage is shaped largely by its geopolitical interests and its support (or rejection) of Western values, the tension between ideological forces and the demand for objectivity and fairness would likely be elevated in the case of 9/11 coverage.

Advertisers

While state-owned media outlets depend on a handful of high officials for their survival, private firms depend on advertisers. Media content may be influenced directly by the particular demands of large corporate advertisers,[21] or indirectly by the general notion that media content must create a "buying mood" among consumers.[22] The advertising dollars of large multinationals or foreign corporations with important ties to the United States market certainly had the potential to influence media coverage of 9/11. Moreover, according to some authors, media firms design content to be predictable while avoiding controversial materials that may disturb or distract the audience from the advertisements.[23] Both the need for advertising revenue and the forces of ideology may reduce the level of press pluralism in liberal capitalist societies.

Ownership

The third influence on the press, which overlaps with the previous two, is media ownership concentration. The individual owners of large media companies may influence content directly by demanding that it become more advertiser-friendly, or more in line with the owner's personal beliefs or values.[24] While there are several famous cases of deliberate manipulation of media content by individual owners, the effects of ownership concentration are more often thought to be indirect and conceptualized at the organizational level. For instance, media ownership concentration may blur the line between the editorial side and the business side of news organizations, particularly when revenues are in decline. Commercial considerations rise in importance as media empires expand. High-level corporate managers become less in tune with the editorial concerns of media workers, and more concerned about increasing revenues. This results in watered-down, homogenized content that reflects the needs of advertisers and corporate executives to produce a culture of consumerism at the expense of the informational and knowledge needs of audiences that would foster diverse and competing viewpoints. The contention that media ownership concentration reduces press pluralism finds ample support in classic and contemporary studies.[25]

Organizational Structure

All members of media organizations, from frontline employees to top-level managers, perform a particular role or function. The roles people fill in media organizations largely determine their views and shape their orientations toward day-to-day routines, including those related to journalistic standards. If the structure of any two media organizations differs, the practices of media workers also differ. In this chapter, I not only consider several newspaper organizations within the given country, but make cross-national comparisons as well. Differences between countries in terms of organizational structure, therefore, may account for differences in the level of press pluralism. Nowhere is this issue more conspicuous than in the case of China, where the structure of state media organizations is controlled by the Chinese authorities and government censors.[26]

The Comparative Approach and the Issue of 9/11

While the relationship between press pluralism and democracy rests on contested ground, much of the controversy is based on studies of Western media systems. In an effort to broaden the debate, this chapter focuses on countries from other regions of the world, including India, China, Colombia, Russia, Lithuania, Egypt, and Germany. As discussed in the previous chapter, the political and economic circumstances in these nations are diverse, providing a fruitful opportunity for comparative analysis and theory development. Comparing the level of press pluralism in nations with high and low levels of democratic development will help us clarify the meaning of this concept and explain why it appears in different forms in different countries.

One of the big challenges of using the comparative approach in media studies, however, is finding press material for which meaningful comparisons can be made. It is rare to find a particular moment in time when the voices of the international press are all talking at once on the same topic. Given the magnitude of the 9/11 attacks and the highly anticipated American response, the days and weeks following the tragedy were certainly one of these moments.

The issues surrounding 9/11 are also ideal for an analysis because they provoked a broad range of viewpoints in the international community. Who carried out the attacks? Why did the attacks occur in the first place? What should be done in response? How should the underlying global conflict be framed or described? The press in each of the project countries offered a variety of answers to these and several other pertinent issues. Marking the beginning of a new and more assertive U.S. foreign policy, 9/11 represented a decisive moment in contemporary world history. Each nation's reaction to the attacks played a role in its future relationship with the United States. President George W. Bush's famous assertion that countries are either "with us or against us" in the war on terrorism only intensified the social and political significance of foreign press representations of 9/11 and the events that followed.

Differentiating Democracy, Press Freedom, and Press Pluralism

Press pluralism has been studied in many different ways. Researchers have analyzed the level of differentiation in society as a whole;[27] the diversity of media ownership;[28] the range of television channels, radio stations, newspapers, magazines, and online publications;[29] the use of diverse sources by media workers; gender and race differences among reporters;[30] the differences in journalistic norms and practices; and the diversity of audiences.[31] In this chapter, the analysis is focused on the level of pluralism in international press content.

As discussed, a *pluralistic* press is often said to play an important role in democratic societies as the embodiment of free expression, as a supplier of vital information to citizens, and as a watchdog that serves the public's interests. In each of these roles, the content of the press is treated as a manifestation of democracy itself. For our purposes, however, these two variables—press pluralism and democracy—have been separated. The relationship between them will not be assumed. It will be tested.

In a similar vein, a distinction between pluralism and "press freedom" should also be made. In the United States and other nations, the freedom of the press has been written into the Bill of Rights and represents an important part of the democratic structure. Possessing this freedom, however, does not necessitate the use of it. At the same time, the absence of freedom does not impede press pluralism on all issues and in all societal contexts. To summarize, press pluralism is defined as newspaper content that contains a wide variety of opposing viewpoints, and conceptualized as something independent from a country's political framework and the level of press freedom.

The events of 9/11 stimulated multiple competing interpretations among scholars, politicians, journalists, and ordinary people in almost every country in the world. At the center of this debate were several important topics, including the threat of international terrorism, the identification of who carried out the attacks, the character of the United States and its foreign policy, the interpretation of why 9/11 occurred, and the views on what actions should be taken in response to 9/11. This chapter examines how the mainstream press in seven countries responded to these and other issues related to the attacks (a total of ten issues were used in this analysis).[32]

To quantify the concept of pluralism, we measured how evenly dispersed were the press's responses across the categories of each issue, using a statistic known as the index of qualitative variation (IQV). The greater the IQV score, the more equally dispersed are the units among each issue's categories. In other words, a high IQV score means that the press offered a highly diverse set of views on the given issue.[33]

Although several studies offer cross-cultural measurements of "democracy,"[34] only the Freedom House Organization's *Freedom in the World* index and the Polity Project's democracy index provide comparative data for all the countries in this project.[35] The Freedom House index is especially appropriate for the present study, because it releases a new data set each year, which allows for an analysis of the two indicators—democracy and press pluralism—during the same time period.[36]

Freedom House is a nonpartisan and broad-based organization that ranks the level of democracy based on two criteria: "political rights" and "civil liberties." The first criterion (political rights) comprises multiple indicators, such as free and fair elections, competition between political parties, and a reasonable level of autonomy for minority groups. The civil liberties criterion refers to free expression, association and organizational rights, the rule of law and human rights, as well as personal autonomy and economic rights.[37]

Press Pluralism by the Numbers

The level of pluralism varied between countries, as well as across the ten different issues. The highest level of pluralism was found in descriptions of the United States. In China, for instance, 52 percent of the press response portrayed the United States with positive words and phrases, such as "united," "adaptable," "economically strong," and "technologically advanced," while 48 percent used negative terms, such as "harsh," "arrogant," and "materialistic" to characterize the country. A similar split was found in Colombia (53 percent positive, 47 percent negative) and India (35 percent positive, 65 percent negative). Egypt and Russia were less pluralistic on this issue. The press in these

countries leaned decisively toward negative images of the United States. Lithuania and Germany were equally biased in the opposite direction, offering predominantly positive descriptions of America. The relatively low IQV ratings in
Germany (.616), Lithuania (.708), Russia (.640), and Egypt (.806) contrasted
with the higher scores found in China (.998), Colombia (.996), and India (.91).
In comparison with other issues, however, the project countries generally offered diverse and competing views when it came to describing and evaluating
the United States.

The lowest level of pluralism was found in articles that described the 9/11
attacks. As discussed in the previous chapter, few authors strayed from decisively negative portrayals of the perpetrators and the act itself. Some authors
used what we considered "neutral" terms to describe the perpetrators, including "educated," "intelligent," and "well organized." President Bush (our reference point for defining categories) never used neutral or positive terms in his
depictions of the attacks or the attackers. The Egyptian press was a clear leader
in offering a neutral portrayal of 9/11 (21 percent of the units fit this category).
With the exceptions of the press in Egypt (.649) and India (.466), the level of
pluralism on this issue was quite low in all the countries—China (.03), Lithuania (.221), Russia (.250), Colombia (.251), and Germany (.275)—especially
when compared with the portrayals of the United States.

Although the level of pluralism varied across the different issues, some
countries consistently offered greater levels of pluralism than others. On average, China (.442), Germany (.570), and Lithuania (.626) offered the lowest
levels of press pluralism on the ten issues surrounding 9/11. Colombia (.689)
and Russia (.726) assumed intermediate positions, while the press in Egypt
(.744) and India (.790) exhibited the highest levels of pluralism.

Correlation analysis was used to assess the associations between the level
of democracy in each country (based on the Freedom House index) and the
level of press pluralism (based on IQV scores for each of the ten issues). As
discussed, many scholars have assumed a positive correlation between these
two variables—that is, the discussion of important issues in the press of democratic nations tends to be more diverse than in nondemocratic nations. This
assumption, however, was supported on only three of the ten issues. Countries
with high democracy scores tended to offer higher levels of pluralism on issue 1 ("How should the U.S. respond to 9/11?"), issue 2 ("How should the

<given country> respond to 9/11?"), and issue 5 ("What caused 9/11?") than countries with low democracy scores. There was no correlation between democracy and pluralism scores on issue 4 ("How should 9/11 be described?"). Democracy was negatively correlated with press pluralism on six of the ten issues.[38] On these six issues, countries with higher democracy scores offered narrower, less balanced interpretations in the press than countries with lower democracy scores.

Conclusion

One of the central assumptions in many studies on democratization is that countries with highly developed democratic institutions generally present robust deliberations on important topics in the mainstream press. In the case of the debates surrounding 9/11, I found only partial support for this conventional wisdom. The press in nations known for their healthy democracies did indeed provide a diverse discussion on some of the issues surrounding 9/11, particularly on the issue of using military force in response to the terrorist attacks. On other issues, however, these nations offered less diverse deliberations than in countries with meager democratic reputations. The mainstream press in democratic nations were less likely to question the immediate assertions made by American officials that Osama bin Laden and Islamic radicals had orchestrated the 9/11 attacks. These media offered a less critical exploration of how the events of 9/11 may have been stimulated by past and present U.S. foreign policies. Discussions of the war in Afghanistan and the broader global conflict brought to light by 9/11 were narrower in democratic nations. The democratic press was also less likely to offer a mixed portrayal of the United States and its policies than the nondemocratic press.

A liberal democracy is not a trophy. It doesn't function very well when it sits on a shelf. Its many parts are meant to move, and when one part begins to slow, the rest are likely to follow. In chapter 6, I showed how the opinion-leading press in the United States was reluctant to move or stray far from the dominant framework established by ruling elites. In this chapter, I argued that the United States was not the only democratic society that failed to produce a rigorous public debate on the issues surrounding 9/11. In many cases, countries known to have weaker democratic institutions produced some of the most lively and controversial discussions on the meaning of terrorism and the appropriate strategies for responding to it.

Deep controversies and conflicts in society, though widely perceived as undesirable, are important for the maintenance of democracy. As Tichenor wrote, "intense controversies may lead to greater realization of a general democratic ideal."[39] While it may seem reasonable for the press in democratic countries to converge and homogenize in times of war and crisis, it is precisely these times when a vigilant press is needed most.

CONCLUSION

Much of what changed after 9/11 stayed changed. At the start of the twenty-first century, two wars began and two wars continued through the end of the decade. As the ten-year anniversary of 9/11 loomed, the number of American troops fighting in Afghanistan was on an upturn, not a decline. Over the years, thousands of American soldiers died and tens of thousands returned home with deep physical and psychological scars. Billions of tax dollars literally went up in smoke as our bombs, missiles, and bullets bombarded far-flung regions of the world. The defense budget more than doubled between 2000 and 2010, from $294.4 billion to $719.2 billion.[1]

When President Obama reached office in 2009, many people believed that a transformation of the war on terrorism was imminent. But then a year passed and the end of war was nowhere in sight. Instead of bringing the consequences of the war on terrorism to the center of public life, the new administration left it in the shadows. At decade's end, serious debate about the human and economic costs of war was simply missing from the political landscape. As pointed out in a *New York Times* op-ed by Tom Brokaw, the candidates in the congressional and Senate races of 2010 clashed on a range of important issues, such as the national debt, jobs, and health care, but few of them took notice of the deaths of American soldiers, the spiraling civilian casualty count, or the nation's vast financial investments in military conflicts.[2]

The increased hurling of lethal projectiles was not the only persistent post-9/11 policy shift. The Bush administration's Patriot Act remained largely intact by decade's end. Barack Obama won the 2008 presidential election on the promise of "change," and yet in May 2011, he still reauthorized some of the Patriot Act's most controversial provisions. With the events of 9/11 fading into history, the government continued violating our past standards of due process as it wiretapped our phones, seized our records and property, and used other intrusive means to search for the enemy among us.

The challenges of being foreign in the United States remained unfalteringly difficult. The number of hate crimes against Arabs and Muslims in the United States rose in the wake of 9/11 and never returned to baseline levels in the ten years that followed. Proponents of stricter immigration laws continued citing the terrorist threat to justify their position in the debate over immigration reform, which only grew more fervent nearing the end of the decade. For instance, lawmakers in Arizona passed a measure in April 2010 that allowed the police to check the documentation of anyone they suspected of being an illegal immigrant.[3] Opponents of the bill warned that it would lead to racial profiling and other abuses. In the new measure's defense, Arizona Governor Jan Brewer said that it was necessary because her state "has been under terrorist attacks . . . with all of this illegal immigration."[4]

As described in chapter 1, numerous social scientists have investigated these and many other changes in American society. The simple question many asked was, "Why?" Why did we react to 9/11 with such eagerness and ferocity? Most of the answers to this question, however, have assumed a rather narrow focus. In recent decades, the scholarly community has broken into small, increasingly isolated segments as the various disciplines responded to society's increasing need for specialized information, not to mention the market demands for tidy, well-packaged *educational* products. Academia has come to look a bit like an outdoor shopping mall. While the disciplines share a common geography, they operate within independent, stand-alone structures. The central aim of this book has been to shop around a bit, bring these structures together, identify the best of what each has to offer, and synthesize the different theories and empirical findings in the hope of providing a more complete explanation of how the terrorist threat influences individuals, groups, and whole societies.

At the individual level, social psychologists have contributed a number of elegant theories that explain our cognitive and affective responses to terrorism. In their book *In the Wake of 9/11,* Pyszczynski, Solomon, and Greenberg trace terrorism's impact on people all the way back to the beginning of humankind.[5] Some early humans, they argue, were well equipped with a particular set of appetites that made them more likely to live longer and have kids. Thanks to natural selection, these life-sustaining characteristics were passed down through the ages. Almost all of us now have a moderately strong ability and desire to evade poisonous snakes, dodge hungry lions, avoid oncoming traffic, and keep breathing.

The proclivity for self-preservation, though a notable endowment of evolution, represents only one of our many special talents as *Homo sapiens*. More clever than our yearning for life is our ability to know we are alive, to think about living, to cogitate upon the process of cogitation, and to figure out the best ways to protect ourselves—and not just our fleshy bodies and bulbous noggins. Each of us has also managed to create, protect, and nurture the "self," the part of us that bruises or blossoms when we evaluate who we are and imagine what others think of us. Staying alive and experiencing a positive sense of self are wonderful things, according to Pyszczynski, Solomon, Greenberg, and other advocates of terror management theory. As they put it, "To be alive and to know it is awesome: grand, breathtaking, tremendous, remarkable, amazing, astounding, and humbling."[6]

Unfortunately, there's a catch to all this spectacular awareness of being: we know equally well that we'll end up otherwise. Death, as we all know, is a real bummer, but so too is low self-esteem. As a result, we spend an awful lot of time worrying about them both. Here's where the "management" in terror management theory comes in. Given the countless happenings of everyday life that jeopardize our physical or metaphysical existence, we must employ a broad array of physical and psychological defenses in order to manage our fears and trepidations.

In more than 150 experimental studies, terror management researchers have shown that just thinking about death (experiencing "mortality salience," to use their terms), or fretting over threats to self-esteem, initiates a predictable set of defense mechanisms. Without doubt, 9/11 was a dramatic induction of mortality salience for many Americans. As we witnessed the destruction of the Twin Towers and other horrifying images of 9/11, it was hard to think about anything besides death. These were "solid fears," as discussed in chapter 2— fears that are still attached to well-established memories and ideas. As a result, we turned inward, reaffirmed our beliefs in country and kin, and went on a rampage to make the villains pay. As Pyszczynski, Solomon, and Greenberg wrote, "One of the most consistent findings from our research has been that reminding Americans of their mortality increases the positivity of their reactions to anyone or anything that praises America and the negativity of their reactions to anyone or anything that criticizes America."[7]

Outside the laboratory, other social scientists used self-administered questionnaires, interviews, and content analysis to document the various social, psychological, and behavioral manifestations of the 9/11 effect. As outlined in chapters 3 and 4, much changed in the American mind-set. The aptness of this conclusion is more convincing when one ponders the scope and variety of small-to-moderate 9/11 effects than when one considers the strength of any one change in the way we see the world. Many of these shifts persisted for one or more years, particularly rally effects and authoritarian tendencies, and their relevance to key public policy issues are beyond question.

In the immediate aftermath, President George W. Bush received a record-high approval rating of 90 percent, which flooded his administration with political capital. The administration's decisive response to 9/11 was further bolstered by increased levels of public trust in government and a rise in patriotism. Americans also placed greater emphasis on security, became more willing to punish those who violate conventional norms and values, and were more attracted to leaders who displayed power, toughness, and an iron determination to confront the enemy.

As concerns about terrorism rose, Americans supported the military actions in Afghanistan and Iraq, as well as the escalation in defense spending. After 9/11, harsh antiterrorism tactics such as torture and assassination and more aggressive law-enforcement procedures no longer seemed as unacceptable to many people. While popular support for the USA PATRIOT Act diminished over time, people were still willing to forfeit civil liberties for a sense of security. Polls showed that the public's willingness to make the civil liberties–security trade-off stood at 11 percent above the pre-9/11 level as late as July 2005. The growing intolerance of many Americans favored those pundits and politicians who wished to place greater restrictions on immigration and politicize anti-Muslim sentiments for political purposes. In short, according to dozens of pre–post 9/11 studies, the attacks brought us together and tore us apart, but mostly it tore us apart.

For many social scientists, this is where the story ends. For some, however, the story has just begun. Let us assume for now that "fear," "perceived threat," "mortality salience," "freaking out," or whatever term for terrible potentialities one prefers is a key piece of the puzzle, that it represents, in fact, the driving force behind America's monumental response to terrorism. Such an explanation, however, does not reveal the particular qualities of terrorism that generate these concerns, nor the aspects of our society and culture that create and sustain them.

Researchers who work in the risk perception tradition in cognitive psychology have much to say about the aspects of terrorism that scare us most. They suggest, to begin with, that hazards of all types reside in our minds as mental constructs, as a set of thoughts and feelings that are fastened together like the beams and floorboards of a house. Once built, these cognitive structures help us make quick decisions about which aspects of our environments are likely to help us and which ones will do us harm. When crossing the street, for instance, we need not spend much time thinking about Newton's laws of motion in order to avoid being run over by an SUV. We can rely instead on our cognitive framework for *traffic*—a sort of stereotype of a dangerous situation that guides our behavior with considerable accuracy and little deliberation.

Using surveys, interviews, and a variety of statistical methods, risk perception scholars have found that not all danger stereotypes are created equal, that some produce greater worries than others, and that our concerns are not always consistent with the probability of being hurt. They have even figured out the particular aspects of hazards that are most likely to produce exaggerated worries and misjudgments. Dangers perceived as *new*, for instance, may evoke higher levels of perceived threat than old or familiar risks, even when the new danger has a slighter chance of causing harm.[8] Tapping into the newness dimension, the framing of terrorism in the media often stressed the uniqueness of the danger, the high-tech weapons that might be used in attacks, the historically unprecedented character of 9/11, and the "new era" of national security. If, instead, the media had regularly described terrorism as an age-old form of violence that has been used for various purposes throughout history by people of all colors, faiths, genders, and nationalities, including by revolutionary forces in the American War of Independence, we might have worried less about terrorism.

Most of us also carried around stereotypical notions of terrorists as "Islamic radicals." Beliefs of this sort would lead us to assume that our enemies have no logical basis for their actions, that their motives are irrational and otherworldly and therefore obstinate and uncontrollable. Perceived *controllability,* meanwhile, is another one of those aspects of danger stereotypes that are known to elevate our risk perceptions. It is likely, for this reason, that as the 24/7 news stream bombarded us with the Islam-terrorism link after 9/11, many of us felt out of control and faced with an intractable threat to our lives and property.

Our perceptions of the terrorist threat have also been colored by the supposed manner of potential attacks. As risk perception scholars tell us, our thinking about how we might be killed influences our estimates of whether we might be killed. Our concerns about being harmed by a shark, for instance, are shaped less by the probability of an attack than by the terrible notion of being ripped apart in a churning froth of blood and saltwater. A dreaded outcome like this one tends to focus our attention on the frightening images and ideas associated with the hazard rather than on the chance of it actually occurring. In such a mental state, we are likely to misjudge the nature of sharks, the risk of attacks, and, perhaps, become more willing to support aggressive measures to reduce the shark population (especially if reputable sources pelt us with suggestions to do so). The same logic may have played out in the public mind as the Bush administration began justifying its call for a preemptive strike against Iraq by regularly linking radical Islamic terrorist groups to Saddam Hussein and his alleged possession of "weapons of mass destruction."

Although risk perception studies have revealed the specific aspects of dangers that tend to frighten us, they have not explained how, why, and under what conditions these frightening aspects appear in our everyday lives, emerge in the public discourse, and thereby creep into our individual minds. The psychology of terrorism, in other words, must be coupled with an analysis of our environments—the social forces behind our responses to terrorism. After all, there is no one type of person or universal individual or single personality out there. Even our seemingly innate predisposition toward self-preservation is not experienced in precisely the same way by all people all the time. If staying alive was the overriding universal force of humankind, no one would choose to fight wars, smoke cigarettes, ride motorcycles, play contact sports, jump off elevated rock formations into rivers of vaguely known depths, or even adopt the risky diet and lifestyle of a typical American college student.

We are not stones. We cannot be understood as a geologist understands the definitive characteristics of metamorphic rocks. We are messy creatures, difficult to study, often erratic, sometimes inventive, inconsistent across various situations, and no doubt prone to misjudge even ourselves, let alone other people. Each of us, nevertheless, has been shaped by a particular social system, a particular culture, a particular set of symbols and ideas that existed prior to our arrival on the planet. For this reason, when we stand back a bit and behold a broad view of society, we see patterns, tendencies, even causal mechanisms that persist, replicate over time, and only gradually transform. We see that our reactions to terrorism were not new or unique or personal or inspired solely by those distinctive psychological and biological elements that make us human.

As discussed in chapter 6, Americans have been fighting a war on terrorism, or something quite like it, throughout much of their history. Conflict is familiar to most of us; militarization is routine; war fits smoothly within the conscious and subconscious norms and roles of American citizenship. After 9/11, the public discussion of international terrorism was unique in several respects, but it tapped into a preexisting cultural script without which none of it would have made sense in the first place.

Before reviewing the details of this script, let's consider a more familiar case: the public discourse on American automobiles—a conversation that is shaped to a great extent by car companies and their endless television commercials. For instance, the Chrysler Group produced a 2010 Super Bowl commercial called "Man's Last Stand." The ad shows a series of men with dull expressions who seem to be plagued by boredom and the onerous strictures of spousal obligation and full-time employment. As their faces appear on the television screen, a second-person voiceover runs through a list of stereotypical concessions that husbands must make for their wives ("I will be civil to your mother. I will put the seat down. I will carry your lip balm. I will watch your vampire TV shows with you"). In the end, the ad's revelation declares that the repressed and anguished life of men is acceptable so long as they get to own fast, black cars with loud engines and drive them on the weekends across open roads with the sun setting on the horizon. A sports car, in other words, represents "man's last stand" against the onslaught of domesticity.

Without culture, of course, the ad has no significance at all, no meaning. Its ideological novelty is nil. The message is only meaningful insofar as we share a preexisting cultural script that clarifies notions of masculinity, marriage, work, and freedom. We are born with zero understanding about what it means to be a man, a husband, a worker, a reluctant viewer of vampire TV shows, or a connoisseur of fast cars and maudlin scenes of sunsets. We don't even know what it means to be free. Such notions are deeply embedded in our institutions and propagated by agents of socialization—the people, groups, organizations, and written rules that dictate our development as human beings. So present are these ideas in our everyday lives that we hardly know it when we see them, when we observe other people carrying them out, when we watch them on television or listen to them on the radio. The car ad and others like it perpetuate these notions, but they won't work in the first place unless a system of meaning already exists.

The goal of both car advertisers and politicians is to figure out what the dominant meaning system looks like, tap into it by producing and disseminating a steady stream of consonant messages, and thereby strengthen the particular parts of the system that sell cars, rouse partisans, and land votes. In the case of terrorism, the consonant set of messages (or "dominant symbolic repertoire") consists of five different news elements, including perilous accounts of the terrorist threat, calls for war as the proper response, the promotion of aggressive security measures, and an ideological position that identifies Islam as the source of the danger. While these messages were more common during the administration of George W. Bush, a similar ideological response to terrorism, as observed in the opinion-leading press, existed during both the Clinton and Obama administrations, which substantiates the theory that culture is stable and U.S. reactions to terrorism are predictable.

Put differently, we're living through the same old story but with new names and slogans. Radical Islamic terrorists, like the communists and Nazis before them, have been cast in a familiar mold: vicious, violent idealists for whom compromise is impossible and to whom violence is the only response. As argued by columnist David Brooks, if the terrorists are "vicious people driven by an insatiable urge to dominate," our only option for dealing with such an enemy is to "fight them to the death."[9]

In the wake of 9/11, it was hard to imagine the terrorists as anything other than inhuman, fanatical agents of destruction, just as it was hard to imagine any other response to 9/11 besides the use of military force. The basis of this difficulty, however, is not to be found in our sublime logic or scientific insight on the nature of terrorism and what to do about it. In fact, we hardly put forth any serious thought at all before the bombs began dropping in Afghanistan (remember that it took us less than one month to begin our endless war). There were certainly no signs of significant debate in the presidential administration, Congress, or the mainstream American news media. We went with our guts. We went with our taken-for-granted, unremarked-upon, externally coordinated understanding of the world—that stable, transparent, uniquely American source of symbolic fuel that drives our values, beliefs, attitudes, and behavior. We went with our culture.

It's difficult to imagine terrorists as logical, friendly, laughing, baby-loving, game-playing, egg-beating, bad-sitcom-watching fellow human beings for the same reasons that it's difficult to imagine a bride dressed in black, a professional baseball park with no hotdogs, a carpeted bowling alley, a major motion picture shown without previews, or the Coyote finally catching and devouring the Road Runner.

This sort of difficulty is one thing we have in common with our enemies. Our understanding of them is, most likely, a mirror reflection of their vision of us. Imagine al Qaeda's version of David Brooks waxing philosophical on the nature of Americans and why they commonly invade foreign countries and blow people up. Would it be difficult for such a pundit to portray us as "vicious people"?[10] Given the capacities of our modern weaponry, most of our fighters have little if any contact with their victims. Some, in fact, deal death blows from 7,500 miles away. As reported in the *Los Angeles Times,* throughout much of the decade following 9/11 there were people sitting in padded chairs somewhere outside Las Vegas who controlled heavily armed drone aircraft soaring over Afghanistan, which, at times, released bombs and missiles that most certainly annihilated human beings.[11] I'm not sure I can think of any scenario more chilling and further removed from the context of death and killing than an Air Force captain dropping off his dress shirts at the drycleaner, stopping by the drive-through for a sausage McMuffin, walking into an office building in Vegas, sitting down in a comfy leather seat, and pulling a little gray trigger that obliterates a dozen people living in a mud hut outside Kandahar.

Our tendency to misunderstand the enemy, dehumanize them with flawed labels and stereotypes, and attribute their behaviors to madness, religious fanaticism, or irrevocable psychological predilections speaks to the need for tracing our response to terrorism to the social, political, and cultural roots of American society. The psychology of terrorism, though essential for understanding 9/11, drops us off at a dead end, leaving us with thoughts of a universal human nature, a primordial life form equipped with standard internal circuitry that comes to life at birth and functions according to design regardless of the temperature or climate. Our behavior, from such a viewpoint, is inevitable, unstoppable, and dislocated from the social circumstances that generations of Americans have chosen to create and sustain.

A rigid psychological perspective on fear disregards the social context that explains why individuals, groups, or whole societies react differently to the same type of threat. As discussed in chapters 7 and 8, international responses to 9/11 varied tremendously across nations. The meaning of these events stretched from "tragedy" to "triumph," and the prescribed reactions to the attacks ranged from the use of overwhelming military force to the termination of America's imperial ambitions. These popular understandings were formed, interestingly enough, virtually without primary sources of information. The actual consequences of terrorism, though seemingly personal and individual, are rarely experienced or observed by individuals firsthand. Therefore, the meanings that people attached to 9/11 depended on the words, images, and symbols they received via the mass media, by listening to elected officials, and through conversations with friends, relatives, and coworkers.

As detailed in the latter chapters of the book, to really understand public reactions to terrorism we need to examine the structure of mass media organizations and the character of the given country's political and economic systems and geopolitical circumstances. Cross-cultural comparisons remind us that the history and inner workings of each society influence the predominant meanings of terrorism and what to do about it. With a global perspective, we not only discover that the dominant symbolic repertoire varies across nations, but also that the social machinery (political economy) that perpetuates these meanings differs from one country to the next.

Media outlets in the United States, for instance, operate within a highly competitive capitalist system that constantly pushes them to produce returns on private investments. When things blow up, or when public officials talk about them blowing up, people watch and listen, leading to greater advertising revenue for media organizations and a better foothold in the marketplace. Fear, in other words, falls in line with the central function of cable news networks and other media: it produces wealth.

American news outlets are also structured in a way that gives top public officials an advantage in the ongoing competition to set the national agenda and focus the public's attention on a particular set of issues. Newsmakers are particularly reliant on the government for information about national security concerns such as terrorism. These circumstances place a great deal of power in the hands of individual politicians. American political figures, meanwhile, operate within a competitive system of their own and therefore wish to identify a strong demand among their constituents and demonstrate their dexterity in responding to it. Fear creates such a demand. It captures our attention, places us on the same ideological page, and primes us, under some conditions, to support the ideas and policies of stalwart leaders who sell themselves as saviors. Our responses to terrorism are responses to a well-monied, magnificently capable, interconnected set of complex organizations. As Mueller aptly put it, "Perhaps the most common reaction to terrorism is the costly stoking of fear and the often even more costly encouragement of overreaction by members of what might be called the 'terrorism industry,' an entity that includes not only various risk entrepreneurs and bureaucrats, but also most of the media and nearly all politicians."[12]

These broad societal factors, meanwhile, exist in different forms throughout the world. As seen in chapter 7, the ways of knowing terrorism are as diverse as the international relations between the United States and other countries. Global reactions to 9/11, though seemingly shaped by universal dismay and antipathy, were affected by preestablished attitudes toward the United States, as well as the broader social context in the given society. Coming to terms with what happened on 9/11 meant coming to terms with America itself, what it stands for, and how it affects the world. If American officials hope to influence whether the international community supports or resists U.S. plans for countering terrorism, they should bear in mind that the common-enemy rationale runs in both directions. While mutually threatened nations tend to coalesce in times of crisis, the strength and longevity of these bonds also depend on the level of mutual understanding, generosity, and respect—sentiments that cannot be gained through unilateralism or heavy-handed geopolitics.

Russia serves as an interesting case in point. As expected, dramatic attacks in both the United States and Russia at the start of the twenty-first century led to increased identification between the two countries. Several analysts pointed out that the mutually perceived threat of terrorism bolstered Russian-American relations during much of the Bush administration.[13] President Vladimir Putin's initial reaction to 9/11 had been, by all accounts, sympathetic, and his solidarity with the United States was strong. Russia quickly became a member of the international antiterrorist coalition, several measures were taken to allow U.S. troops in Central Asia, official relations between the United States and Russia were warmer than at any time since WWII, and there even seemed to be a robust personal friendship between Presidents Bush and Putin. Ultimately, however, other issues would counter these amicable exchanges. Such factors as the expansion of American influence in countries formerly controlled by Moscow, the inclusion of Baltic countries in NATO, and the Russian nationalists' and communists' dislike of American society generated persistent conflicts and controversies between the two nations, and weakened their missions in the fight against violent extremists.

Finally, a few words should be said about chapter 8 and the power of democracy to encourage healthy debates on all matters related to terrorism. When examined from a global perspective, I found that the strength of a country's democratic institutions (as measured by nonpartisan international research groups) did not predict the breadth of public discussion on the key issues surrounding 9/11 (who carried out the attacks, what should be done about them, and so forth). In fact, on most issues, countries with weaker democracies offered the most diverse and least inhibited views on one of this century's most important and complex problems.

For years after 9/11, the discussion of terrorism in the United States was as salient as it was narrow. Much of what commentators, journalists, politicians, and other elites said about the attacks reflected and perpetuated the dominant symbolic repertoire. Reading from the same script, most Americans responded accordingly. We were afraid, as usual; motivated to marginalize outsiders; ready to support harsh, charismatic leaders; and determined to settle the score. Such a mind-set harmonized with the government's aggressive foreign and domestic policies, which were carried out not only in the immediate aftermath of 9/11 but throughout the first post-9/11 decade.

As I sit here in the summer of 2011 typing the final words of this book and thinking about what may come in the next ten years, it's tempting to believe that President Obama, having faltered during his first years in office, will finally make good on his promise to put an end to the politics of fear and create a new paradigm for foreign and domestic policy. The president's most recent steps in Iraq and Afghanistan seem to be moving the country in this direction. A distinct light, if faint, now illuminates the proverbial tunnel. And yet, considering the momentum of war in Afghanistan and Pakistan, it's difficult to know whether we are at the end of something big or at the beginning of it all, whether we are moving straight ahead or merely passing along one side of an arc, whether we will march down a new path or stumble toward our familiar past. In light of history and the ugly realities of American society, it's neither easy nor shrewd to be an optimist. But then, pessimism just isn't much fun. As a compromise, I will end on an ambivalent note and recount the favorite saying of an old friend: "The future is brilliant, but not hopeless."

NOTES

Preface
1. Lydia Saad, "Majority of Americans Think Near-Term Terrorism Unlikely," Gallup, December 2, 2009; Saad, "U.S. Fear of Terrorism Steady after Foiled Christmas Attack," Gallup, January 2010.
2. Andrew R. A. Conway, Linda J. Skitka, Joshua A. Hemmerich, and Trina C. Kershaw, "Flashbulb Memory for 11 September 2001," *Applied Cognitive Psychology* 23, no. 5 (2009): 605–23; Howard Schuman and Willard L. Rodgers, "Cohorts, Chronology, and Collective Memories," *Public Opinion Quarterly* 68, no. 2 (2004): 217–54; David Simpson, *9/11: The Culture of Commemoration* (Chicago: University of Chicago Press, 2006).
3. Laurie Goodstein, "Falwell's Finger-Pointing Inappropriate, Bush Says," *New York Times,* September 15, 2001.
4. See Moore's thesis, which he developed in his 2004 film *Fahrenheit 9/11,* online at www.fahrenheit911.com.
5. For one of Stewart's more thoughtful explanations of his own work, see his interview with the *Bill Moyers Journal* (April 27, 2007) online at www.pbs.org.
6. "Sick Jokes, Healthy Workers," *Psychology Today,* July/August, 1993.
7. Constance Brown Kuriyama, "Chaplin's Impure Comedy: The Art of Survival," *Film Quarterly* 45, no. 3 (1992): 28.
8. Ibid., 29.

Chapter 1. The War on [Insert Enemy Here]
1. For a few examples, see Bruce Hoffman, *Inside Terrorism* (New York: Columbia University Press, 2006); Gus Martin, *Understanding Terrorism: Challenges, Perspectives, and Issues* (Thousand Oaks, CA: Sage, 2006); Michael Ronczkowski, *Terrorism and Organized Hate Crime: Intelligence Gathering, Analysis, and Investigations* (Boca Raton, FL: CRC Press, 2004).
2. See the FBI's website at www.fbi.gov.
3. For a representative of the former group, see Moorthy S. Muthuswamy, *Defeating Political Islam: The New Cold War* (Amherst, NY: Prometheus Books, 2009). An example from the latter group can be found in Pippa Norris, Montague Kern, and Marion Just, eds., *Framing Terrorism: The News Media, the Government, and the Public* (New York: Routledge, 2003).

4. Audrey Kurth Cronin, "Rethinking Sovereignty: American Strategy in the Age of Terrorism," *Survival* 44, no. 2 (2002): 119.
5. Bruce Hoffman, "The Leadership Secrets of Osama bin Laden: The Terrorist as CEO," *Atlantic Monthly* 291, no. 3 (2003): 26–27; Bruce Hoffman, "Al Qaeda, Trends in Terrorism, and Future Potentialities: An Assessment," *Studies in Conflict & Terrorism* 26 (2003): 429–42.
6. Henry Mintzberg, *The Structuring of Organizations: A Synthesis of Research* (Englewood Cliffs, NJ: Prentice-Hall, 1979).
7. Daniel Byman, "Think Again: Al Qaeda," *Foreign Policy,* May 3, 2011, http://www.foreignpolicy.com/articles/2011/05/03/think_again_al_qaeda.
8. Robert Pape, *Dying to Win: The Strategic Logic of Suicide Terrorism* (New York: Random House, 2005).
9. Ibid., 79.
10. George W. Bush, "Address to a Joint Session of Congress and the American People," September 20, 2001 (retrieved online at www.whitehouse.gov); George W. Bush, "Remarks by the President upon Arrival," September 16, 2001 (retrieved online at www.whitehouse.gov).
11. See excerpts from the interview in "Toward the Summit," *New York Times,* May 29, 1988.
12. These are well-known statements that can easily be found in an electronic search of major news outlets (see, for example, Richard Leiby and David Montgomery, "The Conflict Over War: Patriotic Fervor Has Swelled and with It a Wave of Vexing Questions," *Washington Post,* September 16, 2001).
13. R. H. Johnson, *Improbable Dangers: U.S. Conceptions of Threat in the Cold War and After* (New York: St. Martin's Press, 1994); John Mueller, "Simplicity and Spook: Terrorism and the Dynamics of Threat Exaggeration," *International Studies Perspectives* 6, no. 2 (2005): 208–34; Vladimir Shlapentokh, *A Normal Totalitarian Society* (Armonk, NY: M.E. Sharpe, 2001).
14. Joseph S. Nye, "The Decline of America's Soft Power: Why Washington Should Worry," *Foreign Affairs* 83, no. 3 (2004): 16–20.
15. Paul Slovic, "Terrorism as Hazard: A New Species of Trouble," *Risk Analysis* 22, no. 3 (2002): 425–26.
16. For a list of specific predictions of future attacks, see Timothy Noah, "Why No more 9/11s?," *Slate,* March 5, 2009.
17. See the U.S. Food and Drug Administration's report, "Risk Assessment for Food Terrorism and Other Food Safety," October 13, 2003 (retrieved online at www.cfsan.fda.gov).
18. *Safety and Security of Commercial Spent Nuclear Fuel Storage,* National Academies Press, 2005, retrieved online at http://www.laka.org/docu/boeken/pdf/6-01-5-51-91.pdf.
19. Kenneth Katzman, "Al Qaeda: Profile and Threat Assessment," *Congressional Research Service Report for Congress* (August 17, 2005): 1.
20. See Raymond A. Zilinskas's report, "Bioterrorism Threat Assessment and Risk Management Workshop, Monterey Institute of International Studies," June 24, 2003 (retrieved online at http://cns.miis.edu/reports/pdfs/biorisk.pdf).
21. Henry H. Willis, Andrew R. Morral, Terrence K. Kelly, and Jamison Jo Medby, *Estimating Terrorism Risk* (Santa Monica, CA: RAND, 2005).
22. Gordon Woo, "Keynote Lecture Given at the NATO Centre of Excellence: Defense against Terrorism," May 25, 2009, 4 (retrieved online at http://www.rms.com/Publications/GWNATO_052109.pdf).

23. See O'Neill's testimony (October 30, 2001) to the Senate online at http://www
    .treas.gov/press/releases/po743.htm.
24. For the Department of Defense's continually updated casualty report, see the
    online source: http://www.defense.gov/news/casualty.pdf.
25. Bill Hogan, "Alone on the Hill," *Mother Jones,* September 20, 2001.
26. David E. Rosenbaum, "Congressional Leaders Offer Strong Endorsement of
    Attack," *New York Times,* October 8, 2001.
27. Elisabeth Bumiller and Carl Hulse, "Bush Will Use Congress Vote to Press
    U.N." *New York Times,* October 12, 2002.
28. Vladimir Shlapentokh, Joshua Woods, and Eric Shiraev, eds., *America: Sover-
    eign Defender or Cowboy Nation?* (Aldershot, England; Burlington, VT: Ash-
    gate, 2005).
29. Charles V. Pena, "$400 Billion Defense Budget Unnecessary to Fight War on
    Terrorism," *Policy Analysis* 539 (March 28, 2005): 1–25.
30. Ann Scott Tyson, "Bush's Defense Budget Biggest since Reagan Era," *Wash-
    ington Post,* February 6, 2007; Eric Rosenberg, "Bush Pushes to Increase De-
    fense Spending, Jump of 7 Percent Would Top Rest of World's Budgets," *San
    Francisco Chronicle,* February 12, 2006.
31. Sources vary somewhat in their estimates of the total cost of the wars in Iraq and
    Afghanistan. See James Glanz, "The Economic Cost of War," *New York Times,*
    March 1, 2009, and two online sources: www.costofwar.com and www.zfacts.com.
32. Yochi J. Dreazen and August Cole, "Fight Looms on How to Pay for New War
    Plan," *Wall Street Journal,* December 2, 2009.
33. Adam Entous and Julian E. Barnes, "U.S. Boosts Afghan Surge; Pentagon Plans
    to Send 1,400 Extra Marines to Supplement Spring Campaign," *Wall Street
    Journal,* January 4, 2011.
34. Alissa J. Rubin, "Suicide Attack Continues Afghan Trend," *New York Times,*
    February 27, 2011.
35. Taimoor Shah and Alissa J. Rubin, "Taliban Breach Afghan Prison; Hundreds
    Free," *New York Times,* April 26, 2011.
36. Alissa J. Rubin and James Risen, "Bigger Loss Seen at Afghan Bank," *New York
    Times,* January 31, 2011.
37. Alissa J. Rubin and James Risen, "Costly Afghanistan Road Project Is Marred
    by Unsavory Alliances," *New York Times,* May 1, 2011.
38. See the United Nations' report online at http://www.un.org/children/conflict/
    _documents/A-HRC-15-58e.pdf.
39. View the *Frontline* episode ("The Dancing Boys of Afghanistan") at http://
    www.pbs.org/wgbh/pages/frontline/dancingboys/view/?autoplay.
40. Rod Nordland, "Afghans Plan to Stop Recruiting Children as Police," *New York
    Times,* January 29, 2011.
41. Ray Rivera, "Afghan Police Seek to Stop Illicit Trade in Uniforms," *New York
    Times,* April 24, 2011.
42. Christopher Drew, "Audit of Pentagon Spending Finds $70 Billion in Waste,"
    New York Times, March 30, 2011.
43. Gail Makinen, *Economic Effects of 9/11: A Retrospective Assessment* (Wash-
    ington, DC: Congressional Research Service Library, Congressional Research
    Service, 2002), 7.
44. Peter Cohan, "9/11 Didn't 'Change Everything,'" *AOL Money and Finance,*
    September 11, 2006.

45. See the *60 Minutes* interview ("Handouts for the Homeland," April 10, 2005) at www.cbsnews.com.

46. Stephen Kinzer, "Chicago Moving to 'Smart' Surveillance Cameras," *New York Times,* September 21, 2004.

47. For more about the Patriot Act, see David Cole and James X. Dempsey, *Terrorism and the Constitution: Sacrificing Civil Liberties in the Name of National Security* (New York: New Press, 2006); Robert M. Chesney, "The Sleeper Scenario: Terrorism Support Laws and the Demands of Prevention," *Harvard Journal on Legislation* 42, no. 1 (2005): 1–89; Kam C. Wong, "USA Patriot Act and a Policy of Alienation," *Michigan Journal of Minority Rights* 1 (2006): 1–44.

48. Charlie Savage, "Deal Reached on Extension of Patriot Act," *New York Times,* May 19, 2011.

49. See the Office of the Inspector General's report, "The September 11 Detainees" (June 2003) online at http://www.usdoj.gov/oig/special/0306/index.htm.

50. Eric Lichtblau, "Ashcroft Seeks More Power to Pursue Terror Suspects," *New York Times,* June 6, 2003.

51. Center on Law and Security at New York University School of Law, "Terrorist Trial Report Card: September 11, 2001–September 11, 2010," http://www.lawandsecurity.org/Portals/0/documents/01_TTRC2010Final1.pdf.

52. David Stout, "FBI Head Admits Mistakes in Use of Security Act," *New York Times,* March 10, 2007. See the Office of the Inspector General's report ("A Review of the Federal Bureau of Investigation's Use of National Security Letters," March 2007) at www.justice.gov.

53. John Mueller, *Overblown* (New York: Free Press, 2006).

54. James Risen and Eric Lichtblau, "Bush Lets U.S. Spy on Callers without Courts," *New York Times,* December 16, 2005.

55. See an ongoing investigation by the *New York Times* and National Public Radio on the history of the detainee population at the Guantánamo Bay Detention Center online at http://projects.nytimes.com/guantanamo; for more about torture at Guantánamo, see Bob Woodward, "Detainee Tortured, Says U.S. Official," *Washington Post,* January 14, 2009.

56. Linda Greenhouse, "Justices, 5–4, Back Detainee Appeals for Guantánamo," *New York Times,* June 13, 2008.

57. See President Obama's executive orders at www.whitehouse.gov ("President Obama Signs Executive Orders on Detention and Interrogation Policy," January 22, 2009). For further explanation of the Bush administration's antiterrorism campaign, the detention camp at Guantánamo, and the issue of torture, see Jane Mayer, *The Dark Side: The Inside Story of How the War on Terror Turned into a War on American Ideals* (New York: Doubleday, 2008); Gregory Hooks and Clayton Mosher, "Outrages against Personal Dignity: Rationalizing Abuse and Torture in the War on Terror," *Social Forces* 83, no. 4 (2005): 1627–45.

58. Melissa Bell, "WikiLeaks's Guantanamo Bay Files: The Numbers and Names to Know," *Washington Post,* April 25, 2011.

59. The changes were cataloged as follows: "The failure to extend the provision in the Immigration and Nationality Act known as 245(i) that had allowed unauthorized aliens to pay a fine rather than leave the country in order to adjust their status; new enforcement of the requirement that non-citizens report changes of address; an unprecedented involvement of state and local authorities in the enforcement of immigration laws; and restrictions on the acquisition and uses of

various sorts of identification by non-citizens, including driver licenses" (Terri E. Givens, Gary P. Freeman and David L. Leal, eds., *Immigration Policy and Security: U.S., European, and Commonwealth Perspectives* [New York: Routledge, 2009], 5).

60. See the data of the Syracuse research group, known as the Transactional Records Access Clearinghouse, at www.trac.syr.edu.
61. Julia Preston, "States Resisting Program Central to Obama's Immigration Strategy," *New York Times,* May 5, 2011.
62. See the report in an NSF news bulletin at http://www.nsf.gov/news/news_summ .jsp?cntn_id=111036.
63. Susan K. Brown and Frank D. Bean, "Post-9/11 International Graduate Enrollments in the United States: Unintended Consequences of National Security Strategies," in *Immigration Policy and Security,* eds. Givens, Freeman, and Leal 67.
64. The data on America's "most important problem" was taken from the following sources: Lydia Saad, "Americans Have Grown More Concerned in Past Year about Education and Taxes," Gallup, March 31, 2000; Mark Gillespie, "Terrorism Reaches Status of Korean and Vietnam Wars as Most Important Problem, Economy Ranks a Distant Second," Gallup, November 19, 2001; "Most Important Problem," Gallup, October 11–14, 2004.

Chapter 2. Solid Fear
1. Zygmunt Bauman, *Liquid Fear* (Cambridge, UK: Polity Press, 2006).
2. Joshua Woods, "Medieval Security in the Modern State," *Space and Polity* 4, no. 3 (2010): 251–69.
3. Bauman, *Liquid Fear,* 2.
4. Joshua Woods, "What We Talk about When We Talk about Terrorism: Elite Press Coverage of Terrorism Risk from 1997 to 2005," *Harvard International Journal of Press/Politics* 12, no. 3 (2007): 3–20.
5. "Remains of a Day," *Time,* September 9, 2002.
6. Jason Bram, James Orr, and Carol Rapaport, "Measuring the Effects of the September 11 Attack on New York City," *FRBNY Economic Policy Review* 8, no. 2 (2002): 5–20.
7. Woods, "What We Talk about."
8. See the Gallup data in a continually updated report ("Terrorism in the United States") online at www.gallup.com.
9. Ibid.
10. David Bauder, "NY Talk Shows Struggle for Guests," *Washington Post,* October 30, 2001.
11. Darren Davis, *Negative Liberty: Public Opinion and the Terrorist Attacks on America* (New York: Russell Sage Foundation, 2007).
12. Carol Lewis, "The Clash between Security and Liberty in the U.S. Response to Terror," *Public Administration Review* 65, no. 1 (2005): 18–30.
13. Gallup data ("Terrorism in the United States") online at www.gallup.com.
14. The latest available polling data were collected in January 2010. See Saad, "U.S. Fear of Terrorism Steady."
15. Lydia Saad, "Majority in U.S. Say Bin Laden's Death Makes America Safer," Gallup, May 4, 2011."
16. Davis, *Negative Liberty,* 123.

17. S. Galea, J. Ahern, H. Resnick, D. Kilpatrick, M. Bucuvalas, J. Gold, and D. Vlahov, "Psychological Sequelae of the September 11 Terrorist Attacks in New York City," *New England Journal of Medicine* 346, no. 13 (2002): 982–87; C. S. Piotrkowski and S. J. Brannen, "Exposure, Threat Appraisal, and Lost Confidence as Predictors of PTSD Symptoms Following September 11, 2001," *American Journal of Orthopsychiatry* 72, no. 4 (2002): 476–85.

18. D. Herman, C. Felton, and E. Susser, "Mental Health Needs in New York State following the September 11th Attacks," *Journal of Urban Health* 79, no. 3 (2002): 322–31.

19. C. W. Hoven, C. S. Duarte, C. P. Lucas, P. Wu, D. J. Mandell, R. D. Goodwin, M. Cohen, V. Balaban, B. A. Woodruff, F. Bin, G. J. Musa, L. Mei, P. A. Cantor, J. L. Aber, P. Cohen, and E. Susser, "Psychopathology among New York City Public School Children 6 Months after September 11," *Archive of General Psychiatry* 62 (2005): 545–51.

20. Gail Agronick, Ann Stueve, Sue Vargo, and Lydia O'Donnell, "New York City Young Adults' Psychological Reactions to 9/11: Findings from the Reach for Health Longitudinal Study," *American Journal of Community Psychology* 39, nos. 1–2 (2007): 79–90; J. Lawrence Aber, Elizabeth T. Gershoff, Angelica Ware, and Jennifer A. Kotler, "Estimating the Effects of September 11th and Other Forms of Violence on the Mental Health and Social Development of New York City's Youth: A Matter of Context," *Applied Developmental Science* 8, no. 3 (2004): 111–29; Barbara Mowder, Michelle Guttman, Florence Rubinson, and K. Sossin, "Parents, Children, and Trauma: Parent Role Perceptions and Behaviors Related to the 9/11 Tragedy," *Journal of Child and Family Studies* 15, no. 6 (2006): 730–40; Donna A. Gaffney, "The Aftermath of Disaster: Children in Crisis," *Journal of Clinical Psychology* 62, no. 8 (2006): 1001–16.

21. C. Laurel Franklin, Diane Young, and Mark Zimmerman, "Psychiatric Patients' Vulnerability in the Wake of the September 11th Terrorist Attacks," *Journal of Nervous & Mental Disease* 190, no. 12 (2002): 833–38; Roxane Cohen Silver, E. Alison Holman, Daniel N. McIntosh, Michael Poulin, and Virginia Gil-Rivas, "Nationwide Longitudinal Study of Psychological Responses to September 11," *JAMA* 288 (2002): 1235–44; Rose Latino, Barbara Friedman, and Victoria Bellucci, "Treatment with Children and Adolescents Traumatized by the September 11th Attack," *Clinical Social Work Journal* 34, no. 4 (2006): 447–66; Conway Saylor, Virginia DeRoma, and Rhonda Swickert, "College Students with Previous Exposure to Crime Report More PTSD after 9-11-2001," *Psychological Reports* 99, no. 2 (2006): 581–82; J. D. Kinzie, J. K. Boehnlein, C. Riley, and L. Sparr, "The Effects of September 11 on Traumatized Refugees: Reactivation of Posttraumatic Stress Disorder, *Journal of Nervous & Mental Disease* 190, no. 7 (2002): 437–41.

22. John R. Allegra, Farzad Mostashari, Jonathan Rothman, Peter Milano, and Dennis G. Cochrane, "Cardiac Events in New Jersey after the September 11, 2001, Terrorist Attack," *Journal of Urban Health* 82, no. 3 (2005): 358–63; David Vlahov, Sandro Galea, Jennifer Ahern, Heidi Resnick, and Dean Kilpatrick, "Sustained Increased Consumption of Cigarettes, Alcohol, and Marijuana among Manhattan Residents after September 11, 2001," *American Journal of Public Health* 94, no. 2 (2004): 253–54; Judith A. Richman, Joseph S. Wislar, Joseph A. Flaherty, Michael Fendrich, and Kathleen M. Rospenda, "Effects on Alcohol Use and Anxiety of the September 11, 2001, Attacks and Chronic Work

Stressors: A Longitudinal Cohort Study," *American Journal of Public Health* 94, no. 11 (2004): 2010–15.

23. E. Alison Holman, Roxane Cohen Silver, Michael Poulin, Judith Andersen, Virginia Gil-Rivas, and Daniel N. McIntosh, "Terrorism, Acute Stress, and Cardiovascular Health: A 3-Year National Study Following the September 11th Attacks," *Archives of General Psychiatry* 65, no. 1 (2008): 73–80.

24. William E. Schlenger, Juesta M. Caddell, Lori Ebert, B. Kathleen Jordan, Kathryn M. Rourke, David Wilson, Lisa Thalji, J. Michael Dennis, John A. Fairbank, and Richard A. Kulka, "Psychological Reactions to Terrorist Attacks: Findings from the National Study of Americans' Reactions to September 11," *JAMA* 288 (2002): 581–88; C. A. Ford, J. R. Udry, K. Gleiter, and K. Chantala, "Reactions of Young Adults to September 11, 2001," *Archives of Pediatrics and Adolescent Medicine* 157 (2003): 572–78.

25. Mark A. Schuster, Bradley D. Stein, Lisa H. Jaycox, Rebecca L. Collins, Grant N. Marshall, Marc N. Elliott, Annie J. Zhou, David E. Kanouse, Janina L. Morrison, and Sandra H. Berry, "A National Survey of Stress Reactions after the September 11, 2001, Terrorist Attacks," *New England Journal of Medicine* 345, no. 20 (2001): 1507–12.

26. Ford et al.,"Reactions of Young Adults to September 11, 2001."

27. B. D. Stein, M. N. Elliott, L. H. Jaycox, R. L. Collins, S. H. Berry, D. J. Klein, and M. A. Schuster, "A National Longitudinal Study of the Psychological Consequences of the September 11, 2001 Terrorist Attacks: Reactions, Impairment, and Help-seeking," *Psychiatry* 67, no. 2 (2004): 105–17; Cohen Silver et al., "Nationwide Longitudinal Study of Psychological Responses to September 11."

Chapter 3. A Country United . . . Sort Of

1. Alexis de Tocqueville, *Democracy in America,* trans. George Lawrence (New York: Harper & Row, 1966).

2. Robert Bellah, *The Broken Covenant* (New York: Seabury Press, 1975): 112–15.

3. Ibid.

4. Philip Slater, *The Pursuit of Loneliness* (Boston: Beacon Press, 1970), 13.

5. Robert Bellah, Richard Madsen, William Sullivan, Ann Swidler, and Steven Tipton, *Habits of the Heart* (Berkeley: University of California Press, 1985).

6. Robert Putnam, *Bowling Alone* (New York: Simon & Schuster, 2000). For more about the disputes over the "bowling alone" thesis, see Irene Taviss Thomson, "The Theory That Won't Die: From Mass Society to the Decline of Social Capital," *Sociological Forum* 20, no. 3 (2005): 421–48; Dietlind Stolle and Marc Hooghe, "Inaccurate, Exceptional, One-Sided or Irrelevant? The Debate about the Alleged Decline of Social Capital and Civic Engagement in Western Societies," *British Journal of Political Science* 35, no. 1 (2005): 149–67.

7. David Lodge, *Thinks* (New York: Viking, 2001), 100–101.

8. Hal Sider and Cheryl Cole, "The Changing Composition of the Military and the Effect on Labor Force Data," *Monthly Labor Review* 107, no. 7 (1984): 10–13.

9. Paige D. Martin, Gerald Specter, Don Martin, and Maggie Martin, "Expressed Attitudes of Adolescents toward Marriage and Family Life," *Adolescence* 38, no. 150 (2003): 359–67.

10. David J. Harding and Christopher Jencks, "Changing Attitudes toward Premarital Sex: Cohort, Period, and Aging Effects," *Public Opinion Quarterly* 67, no. 2 (2003): 211–26.

11. Joshua Woods, "America: The Archipelago of Almost Fame," *Midwest Quarterly* 48, no. 3 (2007): 359–75.

12. D. Abrams and M. Hogg, "Comments on the Motivational Status of Self-Esteem in Social Identity and Intergroup Discrimination," *European Journal of Social Psychology* 18 (1988): 317–34; Marilynn B. Brewer and Rupert J. Brown, "Intergroup Relations," in *The Handbook of Social Psychology,* vol. 2, ed. Daniel T. Gilbert, Susan T. Fiske, and Gardner Lindzey (New York: McGraw-Hill, 1998).

13. Putnam, *Bowling Alone,* 402.

14. Georg Simmel, *The Sociology of Georg Simmel* (Glencoe, IL: Free Press, 1950).

15. Lewis A. Coser, *The Functions of Social Conflict* (New York: Free Press of Glencoe, 1964).

16. Ibid., 93–94.

17. Henri Tajfel and John Turner, "An Integrative Theory of Intergroup Conflict," in *The Social Psychology of Intergroup Relations,* ed. W. G. Austin and S. Worchel (Monterey, CA: Brooks/Cole, 1979), 33–48.

18. Jeff Greenberg, Sheldon Solomon, and Tom Pyszczynski, "Terror Management Theory of Self-Esteem and Cultural Worldviews: Empirical Assessments and Conceptual Refinements," in *Advances in Experimental Social Psychology,* vol. 29, ed. M. P. Zanna (San Diego, CA: Academic Press, 1997), 61–139.

19. Tom Pyszczynski, A. Abdollahi, Sheldon Solomon, Jeff Greenberg, F. Cohen, and D. Weise, "Mortality Salience, Martyrdom, and Military Might: The Great Satan Versus the Axis of Evil," *Personality and Social Psychology Bulletin* 32 (2006): 526.

20. Sheldon Solomon, Jeff Greenberg, and Tom Pyszczynski, "A Terror Management Theory of Social Behavior: The Psychological Functions of Self-Esteem and Cultural Worldviews," in *Advances in Experimental Social Psychology,* vol. 24, 120.

21. Putnam, *Bowling Alone,* 402.

22. John Mueller, "Presidential Popularity from Truman to Johnson," *American Political Science Review* 64, no. 1 (1970): 18–34.

23. Patricia Bradley, *Slavery, Propaganda, and the American Revolution* (Jackson: University Press of Mississippi, 1998), 52.

24. Robert J. Allison, *The Boston Massacre* (Beverly, MA: Commonwealth Editions, 2006), 64.

25. Robert Putnam, "A Better Society in a Time of War," *New York Times,* October 19, 2001.

26. Ibid.

27. David Levin, *What Happened in Salem? Documents Pertaining to the Seventeenth-Century Witchcraft Trials* (New York: Harcourt, Brace, 1960), xiii.

28. John Demos, "Underlying Themes in the Witchcraft of Seventeenth-Century New England," *American Historical Review* 75, no. 5 (1970): 1311–26.

29. Robert Detweiler, "Shifting Perspectives on the Salem Witches," *History Teacher* 8, no. 4 (1975): 596–610.

30. Centers for Disease Control and Prevention, "Psychological and Emotional Effects of the September 11 Attacks on the World Trade Center: Connecticut, New Jersey and New York," *JAMA* 288, no. 12 (2002): 1467–68.

31. "9/11 by the numbers," *New York Magazine,* September 16, 2002.

32. Theda Skocpol, "Will 9/11 and the War on Terror Revitalize American Civic Democracy?," *PS: Political Science and Politics* 35, no. 3 (2002): 537; Rob-

ert Putnam, "Bowling Together," *The American Prospect,* February 11, 2002, http://prospect.org/cs/articles?articleId=6114.

33. L. Penner, Michael T. Brannick, Shannon Webb, and Patrick Connell, "Effects on Volunteering of the September 11, 2001, Attacks: An Archival Analysis," *Journal of Applied Social Psychology* 35, no. 7, (2005): 1333–60.

34. Michael W. Traugott, Ted Brader, Deborah Coral, Richard Curtin, David Featherman, Robert Groves, Martha Hill, James Jackson, Thomas Juster, Robert Kahn, Courtney Kennedy, Donald Kinder, Beth-Ellen Pennell, Matthew Shapiro, Mark Tessler, David Weir, and Robert Willis, "How Americans Responded: A Study of Public Reactions to 9/11/01," *PS: Political Science and Politics* 35, no. 3 (2002): 511–16.

35. Young-Ok Yum and William Schenck-Hamlin, "Reactions to 9/11 as a Function of Terror Management and Perspective Taking," *Journal of Social Psychology* 145, no. 3 (2005): 265–86; Mario Mikulincer, Victor Florian, and Gilad Hirschberger, "The Existential Function of Close Relationships: Introducing Death into the Science of Love," *Personality and Social Psychology Review* 7, no. 1 (2003): 20–40; C. Peterson and Martin E. P. Seligman, "Character Strengths Before and After September 11," *Psychological Science* 14, no. 4 (2003): 381–84.

36. Tom W. Smith, Kenneth A. Rasinski, and Marianna Toce, *America Rebounds: A National Study of Public Response to the September 11th Terrorist Attacks, Preliminary Findings* (Chicago, IL: National Opinion Research Center, 2001), 4.

37. Not only does trust vary across countries, it is positively correlated with economic growth (Paul J. Zak and Stephen Knack, "Trust and Growth," *Economic Journal* 111, no. 470 [2001]: 295–321).

38. Smith, Rasinski, and Toce, *America Rebounds.*

39. Putnam, "Bowling Together."

40. Ibid.

41. Kenneth A. Rasinski, Jennifer Berktold, Tom W. Smith, and Bethany L. Albertson, *America Recovers: A Follow-Up to a National Study of Public Response to the September 11th Terrorist Attacks* (Chicago, IL: National Opinion Research Center, 2002); Traugott et al., "How Americans Responded"; Ronald J. Burke, "Effects of 9/11 on Individuals and Organizations: Down but Not Out!," *Disaster Prevention and Management* 14, no. 5 (2005): 629–38.

42. Amitai Etzioni and Deirdre Mead, *The State of Society: A Rush to Pre-9/11* (Washington, DC: Communitarian Network, 2003); Kimberly Gross, Sean Aday, and Paul R. Brewer, "A Panel Study of Media Effects on Political and Social Trust after September 11, 2001," *Harvard International Journal of Press/Politics* 9, no. 4 (2004): 49–73; Paul R. Brewer, Sean Aday, and Kimberly Gross, "Do Americans Trust Other Nations? A Panel Study," *Social Science Quarterly* 86, no. 1 (2005): 36–51.

43. Putnam, "Bowling Together."

44. Thomas H. Sander and Robert Putnam, "Walking the Civic Talk after Sept. 11," *Christian Science Monitor,* February 19, 2002; Putnam, "A Better Society in a Time of War."

45. Putnam, "Bowling Together."

46. C. A. Ford, J. R. Udry, K. Gleiter, and K. Chantala, "Reactions of Young Adults to September 11, 2001," *Archives of Pediatrics and Adolescent Medicine* 157 (2003): 572–78.

47. Skocpol, "Will 9/11 Revitalize American Democracy?"

48. Mike Schmierbach, Michael P. Boyle, and Douglas M. McLeod, "Civic Attach-

ment in the Aftermath of September 11," *Mass Communication & Society* 8, no. 4 (2005): 341.

49. Scott L. Althaus, "American News Consumption during Times of National Crisis," *PS: Political Science and Politics* 35, no. 3 (2002): 517–21.
50. Lisa De Moraes, "For an Extraordinary Week, Nielson Puts the Ratings Aside," *Washington Post,* September 20, 2001.
51. Althaus, "American News Consumption during Times of National Crisis."
52. Ibid., 519.
53. Putnam, "Bowling Together."
54. Stanley B. Greenberg, "'We'—not 'me,'" *American Prospect* 12, no. 22 (2001): 25–27.
55. Miguel R. Olivas-Luján, Anne-Wil Harzing, and Scott McCoy, "September 11, 2001: Two Quasi-Experiments on the Influence of Threats on Cultural Values and Cosmopolitanism," *International Journal of Cross Cultural Management* 4, no. 2 (2004): 211–28.
56. Thomas H. Sander and Robert Putnam, "Still Bowling Alone? The Post-9/11 Split," *Journal of Democracy* 21, no. 1 (2010): 11; see a study conducted by the U.S. Higher Education Research Institute online at http://www.gseis.ucla.edu/heri/pr-display.php?prQry=28.
57. Sander and Putnam, "Still Bowling Alone?," 9–16.
58. George H. Gallup, *The Gallup Poll: Public Opinion: 2002* (New York: Rowman & Littlefield, 2003).
59. Brian J. Gaines, "Where's the Rally? Approval and Trust of the President, Cabinet, Congress, and Government since September 11," *PS: Political Science and Politics* 35, no. 3 (2002): 530–36.
60. Neil J. Smelser, "Epilogue: September 11, 2001, as Cultural Trauma," in *Cultural Trauma and Collective Identity,* ed. Jeffrey Alexander, Ron Eyerman, Bernhard Giesen, Neil J. Smelser, and Piotr Sztompka (Berkeley: University of California Press, 2004), 268.
61. "Impact of the Attacks on America," *Gallup News Source,* October 8, 2001 (retrieved online at www.gallup.com).
62. Jonathan McDonald Ladd, "Predispositions and Public Support for the President during the War on Terrorism," *Public Opinion Quarterly* 71, no. 4 (2007): 511–38.
63. Gaines, "Where's the Rally?," 531.
64. Randall Collins, "Rituals of Solidarity and Security in the Wake of Terrorist Attack," *Sociological Theory* 22, no. 1 (2004): 54.
65. M. J. Landau, S. Solomon, J. Greenberg, F. Cohen, T. Pyszczynski, J. Arndt, C. H. Miller, D. M. Ogilvie, and A. Cook, "Deliver Us from Evil: The Effects of Mortality Salience and Reminders of 9/11 on Support for President George W. Bush," *Personality and Social Psychology Bulletin* 30 (2004): 1136–50; M. T. Gailliot, B. J. Schmeichel, and R. F. Baumeister, "Self-Regulatory Processes Defend against the Threat of Death: Effects of Self-Control Depletion and Trait Self-Control on Thoughts and Fears of Dying," *Journal of Personality and Social Psychology* 91 (2006): 49–62; Paul R. Abramson, John H. Aldrich, Jill Rickershauser, and David W. Rohde, "Fear in the Voting Booth: The 2004 Presidential Election," *Political Behavior* 29, no. 2 (2007): 197–220.
66. For more about the *New York Times/CBS News* poll, see James Dao and Dalia Sussman, "Bin Laden Raid Gives President Big Lift in Poll," *New York Times,* May 5, 2011.

67. Virginia A. Chanley, "Trust in Government in the Aftermath of 9/11: Determinants and Consequences," *Political Psychology* 23, no. 3 (2002): 469–83; Putnam, "Bowling Together"; Skocpol, "Will 9/11 Revitalize American Democracy?"; Smith, Rasinski, and Toce, *America Rebounds.*

68. The Gallup organization asked respondents, "How much trust and confidence do you have in our federal government in Washington when it comes to handling ['international problems' / 'domestic problems']—a great deal, a fair amount, not very much, or none at all?" In the September 7–10, 2001, survey, 68 percent of respondents said "a great deal" or "a fair amount" on international problems, 60 percent on domestic problems. These numbers rose to 83 percent and 77 percent, respectively, in the October 11–14 survey (see Gallup's continually updated Pulse of Democracy report at www.galluppoll.com).

69. Ford et al., "Reactions of Young Adults to September 11, 2001," 572–78.

70. Greenberg, "'We'—not 'me,'" 26.

71. Brewer, Aday, and Gross, "Do Americans Trust?"; Paul R. Brewer, Sean Aday, and Kimberly Gross, "Rallies All Around: The Dynamics of Systems Support," in *Framing Terrorism: The News Media, the Government, and the Public,* ed. Pippa Norris, Montague Kern, and Marion Just (New York: Routledge, 2003), 229–53; Marc J. Hetherington and Michael Nelson, "Anatomy of a Rally Effect: George W. Bush and the War on Terrorism," *PS: Political Science and Politics* 36 (2003): 37–42; Rasinski et al., *America Recovers*; Burke, "Effects of 9/11 on Individuals and Organizations," 629–38; Andrew J. Perrin and S. J. Smolek, "Who Trusts? Race, Gender, and the September 11 Rally Effect," *Social Science Research* 38, no. 1 (2009): 134–45.

72. Sophia Moskalenko, Clark McCauley, and Paul Rozin, "Group Identification under Conditions of Threat: College Students' Attachment to Country, Family, Ethnicity, Religion and University Before and After September 11, 2001," *Political Psychology* 27, no. 1 (2006): 77–97.

73. Smith, Rasinski, and Toce, *America Rebounds,* 3.

74. Rasinski et al., *America Recovers.*

75. Joseph Carroll, "Post-9/11 Patriotism Remains Steadfast. Nonwhites Least Likely to Feel Highly Patriotic," Gallup, July 19, 2005.

76. Linda J. Skitka, "Patriotism or Nationalism? Understanding Post–September 11, 2001, Flag-Display Behavior," *Journal of Applied Social Psychology* 35, no. 10 (2005): 1995–2011; D. W. Moore, "War Makes Americans Confident, Sad: Personal Lives Less Affected than during the First Gulf War and 9/11, Gallup, March 26, 2003.

77. Skitka, "Patriotism or Nationalism?"; Carroll, "Post-9/11 Patriotism Remains Steadfast."

78. Randall Collins, "Rituals of Solidarity and Security in the Wake of Terrorist Attack," *Sociological Theory* 22, no. 1 (2004): 53.

Chapter 4. The Authoritarian Turn

1. See the "United States Department of Defense Fiscal Year 2011 Budget Request" online at http://comptroller.defense.gov/defbudget/fy2011/FY2011_Weapons.pdf.

2. W. Seth Carus, *Cruise Missile Proliferation in the 1990s, Washington Paper 159* (Westport, CT: Praeger, 1992), 6.

3. "United States Department of Defense Fiscal Year 2011 Budget Request."

4. The elementary school cost estimate is based on 2008 RSMeans: Reed Construction Data, a leading cost information firm (see http://rsmeans.reedconstruction data.com).
5. See an interactive chart created by the *New York Times* ("Obama's 2011 Budget Proposal") online at http://www.nytimes.com/interactive/2010/02/01/us/budget .html.
6. "United States Department of Defense Fiscal Year 2011 Budget Request."
7. J. H. Stuhmiller, Y. Y. Phillips, and D. R. Richmond, "The Physics and Mechanisms of Primary Blast Injury," in *Textbook of Military Medicine. Conventional Warfare: Blast Ballistic and Burn Injuries,* ed. R. F. Bellamy and R. Zajtchuk (Washington, DC: Department of the Army, Office of the Surgeon General, Borden Institute, 1990), 241–70.
8. Ibid.
9. As General Tommy Franks, commander of U.S. Central Command, told reporters on March 22: "This will be a campaign unlike any other in history—a campaign characterized by shock, by surprise, by flexibility." (Fred Kaplan, "Bush's Many Miscalculations," *Slate,* September 9, 2003).
10. Tajfel and Turner, "An Integrative Theory of Intergroup Conflict"; M. B. Brewer, "Social Identity, Distinctiveness, and In-group Homogeneity," *Social Cognition* 11, no. 1 (1993): 150–64.
11. R. M. Doty, B. E. Peterson, and D. G. Winter, "Threat and Authoritarianism in the United States, 1978–1987," *Journal of Personality and Social Psychology* 61 (1991): 629–40; J. Duckitt, "Authoritarianism and Group Identification: A New View of an Old Construct," *Political Psychology* 10, no. 1 (1989): 63–84; S. Feldman, "Enforcing Social Conformity: A Theory of Authoritarianism," *Political Psychology* 24, no. 1 (2003): 41–74; Jeff Greenberg, Tom Pyszczynski, Sheldon Solomon, A. Rosenblatt, M. Veeder, S. Kirkland, and D. Lyon, "Evidence for Terror Management Theory II: The Effects of Mortality Salience on Reactions to Those who Threaten or Bolster the Cultural Worldview," *Journal of Personality and Social Psychology* 58 (1990): 308–18; Pyszczynski et al., "Mortality Salience, Martyrdom, and Military Might," 525–37; Tom Pyszczynski, Jeff Greenberg, and Sheldon Solomon, *In the Wake of 9/11: The Psychology of Terror* (Washington, DC: American Psychological Association, 2003).
12. T. W. Adorno, E. Frenkl-Brunswik, D. J. Levinson, and R. N. Sanford, *The Authoritarian Personality* (New York: Harper & Row, 1950).
13. G. W. Ladd and E. Cairns, "Children: Ethnic and Political Violence," *Child Development* 67 (1996): 14–18; A. Raviv, A. Sadeh, A. Raviv, O. Silberstein, and O. Diver, "Young Israelis' Reactions to National Trauma: The Rabin Assassination and Terror Attacks," *Political Psychology* 21 (2000): 299–322.
14. Andrew J. Perrin, "National Threat and Political Culture: Authoritarianism, Antiauthoritarianism, and the September 11 Attacks," *Political Psychology* 26, no. 2 (2005): 167–94.
15. Smith, Rasinski, and Toce, *America Rebounds,* 3.
16. Pyszczynski, Greenberg, and Solomon, *In the Wake of 9/11*; F. Cohen, S. Solomon, M. Maxfield, T. Pyszczynski, and J. Greenberg, "Fatal Attraction: The Effects of Mortality Salience on Evaluations of Charismatic, Task-Oriented, and Relationship-Oriented Leaders," *Psychological Science* 15, no. 12 (2004): 846–51; Gaines, "Where's the Rally?"
17. Landau et al.,"Deliver Us from Evil."
18. Ibid., 1146.

19. M. T. Gailliot, B. J. Schmeichel, and R. F. Baumeister, "Self-Regulatory Processes Defend against the Threat of Death: Effects of Self-Control Depletion and Trait Self-Control on Thoughts and Fears of Dying," *Journal of Personality and Social Psychology* 91 (2006): 49–62; Ernestine H. Gordijn and Diederik A. Stapel, "When Controversial Leaders with Charisma Are Effective: The Influence of Terror on the Need for Vision and Impact of Mixed Attitudinal Messages," *European Journal of Social Psychology* 38, no. 3 (2006): 389–411; Abramson, Aldrich, Rickershauser, and Rohde, "Fear in the Voting Booth."

20. Erika Falk and Kate Kenski, "Issue Saliency and Gender Stereotypes: Support for Women as Presidents in Times of War and Terrorism," *Social Science Quarterly* 87, no. 1 (2006): 1–18.

21. Jennifer L. Lawless, "Women, War, and Winning Elections: Gender Stereotyping in the Post-September 11th Era," *Political Research Quarterly* 57, no. 3, (2004): 479–90.

22. Lorraine Dowler, "Women on the Frontlines: Rethinking War Narratives Post 9/11," *GeoJournal* 58, nos. 2–3, (2002): 159–65.

23. Markku Verkasalo, Robin Goodwin, and Irina Bezmenova, "Values Following a Major Terrorist Incident: Finnish Adolescent and Student Values Before and After September 11, 2001," *Journal of Applied Social Psychology* 36, no. 1 (2006): 144–60; S. H. Schwartz, A. Bardi, and G. Bianchi, "Value Adaptation to the Imposition and Collapse of Communist Regimes in Eastern Europe," in *Political Psychology: Cultural and Cross-Cultural Perspectives,* ed. S. A. Renshon and J. Duckitt (London: Macmillan, 2000): 217–37.

24. It should be noted that the study by Verkasalo, Goodwin, and Bezmenova was based on respondents from Finland. On one hand, these results do not directly inform our understanding of 9/11 effects on America. On the other hand, as the authors contend, the study "suggests that even within a relatively 'remote' culture such as Finland, large-scale terrorist attacks may have a significant impact on individual values" (Verkasalo, Goodwin and Bezmenova, "Values Following a Major Terrorist Incident," 158).

25. Olivas-Luján, Harzing, and McCoy, "September 11, 2001," 211–28.

26. Ibid.

27. Ibid., 219.

28. Linda J. Skitka, C. W. Bauman, and E. Mullen, "Political Tolerance and Coming to Psychological Closure Following the September 11, 2001, Terrorist Attacks: An Integrative Approach," *Personality and Social Psychology Bulletin* 30, no. 6 (2004): 743–56; Pyszczynski et al., "Mortality Salience, Martyrdom, and Military Might," 525–37; B. M. Hastings and B. A. Shaffer, "Authoritarianism and Sociopolitical Attitudes in Response to Threats of Terror," *Psychological Reports* 97, no. 2 (2005): 623–30; H. M. Crowson, T. K. Debacker, and S. J. Thoma, "The Role of Authoritarianism, Perceived Threat and Need for Closure or Structure in Predicting Post-9/11 Attitudes and Beliefs," *Journal of Social Psychology* 146, no. 6 (2006): 733–50; Maria Jarymowicz and Daniel Bar-Tal, "The Dominance of Fear over Hope in the Life of Individuals and Collectives," *European Journal of Social Psychology* 36, no. 3 (2006): 367–92.

29. Leoni Huddy, Nadia Khatib, and Theresa Capelos, "Trends: Reactions to the Terrorist Attacks of September 11, 2001," *Public Opinion Quarterly* 66, no. 3 (2002): 418–50.

30. "War on Terrorism," Gallup, November 26–27, 2001 (retrieved online at www.gallup.com).

31. Huddy, Khatib, and Capelos, "Trends," 418–50.

32. Ibid.

33. Ibid.

34. Joseph Carroll, "Slim Majority Supports Anti-Terrorism Action in Afghanistan, Pakistan: Public Continue to Support Military Efforts in Afghanistan," Gallup, August 8, 2007.

35. These ratings were based on general polling questions with dichotomous alternatives, such as "should" or "should not," "favor" or "oppose," and so forth. See P. Everts and P. Isernia, "The War in Iraq," *Public Opinion Quarterly* 69, no. 2 (2005): 264–323.

36. Ibid.

37. Huddy, Khatib and Capelos, "Trends," 418–50; German Marshall Fund, *A World Transformed: Foreign Policy Attitudes of the U.S. Public after September 11,* September 4, 2002 (retrieved online at http://www.worldviews.org/docs/U.S. 9-11v2.pdf).

38. Alessandra Stanley, "As Word Spread about Bin Laden's Death, It Became a TV Moment," *New York Times,* May 3, 2011.

39. Watch footage of both commentators' takes on Osama bin Laden's assignation online at www.mofopolitics.com.

40. Maureen Dowd, "Killing Evil Doesn't Make Us Evil," *New York Times,* May 7, 2011.

41. Arthur Caplan, "Was It Right to Kill bin Laden?," *MSNBC.com,* May 2, 2011.

42. Joseph Carroll, "Perceptions of 'Too Much' Military Spending at 15-Year High: More Americans Also Say the Military Is Not Strong Enough," Gallup, March 2, 2007.

43. George W. Bush, "Remarks by the President Upon Arrival at Barksdale Air Force Base," Barksdale Air Force Base, Louisiana, September 11, 2001, http://www.whitehouse.gov/.

44. George W. Bush, "Statement by the President in His Address to the Nation," September 11, 2001, http://www.whitehouse.gov/.

45. George W. Bush, "Remarks by the President Upon Arrival at Barksdale Air Force Base," Barksdale Air Force Base, LA, September 11, 2001, http://www.whitehouse.gov.

46. Liz Sidoti, "9/11 Brought Us Together, But Was It Unity?" Associated Press, September 6, 2011.

47. George W. Bush, "Remarks by the President In Photo Opportunity with the National Security Team," September 12, 2001, http://www.whitehouse.gov.

48. George W. Bush, "Gov. Ridge Sworn-In to Lead Homeland Security," October 8, 2001, http://www.whitehouse.gov.

49. Barry Glassner, *The Culture of Fear: Why Americans are Afraid of the Wrong Things* (New York: Basic Books, 1999).

50. Edward C. Stewart and Milton J. Bennett, *American Cultural Patterns: A Cross-Cultural Perspective* (Chicago: Intercultural Press, 1991).

51. This figure (69 percent) represents an average across six national polls that used comparable questions; the findings from the individual polls included 74, 61, 55, 63, and 79 percent (Huddy, Khatib and Capelos, "Trends," 418–50). For related findings, see Leonie Huddy, Stanley Feldman, Charles Tabar, and Gallya Lahav, "Threat, Anxiety, and Support of Antiterrorism Policies," *American Journal of Political Science* 49, no. 3 (2005): 593–608; M. Greenberg, P. Craighill, and A. Greenberg, "Trying to Understand Behavioral Responses to

Terrorism: Personal Civil Liberties, Environmental Hazards, and U.S. Resident Reactions to the September 11, 2001 Attacks," *Human Ecology Review* 11, no. 2 (2004): 165–76.

52. Samuel J. Best, Brian S. Krueger, and Jeffrey Ladewig, "Privacy in the Information Age," *Public Opinion Quarterly* 70, no. 3 (2006): 375–401.

53. Ibid.

54. Ibid.

55. Davis, *Negative Liberty*.

56. Ibid., 119.

57. Greenberg, Craighill, and Greenberg, "Trying to Understand Behavioral Responses to Terrorism," 165–76.

58. For FBI hate crime statistics, see http://www.fbi.gov/ucr/ucr.htm#hate; for a study of hate crime in the wake of 9/11, see Bryan Byers and James Jones, "The Impact of the Terrorist Attacks of 9/11 on Anti-Islamic Hate Crime," *Journal of Ethnicity in Criminal Justice* 5, no. 1 (2007): 43–56.

59. See FBI hate crime statistics

60. Jack Levin and Jim Nolan, *The Violence of Hate: Confronting Racism, Anti-Semitism, and Other Forms of Bigotry* (Boston: Pearson Allyn and Bacon, 2010).

61. American-Arab Anti-Discrimination Committee, "Report on Hate Crimes and Discrimination against Arab Americans: The Post–September 11 Backlash, September 11, 2001–October 11, 2002," available online at http://www.adc.org/PDF/hcr02.pdf. See also Human Rights Watch, "We Are Not the Enemy: Hate Crimes against Arabs, Muslims, and Those Perceived to be Arab or Muslim after September 11," *Human Rights Watch* 14, no. 6 (2002): 1–41.

62. The U.S. Equal Employment Opportunity Commission's discrimination data are available online at www.eeoc.gov.

63. Steven Greenhouse, "Offended Muslims Speak Up," *New York Times,* September 24, 2010.

64. Costas Panagopoulos, "The Polls—Trends: Arab and Muslim Americans and Islam in the Aftermath of 9/11," *Public Opinion Quarterly* 70, no. 4 (2006): 608–24.

65. Frank Newport, "Americans Still Say Muslims Have Negative View of U.S.," Gallup, June 3, 2009.

66. Chelsea E. Schafer and Greg M. Shaw, "Tolerance in the United States," *Public Opinion Quarterly* 73, no. 2 (2009): 404–31.

67. Ibid.

68. Gallup Center for Muslim Studies, "In U.S., Religious Prejudice Stronger against Muslims," Gallup, January 21, 2010.

69. Jack G. Shaheen, "Reel Bad Arabs: How Hollywood Vilifies a People," *Annals of the American Academy of Political and Social Science* 588, no. 1 (2003): 171–93.

70. Gallup's Pulse of Democracy: Immigration, accessed online on October 5, 2007 at www.galluppoll.com.

71. See a continually updated survey at ibid.

72. Francine Segovia and Renatta Defever, "American Public Opinion on Immigrants and Immigration Policy," *Public Opinion Quarterly* 74, no. 2 (2010): 375–94.

73. Pew Research Center, "No Consensus on Immigration Problem or Proposed Fixes," March 30, 2006 (retrieved online at http://people-press.org); Frank Newport, "Americans Have Become More Negative on Impact of Immigrants," Gallup, July 13, 2007; Jeffrey M. Jones, "Only 4 in 10 Americans Satisfied

with Treatment of Immigrants," Gallup, August 15, 2007; Kathleen M. Moore, "'United We Stand': American Attitudes toward (Muslim) Immigration Post-September 11," *Muslim World* 92, nos. 1–2 (2002): 39–57; Panagopoulos, "Polls—Trends"; V. M. Esses, J. F. Dovidio, and G. Hodson, "Public Attitudes toward Immigration in the United States and Canada in Response to the September 11, 2001 'Attack on America,'" *Analysis of Social Issues and Public Policy* 2, no. 1 (2002): 69–85; C. R. Nagel, "Geopolitics by Another Name: Immigration and the Politics of Assimilation," *Political Geography* 21, no. 8 (2002): 971–87.

74. William J. Dobson, "The Day Nothing Much Changed," *Foreign Policy* 156 (Sept./Oct. 2006): 22.

75. Jon Stewart, Ben Karlin, and David Javerbaum, *America (The Book): A Citizen's Guide to Democracy Inaction* (New York: Warner Books, 2004), 24. The use of sarcasm on this decidedly unplayful topic may serve a reasonable purpose. Humor, as the philosopher Simon Critchley suggests, can change the situation in a way that encourages people to take a critical view of accepted practices. A joke may allow us to inventory our problems and take a reflexive glimpse at past failures (see Simon Critchley, *On Humour* [London: Routledge, 2002], 10). How else but through comic deprecation can we fully grasp the nation's insistence on violent retribution and the brutality of American political culture?

76. Rachel J. Chen and Joseph S. Chen, "Terrorism Effects on Travel Arrangements and Tourism Practices," *International Journal of Hospitality & Tourism Administration* 4, no. 3 (2003): 49–63; Tony Carter, *Many Thin Companies: The Change in Customer Dealings and Managers since September 11, 2001* (New York: Best Business Books, 2004); G. Gigerenzer, "Out of the Frying Pan into the Fire: Behavioral Reactions to Terrorist Attacks," *Risk Analysis* 26, no. 2 (2006): 347–51; G. Gigerenzer, "Dread Risk, September 11, and Fatal Traffic Accidents," *Psychological Science* 15, no. 4 (2004): 286–87; Makinen, *Economic Effects of 9/11*.

77. Scott Burns, "Did Terrorists Cause the Housing Mess?," *MSN Money Central,* February 13, 2008.

78. A. Wrzesniewski, "'It's Not Just a Job': Shifting Meanings of Work in the Wake of 9/11," *Journal of Management Inquiry* 11, no. 2 (2002): 230–34; Burke, "Effects of 9/11 on Individuals and Organizations," 629–38.

79. R. J. Blendon, K. Scoles, C. DesRoches, J. Young, M. Herrmann, J. Schmidt, and M. Kim, "Americans' Health Priorities Revisited after September 11," *Health Affairs,* November 13, 2001.

80. Brenda Eskenazi, Amy R. Marks, Ralph Catalano, Tim Bruckner, and Paolo G. Toniolo, "Low Birth Weight in New York City and Upstate New York following the Events of September 11," *Human Reproduction* 22, no. 11 (2007): 3013–20.

81. David L. Altheide, "Consuming Terrorism," *Symbolic Interaction* 27, no. 3 (2004): 289–308.

82. Stan A. Kaplowitz and Toby A. Ten Eyck, "Attitudes of the Food Industry towards Safety Regulations: Descriptive Statistics and Some Major Predictors," *Human Ecology Review* 13, no. 1 (2006): 11–22.

83. P. Fischer, T. Greitemeyer, A. Kastenmüller, D. Frey, and S. Osswald, "Terror Salience and Punishment: Does Terror Salience Induce Threat to Social Order?," *Journal of Experimental Social Psychology* 43, no. 6 (2007): 964–71.

84. John S. Seiter and Robert H. Gass, "The Effect of Patriotic Messages on Restaurant Tipping," *Journal of Applied Social Psychology* 35, no. 6 (2005): 1197–1205.

85. Jeffrey M. Jones, "Halloween Festivities Largely Unaffected by Terrorism Concerns," Gallup, October 30, 2001.
86. Matthew Nisbet and Teresa Myers, "The Polls—Trends: Twenty Years of Public Opinion about Global Warming," *Public Opinion Quarterly* 71, no. 3 (2007): 444–70.
87. Thomas L. Friedman, "The Power of Green," *New York Times Magazine,* April 15, 2007; Matthew Nisbet, "Going Nuclear: Frames and Public Opinion about Atomic Energy," *Science and the Media,* June 1, 2006; Robert F. Kennedy, "Better Gas Mileage, Greater Security," *New York Times,* November 24, 2001.
88. L. Lundy and T. Irani, "Media Framing of Agricultural Biotechnology Surrounding 9/11," in *Terrorism, Media, Society,* ed. Tomas Pludowski (Warsaw and Torun, Poland: Collegium Civitas Press and Adam Marszalek, 2006).
89. Duncan Green and Matthew Griffith, "Globalization and Its Discontents," *International Affairs* 78, no. 1 (2002): 49–68; Gregory M. Maney, Lynne M. Woehrle, and Patrick G. Coy, "Harnessing and Challenging Hegemony: The U.S. Peace Movement after 9/11," *Sociological Perspectives* 48, no. 3 (2005): 338–57; Bruce Barcott, "From Tree-Hugger to Terrorist," *New York Times,* April 7, 2002.
90. Altheide, "Consuming Terrorism"; Tom W. Smith, *Public Attitudes towards the Regulation of Firearms* (Chicago: National Opinion Research Center, 2007).
91. Jason Sunshine and Tom R. Tyler, "The Role of Procedural Justice and Legitimacy in Shaping Public Support for Policing," *Law & Society Review* 37, no. 3 (2003): 513–49.
92. M. Coleman, "U.S. Statecraft and the U.S.-Mexico Border as Security/Economy Nexus," *Political Geography* 24 (2005): 185–209; Jason Ackleson, "Directions in Border Security Research," *Social Science Journal* 40 (2003): 573–81.
93. Richard C. Eichenberg, "Gender Differences in Public Attitudes toward the Use of Force by the United States, 1990–2003," *International Security* 28, no. 1 (2003): 110–41.
94. Davis, *Negative Liberty.*
95. Brewer, Aday, and Gross, "Do Americans Trust?"
96. German Marshall Fund, *A World Transformed: Foreign Policy Attitudes of the U.S. Public after September 11,* September 4, 2002 (retrieved online at http://www.worldviews.org/docs/U.S.9-11v2.pdf).
97. Kareem Fahim, "Where Candy Machines Are Eyed with Suspicion," *New York Times,* October 12, 2007.

Chapter 5. Radical Islam, Loose Nukes, and Other Reasons to Freak Out

1. Mueller, *Overblown.*
2. National Institutes of Health, "Morbidity & Mortality: 2009 Chart Book on Cardiovascular, Lung, and Blood Disease" (available online at http://www.nhlbi.nih.gov/resources/docs/2009_ChartBook.pdf).
3. Ibid.
4. See, for instance, Norris, Kern, and Just, eds., *Framing Terrorism*; Amy Fried, "Terrorism as a Context of Coverage before the Iraq War," *Harvard International Journal of Press/Politics* 10, no. 3 (2005): 125–32; R. M. Entman, "Cascading Activation: Contesting the White House's Frame after 9/11," *Political Communication* 20, no. 4 (2003): 415–32; R. M. Entman, *Projections of Power: Framing News, Public Opinion and U.S. Foreign Policy* (Chicago: University of Chicago Press, 2004); Susan Moeller, *Media Coverage of Weapons of Mass Destruction* (College Park: Center for International and Security Studies at Maryland, University of Maryland at College Park, 2004).

5. Woods, "What We Talk about When We Talk about Terrorism."
6. Without delving into great detail, it should be noted that few areas of social science have inspired as much critical examination and blunt disagreement as the academic discussion of what news frames are and how they function in communicative texts (see D. A. Scheufele, "Framing as a Theory of Media Effects," *Journal of Communication* 49 [1999]: 103–19; R. M. Entman, "Framing: Toward Clarification of a Fractured Paradigm," *Journal of Communication* 43, no. 4 [1993]: 51–58; P. D'Angelo, "News Framing as a Multiparadigmatic Research Program: A Response to Entman." *Journal of Communication,* 52, no. 4 [2002]: 870–88). And yet, in spite of the ivory-tower tumult, the concept of framing remains extremely popular.
7. Entman, "Framing."
8. The early development of framing as an area of research is often associated with sociologist Erving Goffman, who applied the concept to a variety of social phenomena, non-mass-mediated social interaction in particular (Erving Goffman, *Frame Analysis: An Essay on the Organization of the Experience* [New York: Harper Colophon, 1974]; see Robert D. Benford and David A. Snow, "Framing Processes and Social Movements: An Overview and Assessment," *Annual Review of Sociology,* 26 [2000]: 611–39).
9. David A. Snow and Scott C. Byrd, "Ideology, Framing and the Islamic Terrorist Movement," *Mobilization: An International Quarterly Review* 12, no. 1 (2007): 119–36.
10. Matthew Aaron Gentzkow and Jesse M. Shapiro, "What Drives Media Slant? Evidence from U.S. Daily Newspapers," November 13, 2006, retrieved online at Social Science Research Network (SSRN), http://ssrn.com/abstract=947640.
11. David L. Altheide, *Terrorism and the Politics of Fear* (Lanham, MD: AltaMira Press, 2006); Altheide, *Creating Fear: News and the Construction of Crisis* (New York: Aldine de Gruyter, 2002); Norris, Kern, and Just, eds., *Framing Terrorism*; Entman, "Cascading Activation"; Xigen Li and Ralph Izard, "9/11 Attack Coverage Reveals Similarities, Differences," *Newspaper Research Journal* 24, no. 1 (2003): 204–19; Project for Excellence in Journalism, "Return to Normalcy? How the Media Have Covered the War on Terrorism," released January 28, 2002, http://www.journalism.org/resources/research/reports/normalcy/default.asp.
12. Myra Ferree, William Gamson, Jürgen Gerhards, and Dieter Rucht, *Shaping Abortion Discourse: Democracy and the Public Sphere in Germany and the United States* (Cambridge, UK: Cambridge University Press, 2002).
13. David A. Snow, Rens Vliegenthart, and Catherine Corrigall-Brown, "Framing the French Riots: A Comparative Study of Frame Variation," *Social Forces* 86, no. 2 (2007): 385–415.
14. J. N. Druckman, "The Implications of Framing Effects for Citizen Competence," *Political Behavior* 23, no. 3 (2001): 226; T. E. Nelson and D. R. Kinder, "Issue Frames and Group-centrism in American Public Opinion," *Journal of Politics* 58, no. 4 (1996): 1055–78; P. M. Sniderman and S. M. Theriault, "The Structure of Political Argument and the Logic of Issue Framing," in *Studies in Public Opinion: Attitudes, Nonattitudes, Measurement Error, and Change,* ed. W. E. Saris and P. M. Sniderman (Princeton: Princeton University Press, 2004), 136.
15. D. Kahneman and A. Tversky, "Choices, Values, and Frames," *American Psychologist* 39 (1984): 73–103; see B. McNeil, S. Pauker, H. Sox, and A. Tversky, "On the Elicitation of Preferences for Alternative Therapies," *New England Journal of Medicine* 306 (1982): 1259–62.

16. Jon Hurwitz and Mark Peffley, "Playing the Race Card in the Post–Willie Horton Era: The Impact of Racialized Code Words on Support for Punitive Crime Policy," *Public Opinion Quarterly* 69, no. 1 (2005): 99–112.
17. Sniderman and Theriault, "Structure of Political Argument and the Logic of Issue Framing."
18. Herbert J. Gans, "Reopening the Black Box: Toward a Limited Effects Theory," *Journal of Communication* 43, no. 4 (1993): 31.
19. W. A. Gamson, D. Croteau, W. Hoynes, and T. Sasson, "Media Images and the Social Construction of Reality," *Annual Review of Sociology* 18 (1992): 373–93.
20. Paul Slovic, *The Perception of Risk* (London; Sterling, VA: Earthscan, 2004).
21. Leonie Huddy, Stanley Feldman, and Christopher Weber, "The Political Consequences of Perceived Threat and Felt Insecurity," *Annals of the American Academy of Political and Social Science* 614 (2007): 131–53; Huddy et al., "Threat, Anxiety, and Support of Antiterrorism Policies."
22. H. A. Cooper, "Terrorism: The Problem of Definition Revisited," *American Behavioral Scientist* 44, no. 6 (2001): 881–93.
23. Ziva Kunda, *Social Cognition: Making Sense of People* (Cambridge, MA: MIT Press, 1999).
24. Norris, Kern, and Just, eds., *Framing Terrorism.*
25. B. Fischhoff, P. Slovic, S. Lichtenstein, S. Read, and B. Combs, "How Safe Is Safe Enough? A Psychometric Study of Attitudes towards Technological Risks and Benefits," *Policy Sciences* 9 (1978): 127–52; Lennart Sjöberg, "The Perceived Risk of Terrorism," *Risk Management: An International Journal* 7 (2005): 43–61; V. T. Covello, "Risk Communication: An Emerging Area of Health Communication Research," in *Communication Yearbook,* ed. S. Deetz, 15th ed. (Newbury Park, CA: Sage, 1992); Slovic, *Perception of Risk.*
26. See U.S. Department of Transportation, Traffic Safety Facts 2001, available online at http://www-nrd.nhtsa.dot.gov/Pubs/809476.PDF.
27. Race research in sociology and social psychology relies on a similar line of theorizing (see, for example, Thomas E. Ford, "Effects of Stereotypical Television Portrayals of African-Americans on Person Perception," *Social Psychology Quarterly* 60, no. 3 [1997]: 266–75).
28. Brigitte L. Nacos and Oscar Torres-Reyna, "Framing Muslim-Americans Before and After 9/11," in *Framing Terrorism: The News Media, the Government, and the Public,* ed. Pippa Norris, Montague Kern, and Marion Just (New York: Routledge, 2003); Brigette L. Nacos, *Terrorism and the Media: From the Iran Hostage Crisis to the World Trade Center Bombing* (New York: Columbia University Press, 1994); Michael W. Traugott and Ted Brader, "Explaining 9/11," in *Framing Terrorism,* ed. Norris, Kern, and Just.
29. Panagopoulos, "Polls—Trends"; Young-Ok Yum and William Schenck-Hamlin, "Reactions to 9/11 as a Function of Terror Management and Perspective Taking," *Journal of Social Psychology* 145, no. 3 (2005): 265–86.
30. Pape, *Dying to Win.*
31. Fischhoff et al., "How Safe Is Safe Enough?"
32. Paul Slovic, M. L. Finucane, E. Peters, and D. G. McGregor, "The Affect Heuristic: Rational Actors or Rational Fools? Implications of the Affect Heuristic for Behavioral Economics," in *Heuristics and Biases: The Psychology of Intuitive Judgment,* ed. D. Griffin, D. Kahneman, and T. Gilovich (Cambridge, UK: Cambridge University Press, 2002); Melissa Finucane, Ali Alhakami, Paul Slovic, and Stephen M. Johnson, "The Affect Heuristic in Judgments of Risks

and Benefits," *Journal of Behavioral Decision Making* 13 (2000): 1–17; E. J. Johnson and A. Tversky, "Affect, Generalization, and the Perception of Risk," *Journal of Personality and Social Psychology* 45 (1983): 20–31; Cass Sunstein, "Terrorism and Probability Neglect," *Journal of Risk and Uncertainty* 26, nos. 2/3 (2003): 121–36.

33. D. M. Cress and D. A. Snow, "The Outcomes of Homeless Mobilization: The Influence of Organization, Disruption, Political Mediation, and Framing," *American Journal of Sociology* 105 (2000): 1063–1104; Robert D. Benford and David A. Snow, "Framing Processes and Social Movements: An Overview and Assessment," *Annual Review of Sociology* 26 (2000): 611–39; W. A. Gamson, D. Croteau, W. Hoynes and T. Sasson, "Media Images and the Social Construction of Reality," *Annual Review of Sociology* 18 (1992): 373–93.

34. Slovic, *Perception of Risk.*

35. Sunstein, "Terrorism and Probability Neglect," 121–36.

36. A detailed report, including the data from this experiment, is forthcoming in *Critical Studies on Terrorism* under the title "Framing Terror: An Experimental Framing Effects Study of the Perceived Threat of Terrorism."

37. Sunstein, "Terrorism and Probability Neglect," 121–36.

38. Cress and Snow, "Outcomes of Homeless Mobilization," 1063–1104; Benford and Snow, "Framing Processes and Social Movements," 611–39; W. A. Gamson, D. Croteau, W. Hoynes, and T. Sasson, "Media Images and the Social Construction of Reality," *Annual Review of Sociology* 18 (1992): 373–93.

39. Davis, *Negative Liberty.*

40. Miroslav Nincic and Donna J. Nincic, "Race, Gender, and War," *Journal of Peace Research* 39, no. 5 (2002): 547–68; Pamela Johnston Conover and Virginia Sapiro, "Gender, Feminist Consciousness, and War," *American Journal of Political Science* 37, no. 4 (1993): 1079–99.

41. For more about the case of Bruce Ivins, who committed suicide in 2008 before he was formally charged by the FBI for the 2001 anthrax attacks, see David Freed, "The Wrong Man," *Atlantic Monthly* 305, no. 4 (2010): 46–57; Scott Shane, "Panel of Psychiatrists Backs F.B.I.'s Finding that Scientist Sent Anthrax Letters," *New York Times,* March 24, 2011.

42. Mike Carter, "Alleged Neo-Nazi Charged with Hate Crime in Spokane Bomb Plot," *Seattle Times,* April 21, 2011.

43. Nancy Gibbs, "George Tiller," *Time,* June 15, 2009.

44. Shaila Dewan, "Olympics Bomber Apologizes and Is Sentenced to Life Terms," *New York Times,* August 23, 2005.

45. Harvey W. Kushner, *Encyclopedia of Terrorism* (Thousand Oaks, CA: Sage, 2002).

46. Scott Shane, "Words as Weapons: Dropping the 'Terrorism' Bomb," *New York Times,* April 3, 2010.

47. For FBI hate crime statistics, see http://www.fbi.gov/ucr/ucr.htm#hate; for a study of hate crime in the wake of 9/11, see Bryan Byers and James Jones, "The Impact of the Terrorist Attacks of 9/11 on Anti-Islamic Hate Crime," *Journal of Ethnicity in Criminal Justice* 5, no. 1 (2007): 43–56.

48. Panagopoulos, "Polls—Trends."

49. Altheide, *Terrorism and the Politics of Fear.*

50. Fried, "Terrorism as a Context of Coverage before the Iraq War," 125–32; Entman, *Projections of Power*; Moeller, *Media Coverage of Weapons of Mass Destruction*; Amy Gershkoff and Shana Kushner, "Shaping Public Opinion: The 9/11-Iraq Connection in the Bush Administration's Rhetoric," *Perspectives on Politics* 3, no. 3 (2005): 525–38.

51. See "The Times and Iraq," *New York Times,* May 26, 2004.
52. Roger W. Cobb, "The Belief-Systems Perspective: An Assessment of a Framework," *Journal of Politics* 35, no. 1 (1973): 121–53.
53. Philip Converse, "The Nature of Belief Systems in Mass Publics," in *Ideology and Discontent,* ed. David Apter (Glencoe, IL: Free Press, 1964)
54. Finucane et al.,"The Affect Heuristic in Judgments of Risks and Benefits," 1–17; Robert B. Zajonc, "Feeling and Thinking: Preferences Need No Inferences," *American Psychologist* 35 (1980): 151–75; A. R. Damasio, *Descartes' Error: Emotion, Reason, and the Human Brain* (New York: Avon, 1994); S. Epstein, "Integration of the Cognitive and Psychodynamic Unconscious," *American Psychologist* 49 (1994): 709–24.

Chapter 6. The Fear Factory under Three Presidents

1. M. M. Dewey and L. Barr, "A Study of the Structure and Distribution of the Nexus," *Journal of Cell Biology* 23 (1964): 553–85.
2. William A. Gamson and Andre Modigliani, "Media Discourse and Public Opinion on Nuclear Power: A Constructionist Approach," *American Journal of Sociology* 95, no. 1 (1989): 1–37.
3. Altheide, *Terrorism and the Politics of Fear*; Fried, "Terrorism as a Context of Coverage before the Iraq War," 125–32; Entman, *Projections of Power*; Moeller, *Media Coverage of Weapons of Mass Destruction*; Gershkoff and Kushner, "Shaping Public Opinion," 525–38; Norris, Kern, and Just, eds., *Framing Terrorism.*
4. Rhys H. Williams, "From the 'Beloved Community' to 'Family Values': Religious Language, Symbolic Repertories, and Democratic Culture," in *Social Movements: Identity, Culture, and the State*, ed. N. Whittier, D. Meyer, and B. Robnett (New York: Oxford University Press, 2002), 247–65; Lynne Woehrle, Patrick Coy, and Gregory Maney, *Contesting Patriotism: Culture, Power and Strategy in the Peace Movement* (New York: Rowman & Littlefield, 2008).
5. Gregory M. Maney, Lynne M. Woehrle, and Patrick G. Coy, "Harnessing and Challenging Hegemony: The U.S. Peace Movement after 9/11," *Sociological Perspectives* 48, no. 3 (2005): 358.
6. Entman, "Cascading Activation."
7. A. Rachlin, *News as Hegemonic Reality: American Political Culture and the Framing of News Accounts* (New York: Praeger, 1988); E. Augelli and C. Murphy, *Quest for Supremacy in the Third World: A Gramscian Analysis* (London: Pinter, 1988); E. S. Herman and Noam Chomsky, *Manufacturing Consent: The Political Economy of the Mass Media* (New York: Pantheon Books, 2002); Antonio Gramsci, *Selections from Prison Notebooks* (London: New Left Books, 1971).
8. Maney, Woehrle, and Coy, "Harnessing and Challenging Hegemony," 358.
9. Erika G. King and Mary deYoung, "Imag(in)ing September 11: Ward Churchill, Frame Contestation, and Media Hegemony," *Journal of Communication Inquiry* 32, no. 2 (2008): 123–39.
10. Marc Steinberg, "The Talk and Back Talk of Collective Action: A Dialogic Analysis of Repertoires of Discourse among Nineteenth-Century English Cotton Spinners," *American Journal of Sociology* 105, no. 3 (1999): 746.
11. Stuart Hall, "The Rediscovery of 'Ideology': Return of the Repressed in Media Studies," in *Culture, Society, and the Media*, ed. M. Gurevitch, T. Bennett, J. Curran, and J. Wollacott (London: Methuen, 1982), 56–90; Denis McQuail, *Mass Communication Theory* (London; Thousand Oaks, CA: Sage, 2000).

12. Maney, Woehrle, and Coy, "Harnessing and Challenging Hegemony," 338–57.

13. Altheide, *Creating Fear* and *Terrorism and the Politics of Fear.*

14. Ruud Koopmans, "The Dynamics of Protest Waves: West Germany, 1965 to 1989," *American Sociological Review* 58 (1993): 637–58; Hanspeter Kriesi, Ruud Koopmans, Jan W. Dyvendak, and Marco G. Giugni, *New Social Movements in Western Europe: A Comparative Analysis* (Minneapolis: University of Minnesota Press, 1995).

15. Fischhoff et al., "How Safe Is Safe Enough?"; Sjöberg, "Perceived Risk of Terrorism"; Covello, "Risk Communication"; Slovic, *Perception of Risk.*

16. Fischhoff et al., "How Safe Is Safe Enough?"

17. Slovic, *Perception of Risk.*

18. Amos Tversky and Daniel Kahneman, "Judgment under Uncertainty: Heuristics and Biases," *Science* 185 (1974): 1124–31; Cass Sunstein, "Fear and Liberty," *Social Research* 71, no. 4 (2004): 976–96.

19. Kristie Bunton, "Social Responsibility in Covering Community: A Narrative Case Analysis," *Journal of Mass Media Ethics* 13, no. 4 (1998): 232–46.

20. Kim Witte and Mike Allen, "A Meta-Analysis of Fear Appeals: Implications for Effective Public Health Campaigns," *Health Education & Behavior* 27, no. 5 (2000): 591–615.

21. Jonathan D. Brown and Judith M. Siegel, "Attributions for Negative Life Events and Depression: The Role of Perceived Control," *Journal of Personality and Social Psychology* 54 (1988): 316–22.

22. See the article "Vice President's Remarks and Q&A at a Town Hall Meeting in Minnesota," available online in the White House archives (http://georgewbush-whitehouse.archives.gov).

23. Marta Lagos, "Terrorism and the Image of the United States in Latin America," *International Journal of Public Opinion Research* 15, no. 1 (2003): 95–101.

24. Herbert J. Gans, *Deciding What's News: A Study of CBS Evening News, NBC Nightly News, Newsweek, and Time* (New York: Pantheon Books, 1979); Bernard C. Cohen, *The Press and Foreign Policy* (Princeton, NJ: Princeton University Press, 1963); Lance W. Bennett, "The News about Foreign Policy," in *Taken by Storm: The Media, Public Opinion and U.S. Foreign Policy in the Gulf War,* ed. Lance W. Bennett and David L. Paletz (Chicago: University of Chicago Press, 1994); Li and Izard, "9/11 Attack Coverage Reveals Similarities, Differences," 204–19; Project for Excellence in Journalism, "Return to Normalcy?" (available online at www.journalism.org/resources/research/reports/normalcy/default.asp).

25. National Security Strategy of the United States of America (2002), released by the White House in September 2002 (http://www.whitehouse.gov/nsc/nss.pdf); Ivo H. Daalder, James M. Lindsay, and James B. Steinberg, "Hard Choices: National Security and the War on Terrorism," *Current History* 101, no. 659 (2002): 409–13; Richard C. Leone and Greg Anrig Jr., eds., *The War on Our Freedoms: Civil Liberties in an Age of Terrorism.* (New York: BBS Public Affairs, 2003); Thomas E. Baker and John F. Stack, *At War with Civil Rights and Civil Liberties* (Lanham, MD: Rowman & Littlefield, 2006); Cole and Dempsey, *Terrorism and the Constitution*; Doris A. Graber, "Terrorism, Censorship, and the First Amendment: In Search of Policy Guidelines," in *Framing Terrorism: The News Media, the Government, and the Public,* ed. Pippa Norris, Montague Kern, and Marion Just (New York: Routledge, 2003); Sunstein, "Fear and Liberty," 976–96.

26. George W. Bush, "Islam is Peace," remarks by the President at Islamic Center of

Washington, DC, September 17, 2001 (available online at: http://georgewbush
-whitehouse.archives.gov).

27. Bush, "Address to a Joint Session of Congress and the American People" (http://
georgewbush-whitehouse.archives.gov).

28. Though Ashcroft would later deny making this statement, the columnist who
took the quote claimed that he had read it back to both Ashcroft and his communications director to confirm its accuracy and received no correction at the time
(Nat Hentoff, "Ashcroft's Rhetorical Jihad on Islam: Attorney General Gets
Grief for His Reported Remarks," *Washington Times,* March 11, 2002).

29. Alan Cooperman, "Pipes to Be Named to Think Tank; Controversial Mideast
Scholar Will Be Recess Appointment," *Washington Post,* August 22, 2003.

30. American-Arab Anti-Discrimination Committee, "Report on Hate Crimes and
Discrimination against Arab Americans," 122.

31. Daniel Pipes, "We're going to Conquer America," *New York Post,* September
12, 2001.

32. Nacos and Torres-Reyna, "Framing Muslim-Americans Before and After 9/11";
Nacos, *Terrorism and the Media;* Traugott and Brader, "Explaining 9/11"; Pew
Research Center, "Views of Islam Remain Sharply Divided: Plurality Sees Is-
lam as More Likely to Encourage Violence," September 9, 2004 (retrieved on-
line at www.people-press.org); D. W. Moore, "Terrorism, Spread of Weapons
of Mass Destruction Most Critical Threats: Few Partisan and Socioeconomic
Differences on Rankings of Threats," Gallup, March 8, 2004; Moore, "'United
We Stand,'" 39–57.

33. Carl Hulse, "G.O.P. Seizes on Mosque Issue Ahead of Elections," *New York
Times,* August 16, 2010.

34. See an interview of Mr. King by CNN's Candy Crowley, http://transcripts.cnn
.com/TRANSCRIPTS/1103/06/sotu.01.html.

35. Akbar Ahmed, "Fair to Muslims?," *New York Times,* March 9, 2011. See a clip
about the controversy that includes Bill O'Reilly's reaction at http://www.you
tube.com/watch?v=ljzGWkjJYtk.

36. See the CNN report online at http://www.youtube.com/watch?v=H7ceyrBw50Y,
and discussion of Tancredo's statements in Electa Draper, "Denver Lawyer Says
Prejudice against Muslim Americans Has Grown," *Denver Post,* June 5, 2011.

37. Martin Peretz, "The New York Times Laments 'A Sadly Wary Misunderstand-
ing of Muslim-Americans': But Really Is It 'Sadly Wary' or a 'Misunderstand-
ing' At All? (blog post), *New Republic,* September 4, 2010.

38. For a detailed summary of President Obama's statements about terrorism during
his first year in office, see Peter Baker, "Inside Obama's War on Terrorism,"
New York Times, January 17, 2010.

39. Helene Cooper and Sheryl Gay Stolberg, "Obama Declares an End to Combat
Mission in Iraq," *New York Times,* August 31, 2010.

40. Thom Shanker and Christopher Drew, "Pentagon Anticipates Deep Budget
Cuts," *New York Times,* January 7, 2011; Paul Tait, "Time Running Out to Pre-
pare Afghan Security Forces," *Reuters,* May 9, 2011.

41. See the transcript of the White House Press Briefing by Press Secretary Robert
Gibbs on April 9, 2009 (retrieved online at www.whitehouse.gov).

42. Baker, "Inside Obama's War on Terrorism."

43. See, for instance, "Lethal Force under Law," *New York Times,* October 10, 2010.

44. Sharon Begley, "The Roots of Fear," *Newsweek,* December 24, 2007.

45. A detailed version of this study, which includes the data from the content analysis,

is currently under review at a peer-reviewed journal. For questions, or to receive a copy of the manuscript, please contact the author at joshua.woods@mail.wvu .edu.

46. Toby A. Ten Eyck and M. Williment, "The National Media and Things Genetic," *Science Communication* 25, no. 2 (2003): 129–52; Beverly Horvit, "Combat, Political Violence Top International Categories," *Newspaper Research Journal* 24, no. 2 (2003): 22–35; K. A. Swain, "Proximity and Power Factors in Western Coverage of the Sub Saharan AIDS Crisis," *Journalism and Mass Communication Quarterly* 80, no. 1 (2003): 145 65; James K. Hertog, "Elite Press Coverage of the 1986 U.S.-Libya Conflict: A Case Study of Tactical and Strategic Critique," *Journalism and Mass Communication Quarterly* 77, no. 3 (2000): 612–27.

47. Todd Gitlin, *The Whole World Is Watching: Mass Media in the Making & Unmaking of the New Left* (Berkeley: University of California Press, 1980); Gans, *Deciding What's News*.

48. Tim Groseclose and Jeffrey Milyo, "A Measure of Media Bias," *Quarterly Journal of Economics* 120, no. 4 (2005): 1191–1237.

49. Moreover, these two newspapers were used in a similar study of terrorism coverage, which may offer an opportunity for cross-study comparisons; see Li and Izard, "9/11 Attack Coverage Reveals Similarities, Differences," 204–19.

50. Articles that contained one of several search terms related to the threat of terrorism were collected and archived. The terms included: threat of terror!; terror! threat; war on terror!; terror! risk; terror! alert (the exclamation point represents a wildcard function that allows the search engine to find all variations of the term "terror," including terrorism, terrorist, and terrorists).

51. Efforts were taken to measure the reliability of the coding procedures. The percentage of agreement between coders was shown to be very high, ranging from 89 to 100 percent.

52. Bennett, "News about Foreign Policy."

53. Steinberg, "Talk and Back Talk of Collective Action," 746; Mark Gottdiener, *Postmodern Semiotics: Material Culture and the Forms of Postmodern Life* (Oxford: Blackwell, 1995); Gans, "Reopening the Black Box."

54. Samuel P. Huntington, *The Clash of Civilizations and the Remaking of the World* (New York: Simon & Schuster, 2003).

Chapter 7. Global Responses to Terror

1. As just one example of his work on this subject, see Ernest Becker, *The Birth and Death of Meaning: An Interdisciplinary Perspective on the Problem of Man* (New York: Free Press, 1971).

2. Becker, *The Denial of Death* (New York: Free Press, 1973), ix.

3. Many social scientists, sociologists in particular, would refute some of Becker's claims. They would argue, in contrast, that the fear of death, whether caused by terrorism or old age, is a learned emotion, a psychological manifestation of the culture within which a person is born and raised. Similar thoughts of dying may produce very different responses in people depending on the given cultural meanings they attach to death. See, for instance, Glenn M. Vernon, *The Sociology of Death: An Analysis of Death-Related Behavior* (New York: Ronald, 1970).

4. B. Fischhoff, R. M. Gonzalez, D. A. Small, and J. S. Lerner, "Judged Terror Risk and Proximity to the World Trade Center," *Journal of Risk and Uncertainty* 26, nos. 2/3 (2003): 137–51.

5. Joshua Woods, Toby A. Ten Eyck, Stan A. Kaplowitz, and Vladimir Shlapentokh, "Terrorism Risk Perceptions and Proximity to Primary Terrorist Targets:
   How Close Is Too Close?," *Human Ecology Review* 15, no. 1 (2008): 63–70.
6. Richard Overy, *Why the Allies Won* (London: Jonathan Cape, 1995), 325.
7. Denis Lacorne and Jacques Rupnik, "France Bewitched by America," in *The
   Rise and Fall of Anti-Americanism,* ed. Denis Lacorne, Jacques Rupnik, and
   Marie-France Toinet (New York: St. Martin's Press, 1990).
8. Jeffrey Brooks, *Thank You, Comrade Stalin!* (Princeton, NJ: Princeton University Press, 2000).
9. William Buchanan and Hadley Cantril, *How Nations See Each Other* (Urbana:
   University of Illinois Press, 1953).
10. Fareed Zakaria, "The Arrogant Empire," *Newsweek,* March 24, 2003; see a re-
    lated article by *New York Times* columnist Thomas Friedman ("Let Them Come
    to Berlin," *New York Times,* November 7, 2002).
11. W. J. Severin, *Communication Theories: Origins, Methods, and Uses in the
    Mass Media* (New York: Longman, 1991); M. D. Slater, "Integrating Applica-
    tion of Media Effects, Persuasion, and Behavior Change Theories to Commu-
    nication Campaigns: A Stages-of-Change Framework," *Health Communication*
    11, no. 4 (1999): 335–54.
12. P. Monge and S. A. Matei, "The Role of the Global Telecommunications Net-
    work in Bridging Economic and Political Divides, 1989 to 1999," *Journal of
    Communication* 54 (2004): 511–31.
13. Coser, *Functions of Social Conflict.*
14. John D. DeLamater and Daniel J. Myers, *Social Psychology,* 6th ed. (Blemont,
    CA: Thompson Wadsworth, 2007).
15. See Fritz Heider, "Attitudes and Cognitive Organization," *Journal of Psychol-
    ogy* 21 (1946): 107–12; Heider, *The Psychology of Interpersonal Relations*
    (New York: Wiley, 1958). Heider's "balance theory" (or variants of it) has been
    supported by numerous other empirical studies (J. A. Krosnick, "Americans'
    Perceptions of Presidential Candidates: A Test of the Projection Hypothesis,"
    Journal of Social Issues 46, no. 2 [1990]: 159–82; V. Ottati, M. Fishbein, and S.
    E. Middlestadt, "Determinants of Voters' Beliefs about the Candidates' Stands
    on Issues: The Role of Evaluative Bias Heuristics and the Candidates' Expressed
    Message," *Journal of Personality and Social Psychology* 55 [1988]: 517–29;
    T. M. Newcomb, *The Acquaintance Process* [New York: Holt, Rinehart and
    Winston, 1961]; E. Aronson and V. Cope, "My Enemy's Enemy Is My Friend,"
    Journal of Personality and Social Psychology 8 [1968]: 34–38).
16. A. H. Eagly and S. Chaiken, "Attitude Structure and Function," in *The Hand-
    book of Social Psychology,* ed. D. T. Gilbert, S. T. Fiske, and G. Lindzey (Boston:
    McGraw-Hill, 1998).
17. T. M. Newcomb, "Interpersonal Balance," in *Theories of Cognitive Consisten-
    cy: A Sourcebook,* ed. R. P. Abelson (Chicago: Rand McNally, 1968).
18. Fred Kaplan, "Bush's Many Miscalculations," *Slate,* September 9, 2003.
19. Thomas L. Friedman, "Tone It Down a Notch," *New York Times,* October 2, 2002.
20. Suzanne Daley, "First Time, NATO Invokes Joint Defense Pact with U.S.," *New
    York Times,* September 13, 2001.
21. "The Blair Years: In His Own Words," *Guardian,* May 11, 2007.
22. Pew Research Center, "A Year after Iraq War: Mistrust of America in Europe
    Ever Higher, Muslim Anger Persists," March 16, 2004 (retrieved online at
    http://people-press.org).

23. See longitudinal data from the "Voice of the People Survey" online at http://www.voice-of-the-people.net.
24. See two reports by the Pew Research Center: "American Character Gets Mixed Reviews: U.S. Image up Slightly, but Still Negative," June 23, 2005, and "Global Opinion: The Spread of Anti-Americanism: A Review of Pew Global Attitudes Project Findings," January 24, 2005 (both retrieved online at http://people-press.org).
25. Pew Research Center, "Obama More Popular Abroad than at Home, Global Image of U.S. Continues to Benefit," June 17, 2010 (retrieved online at http://people-press.org).
26. Ibid.
27. The group of countries selected for the project reflected a "purposive sample" based on several criteria, including geopolitical significance, nuclear capability, as well as our interest in particular cultural, economic, and political differences between these nations. Russia, India, and China are three of the largest foreign countries that possess nuclear weapons, and have strong geopolitical influences. Germany and Lithuania represent Western and Eastern European culture and politics, respectively. Colombia was selected as the representative from Latin America, and Egypt represents the Muslim world. Although these countries represent distinct regions of the world—the Middle East, Latin America, Asia, Eastern and Western Europe—generalizations across these regions should be made only with caution, and even then they will remain impressionistic to some extent. However, our total sample does comprise a sizable portion of the world's population, and each country plays a unique and oftentimes powerful role in the regional and global political arenas. Moreover, in the wake of 9/11, there was a notable similarity in public opinion of the United States across the countries in these regions, particularly in the Muslim world and in Western Europe, according to the Pew Research Center (http://people-press.org; Pew Research Center, 2005).
28. Any article that contained the views of more than one person on one of our topics of interest was broken into separate units of analysis. For this reason, the sample included a total of 2,856 units, but only 2,369 articles.
29. For a detailed explanation of the methods used in this project, see Shlapentokh, Woods, and Shiraev, eds., *America*.
30. The issues included (a) depictions of 9/11, (b) the identification of the prime suspects, (c) suggestions on how the United States should respond to the attacks, and (d) general descriptions of America itself. For each of these issues, an extensive list of response options was compiled. A combined total of 111 alternatives were included in the codebook. In addition to these four quantitative indicators, the coders were also asked to give their own assessment of each respondent in the sample ("respondents" were either the byline author of an article, or someone quoted in an article). Estimates ranged from 1 ("completely favorable toward the U.S.") to 5 ("completely unfavorable toward the U.S.").
31. For an explanation of the factor analysis used to combine the variables, see Joshua Woods, "The Common Enemy Rationale: An Attempt to Apply Concepts of Cognitive Consistency to the Portrayals of the United States in the Foreign Press," *Global Media Journal* 4, no. 7 (2005), http://lass.calumet.purdue.edu/cca/gmj/fa05/gmj-fa05-woods.htm
32. By "favorability," then, we mean "agreement" with the official U.S. position as articulated by the president. The official opinion was determined using a content

analysis of forty-six public speeches made by President Bush after 9/11. The speeches were published on the White House website September 11–25 and October 7–21, 2001 (see www.whitehouse.gov).

33. Ursula Kelders, commentary in *Westdeutsche Allgemeine Zeitung,* September 12, 2001.
34. Ahmad Almajhop, commentary in *Afaq Arabia,* September 15, 2001.
35. Frank Newport, "Americans Continue to be Strongly behind Retaliatory Military Actions," Gallup, September 24, 2001.
36. Leonid Shebarshin, commentary in *Argumenty i Fakty,* September 11–17, 2001; see David R. Farber, *What They Think of Us: International Perceptions of the United States since 9/11* (Princeton, NJ: Princeton University Press, 2007).
37. Newport, "Americans Continue to Be Strongly behind Retaliatory Military Actions."
38. Leonid Ivashov, commentary in *Nezavisimaya Gazeta,* October 10, 2001.
39. For a more detailed explanation of these findings and an expanded discussion of the social and historical context of the press in each of the project countries, see Shlapentokh, Woods, and Shiraev, eds., *America.*

Chapter 8. Democracy on the Fritz

1. Gamson et al.,"Media Images and the Social Construction of Reality," 2.
2. Siebert and his colleagues suggest that the libertarian model has the potential for allowing economic constraints to influence the press, but they quickly justify the model by discussing its close variant, the "social responsibility" model. Social responsibility theory holds "that the power and near monopoly position of the media impose on them an obligation to be socially responsible, to see that all sides are fairly presented and that the public has enough information to decide" (Fred S. Siebert, Theodore Peterson, and Wilbur Schramm, *Four Theories of the Press: The Authoritarian, Libertarian, Social Responsibility, and Soviet Communist Concepts of What the Press Should Be and Do* [Urbana: University of Illinois Press, 1956], 5).
3. Daniel C. Hallin and Paolo Mancini, *Comparing Media Systems: Three Models of Media and Politics* (Cambridge, UK; New York: Cambridge University Press, 2004), 7.
4. Denis McQuail, *Mass Communication Theory* (London; Thousand Oaks, CA: Sage Publications, 2000).
5. Ibid., 70.
6. Siebert, Peterson, and Schramm, *Four Theories of the Press.*
7. Frances Millard, "Democratization and the Media in Poland," in *Democratization and the Media,* ed. Vicky Randall (London; Portland, OR: Frank Cass, 1998).
8. Ellen Propper Mickiewicz, *Changing Channels: Television and the Struggle for Power in Russia* (Durham, NC: Duke University Press, 1999).
9. H. Davis, P. Hammond, and L. Nizamova, "Changing Identities and Practices in Post-Soviet Journalism: The Case of Tatarstan," *European Journal of Communication* 13, no. 1 (1998): 77–98.
10. M. Sukosd, "Democratic Transformation and the Mass Media in Hungary: From Stalinism to Democratic Consolidation," in *Democracy and the Media: A Comparative Perspective,* ed. Richard Gunther and Anthony Mughan (Cambridge, UK: Cambridge University Press, 2000).
11. T. A. Mollison, "Television Broadcasting Leads Romania's March toward an Open,

Democratic Society," *Journal of Broadcasting & Electronic Media* 42, no. 1 (1998): 128–41.

12. R. Bresnahan, "The Media and the Neoliberal Transition in Chile: Democratic Promise Unfulfilled," *Latin American Perspectives* 30, no. 6 (2003): 39–68.
13. G. D., Rawnsley and M. T. Rawnsley, "Regime Transition and the Media in Taiwan," in *Democratization and the Media*, ed. Randall.
14. V. Randall, "Introduction," in *Democratization and the Media*.
15. McQuail, *Mass Communication Theory*.
16. Jennifer L. Merolla and Elizabeth J. Zechmeister, *Democracy at Risk: How Terrorist Threats Affect the Public* (Chicago: University of Chicago Press, 2009).
17. Ibid., 195.
18. Ibid., 196.
19. Pamela J. Shoemaker and Stephen D. Reese, *Mediating the Message: Theories of Influences on Mass Media Content* (White Plains, NY: Longman, 1996), 228. Many of the authors who support this position draw on the Marxist tradition. As Parenti wrote, citing Marx directly, "Those who control the material means of production also control the mental means of production." See Michael Parenti, *Inventing Reality: Politics and the Mass Media* (New York: St. Martin's Press, 1986), 32.
20. H. Molotch and M. Lester, "News as Purposive Behavior: On the Strategic Use of Routine Events, Accidents and Scandals," *American Sociological Review* 39 (1974): 101–12; P. Bachrach and M. Baratz, "Two Faces of Power," *American Political Science Review* 56 (1962): 947–52; J. Herbert Altschull, *Agents of Power: The Media and Public Policy* (White Plains, NY: Longman, 1995).
21. Gloria Steinem, "Sex, Lies, and Advertising," *Ms,* July/August 1990, 18–28; C. Edwin Baker, *Media, Markets, and Democracy* (Cambridge, UK; New York: Cambridge University Press, 2002).
22. Herman and Chomsky, *Manufacturing Consent*.
23. Gamson, Croteau, Hoynes, and Sasson, "Media Images and the Social Construction of Reality," 373–93.
24. Shoemaker and Reese, *Mediating the Message*.
25. For examples of such studies, see John H. McManus, *Market-driven Journalism: Let the Citizen Beware?* (Thousand Oaks, CA: Sage, 1994); Baker, *Media, Markets, and Democracy*; Ben H. Bagdikian, *The Media Monopoly* (Boston: Beacon Press, 2000); Dean Alger, *Megamedia: How Giant Corporations Dominate Mass Media, Distort Competition, and Endanger Democracy* (Lanham, MD: Rowman & Littlefield, 1998). It should be noted, at the same time, that studies on the negative influences of ideology, advertisers, and ownership concentration on press pluralism or "media diversity" have been contested in the literature. See M. E. McCombs, "Concentration, Monopoly, and Content," in *Press Concentration and Monopoly: New Perspectives on Newspaper Ownership and Operation*, ed. Robert G. Picard (Norwood, NJ: Ablex, 1988); D. F. Hale, "Editorial Diversity and Ad Concentration," in *Press Concentration and Monopoly*; David P. Demers, *The Menace of the Corporate Newspaper: Fact or Fiction?* (Ames: Iowa State University Press, 1996); G. L. Grotta, "Consolidation of Newspapers: What Happens to the Consumer?," *Journalism Quarterly* 48 (1971): 245–50. In her book on television diversity, Einstein offers ample evidence to reject the "prevailing wisdom that the more concentrated the media industry, the less diverse the communication landscape" (Mara Einstein, *Media Diversity: Economics, Ownership, and the FCC* [Mahwah, NJ: L. Erl-

baum, 2004], vii). In a classic study on radio broadcasting, Peter Steiner argued that media ownership concentration actually produces more diversity, because when radio channels compete they tend to produce similar content as they strive for the largest share of the market ("Program Patterns and Preferences, and the Workability of Competition in Radio Broadcasting," *Quarterly Journal of Economics* 66 [1952]: 194–223).

26. Yuezhi Zhao, *Media, Market, and Democracy in China: Between the Party Line and the Bottom Line* (Urbana: University of Illinois Press, 1998); A. Fung, "China and Hong Kong Reporting on the United States: Ambivalence and Contradictions," in *America*; X. Liu and J. Wu, "Chinese Public Opinion in Response to the 9/11 Events," in *America*.

27. Shoemaker and Reese, *Mediating the Message*; Pierre Bourdieu, *Acts of Resistance: Against the Tyranny of the Market,* trans. Richard Nice (New York: New Press, 1998); Emile Durkheim, *The Rules of Sociological Method* (New York: Free Press, 1964).

28. Einstein, *Media Diversity*; Baker, *Media, Markets, and Democracy*; Bagdikian, *Media Monopoly*.

29. Sakae Ishikawa, ed., *Quality Assessment of Television* (Luton, Bedfordshire: University of Luton Press, 1996); H. Hellman, "Diversity, an End in Itself? Developing a Multi-measure Methodology of Television Programme Variety Studies," *European Journal of Communication* 16, no. 2 (2001): 181–208.

30. L. M. Zoch and J. V. Turk, "Women Making News: Gender as a Variable in Source Selection and Use," *Journalism and Mass Communication Quarterly* 75 (Winter 1998): 762–75.

31. McQuail, *Media Performance*.

32. For a full explanation of the methodology of this project, see Joshua Woods, "Democracy and the Press: A Comparative Analysis of Pluralism in the International Print Media," *Social Science Journal* 44, no. 2 (2007): 213–30.

33. The highest value of IQV is always 1.0 whenever cases are equally spread over the categories. For instance, if a given issue related to 9/11 had four categories and an equal number of content units fell in each category, the IQV score would be calculated as follows: IQV = $[1-(.25^2 + .25^2 + .25^2 + .25^2)] / (.75) = 1$. If all of the units fell in one category, the equation would give the lowest possible IQV value, 0.

34. See, for example, Seymour M. Lipset and Jason M. Lakin, *The Democratic Century* (Norman: University of Oklahoma Press, 2004); Robert A. Dahl, *Polyarchy: Participation and Opposition* (New Haven, CT: Yale University Press, 1971); Dahl, *On Democracy* (New Haven, CT: University Press, 1998); Z. Elkins, "Gradations of Democracy? Empirical Test of Alternative Conceptualizations," *American Journal of Political Science* 44, no. 2 (2000): 293–300.

35. Polity Project is a joint research project conducted by the University of Maryland's Center for International Development and Conflict Management and George Mason University's Center for Global Policy. The Polity database is available online at http://www.cidcm.umd.edu/inscr/polity.

36. See the Freedom House data online at www.freedomhouse.org. Several studies have drawn on these data for measuring democracy. See D. Collier and R. Adcock, "Democracy and Dichotomies: A Pragmatic Approach to Choices about Concepts," *Annual Review of Political Science* 2 (1999): 537–65; T. Vanhanen, "A New Dataset for Measuring Democracy, 1810–1998," *Journal of Peace Research* 37, no. 2 (2000): 251–65; J. Isham, D. Kaufmann, and L. H. Pritchett,

"Civil Liberties, Democracy, and the Performance of Government Projects," *World Bank Economic Review* 11, no. 2 (1997): 219–42; C. C. Gibson, "Of Waves and Ripples: Democracy and Political Change in Africa in the 1990s," *Annual Review of Political Science* 5 (2002): 201–21. At the same time, the Freedom House project is not immune to critiques and must contend with the methodological difficulties associated with conducting extensive cross-national research. For critiques, see K. A. Bollen and P. Paxton, "Subjective Measures of Liberal Democracy," *Comparative Political Studies* 33, no. 1 (2000): 58–86; Sara McLaughlin, Scott Gates, Havard Hegre, Ranveig Gissinger, and Nils Petter Gleditsch, "Timing the Changes in Political Structures: A New Polity Database," *Journal of Conflict Resolution* 42, no. 2 (1998): 231–42.

37. Freedom House website.
38. The six issues included: Who is the prime suspect of 9/11? How should the global conflict of 9/11 be described? Why did the U.S. carry out military actions in Afghanistan? How should the U.S.-led war in Afghanistan be evaluated? What terms should be used to describe the U.S.? The sixth issue consisted of the coder's subjective assessment of the article's view of the United States. For more details on these issues and how they were analyzed, see Woods, "Democracy and the Press."
39. Phillip J. Tichenor, *Community Conflict and the Press* (Beverly Hills, CA: Sage, 1980), 23.

Conclusion

1. See data from the Defense Department in "Our View on Defense Spending: It's Time to Put a Hold on the Pentagon's Blank Check," *USA Today,* May 20, 2010.
2. Tom Brokaw, "The Wars That America Forgot About," *New York Times,* October 17, 2010. See Andrew Bacevich, *Washington Rules: America's Path to Permanent War* (New York: Metropolitan Books, 2010); Clyde Haberman, "For Many, Wars Are Out of Sight, Out of Mind and Out of the Debate," *New York Times,* October 26, 2010.
3. "Arizona Passes Tough Illegal Immigration Law," *Reuters,* April 19, 2010.
4. See a video of Governor Brewer's statements online at http://thinkprogress .org/2010/04/30/brewer-terrorist-attacks.
5. Pyszczynski, Greenberg, and Solomon, *In the Wake of 9/11.*
6. Ibid., 15.
7. Ibid., 9.
8. Fischhoff et al., "How Safe Is Safe Enough?"; Sjöberg, " Perceived Risk of Terrorism"; Covello, "Risk Communication"; Slovic, *Perception of Risk.*
9. David Brooks, "Columbine Killers," *New York Times,* April 24, 2004.
10. Ibid.
11. David Zucchino, "Drone Pilots Have a Front-row Seat on War, from Half a World Away," *Los Angeles Times,* February 21, 2010.
12. Mueller, *Overblown,* 33.
13. See, for instance, a Russian newspaper's interview with Nikolai Zlobin, director of Russian and Asian Programs at the Center for Defense Information in the United States (*Izvestia,* August 28, 2003).

SELECTED BIBLIOGRAPHY

"9/11 by the numbers," *New York Magazine,* September 16, 2002.

Abrams, D., and M. Hogg. "Comments on the Motivational Status of Self-esteem in Social Identity and Intergroup Discrimination." *European Journal of Social Psychology* 18 (1988): 317–34.

Abramson, Paul R., John H. Aldrich, Jill Rickershauser, and David W. Rohde. "Fear in the Voting Booth: The 2004 Presidential Election." *Political Behavior* 29, no. 2 (2007): 197–220.

Adorno, T. W., E. Frenkl-Brunswik, D. J. Levinson, and R. N. Sanford. *The Authoritarian Personality.* New York: Harper & Row, 1950.

Alger, Dean. *Megamedia: How Giant Corporations Dominate Mass Media, Distort Competition, and Endanger Democracy.* Lanham, MD: Rowman & Littlefield, 1998.

Althaus, Scott L. "American News Consumption during Times of National Crisis." *PS: Political Science and Politics* 35, no. 3 (2002): 517–21.

Altheide, David L. "Consuming Terrorism." *Symbolic Interaction* 27, no. 3 (2004): 289–308.

———. *Creating Fear: News and the Construction of Crisis.* New York: Aldine de Gruyter, 2002.

———. *Terrorism and the Politics of Fear.* Lanham, MD: AltaMira Press, 2006.

Altschull, J. Herbert. *Agents of Power: The Media and Public Policy.* White Plains, NY: Longman, 1995.

Aronson, E., and V. Cope. "My Enemy's Enemy Is My Friend." *Journal of Personality and Social Psychology* 8 (1968): 34–38.

Bachrach, P., and M. Baratz. "Two Faces of Power." *American Political Science Review* 56 (1962): 947–52.

Bagdikian, Ben H. *The Media Monopoly.* Boston: Beacon Press, 2000.

Baker, C. Edwin *Media, Markets, and Democracy.* New York: Cambridge University Press, 2002.

Baker, Peter. "Inside Obama's War on Terrorism." *New York Times,* January 17, 2010.

Barber, B. R. "Beyond Jihad vs. McWorld." *Nation,* January 21, 2002.

Bauman, Zygmunt. *Liquid Fear*. Cambridge, UK: Polity Press, 2006.

Becker, Ernest. *The Birth and Death of Meaning: An Interdisciplinary Perspective on the Problem of Man.* New York: Free Press, 1971.

————. *The Denial of Death.* New York: Free Press, 1973.

Bellah, Robert, Richard Madsen, William Sullivan, Ann Swidler, and Steven Tipton. *Habits of the Heart.* Berkeley: University of California Press, 1985.

Benford, Robert D., and David A. Snow. "Framing Processes and Social Movements: An Overview and Assessment." *Annual Review of Sociology* 26 (2000): 611–39.

Bennett, Lance W. "The News about Foreign Policy." *Taken by Storm: The Media, Public Opinion and U.S. Foreign Policy in the Gulf War.* Edited by Lance W. Bennett and David L. Paletz. Chicago: University of Chicago Press, 1994.

Best, Samuel J., Brian S. Krueger, and Jeffrey Ladewig. "Privacy in the Information Age." *Public Opinion Quarterly* 70, no. 3 (2006): 375–401.

Bourdieu, Pierre. *Acts of Resistance: Against the Tyranny of the Market.* Translated by Richard Nice. New York: New Press, 1998.

Brewer, Marilynn B., and Rupert J. Brown. "Intergroup Relations." *The Handbook of Social Psychology,* vol. 2. Edited by Daniel T. Gilbert, Susan T. Fiske, and Gardner Lindzey. New York: McGraw-Hill, 1998.

Brewer, Paul R., Sean Aday, and Kimberly Gross. "Do Americans Trust Other Nations? A Panel Study." *Social Science Quarterly* 86, no. 1 (2005): 36–51.

Byers, Bryan, and James Jones. "The Impact of the Terrorist Attacks of 9/11 on Anti-Islamic Hate Crime." *Journal of Ethnicity in Criminal Justice* 5, no. 1 (2007): 43–56.

Carragee, Kevin M., and Wim Roefs. "The Neglect of Power in Recent Framing Research." *Journal of Communication* 54, no. 2 (2004): 214–33.

Chanley, Virginia A. "Trust in Government in the Aftermath of 9/11: Determinants and Consequences." *Political Psychology* 23, no. 3 (2002): 469–83.

Chomsky, Noam. *9-11.* New York: Seven Stories Press, 2001.

Cohen, Bernard C. *The Press and Foreign Policy.* Princeton, NJ: Princeton University Press, 1963.

Cohen, F., S. Solomon, M. Maxfield, T. Pyszczynski, and J. Greenberg. "Fatal Attraction: The Effects of Mortality Salience on Evaluations of Charismatic, Task-Oriented, and Relationship-Oriented Leaders." *Psychological Science* 15, no. 12 (2004): 846–51.

Cole, David, and James X. Dempsey. *Terrorism and the Constitution: Sacrificing Civil Liberties in the Name of National Security.* New York: New Press, 2006.

Collins, Randall. "Rituals of Solidarity and Security in the Wake of Terrorist Attack." *Sociological Theory* 22, no. 1 (2004): 53–87.

Converse, Philip. "Nonattitudes and American Public Opinion: Comment—The Status of Nonattitudes." *American Political Science Review* 68 (1974): 650–66.

Cooper, H. A. "Terrorism: The Problem of Definition Revisited." *American Behavioral Scientist* 44, no. 6 (2001): 881–93.

Coser, Lewis A. *The Functions of Social Conflict.* New York: Free Press of Glencoe, 1964.

Dahl, Robert A. *On Democracy.* New Haven, CT: Yale University Press, 1998.

Davis, Darren W. *Negative Liberty: Public Opinion and the Terrorist Attacks on America.* New York: Russell Sage Foundation, 2007.

Doty, R. M., B. E. Peterson, and D. G. Winter. "Threat and Authoritarianism in the United States, 1978–1987." *Journal of Personality and Social Psychology* 61 (1991): 629–40.

Dowler, Lorraine. "Women on the Frontlines: Rethinking War Narratives Post 9/11." *GeoJournal* 58, nos. 2–3 (2002): 159–65.

Druckman, J. N. "The Implications of Framing Effects for Citizen Competence." *Political Behavior* 23, no. 3 (2001): 225–56.

Durkheim, Emile. *The Rules of Sociological Method.* New York: Free Press, 1964.

Eagly, A. H., and S. Chaiken. "Attitude Structure and Function." *The Handbook of Social Psychology.* Edited by Daniel T. Gilbert, Susan T. Fiske, and Gardner Lindzey. Boston: McGraw-Hill, 1998.

Entman, Robert M. "Cascading Activation: Contesting the White House's Frame after 9/11." *Political Communication* 20, no. 4 (2003): 415–32.

————. *Democracy Without Citizens: Media and the Decay of American Politics.* New York: Oxford University Press, 1989.

————. "Framing: Toward Clarification of a Fractured Paradigm." *Journal of Communication* 43, no. 4 (1993): 51–58.

————. *Projections of Power: Framing News, Public Opinion and U.S. Foreign Policy.* Chicago: University of Chicago Press, 2004.

Esses, V. M., J. F. Dovidio, and G. Hodson. "Public Attitudes toward Immigration in the United States and Canada in Response to the September 11, 2001 'Attack on America.'" *Analysis of Social Issues and Public Policy* 2, no. 1 (2002): 69–85.

Etzioni, Amitai. *How Patriotic Is the Patriot Act? Freedom Versus Security in the Age of Terrorism.* New York: Routledge, 2004.

————, and Deirdre Mead. *The State of Society: A Rush to Pre-9/11.* Washington, DC: Communitarian Network, 2003.

Everts, P., and P. Isernia. "The War in Iraq." *Public Opinion Quarterly* 69, no. 2 (2005): 264–323.

Farber, David R. *What They Think of Us: International Perceptions of the United States since 9/11.* Princeton, NJ: Princeton University Press, 2007.

Finucane, Melissa L., Ali Alhakami, Paul Slovic, and Stephen M. Johnson. "The Affect Heuristic in Judgments of Risks and Benefits." *Journal of Behavioral Decision Making* 13 (2000): 1–17.

Fischer, P., T. Greitemeyer, A. Kastenmüller, D. Frey, and S. Osswald. "Terror Salience and Punishment: Does Terror Salience Induce Threat to Social Order?" *Journal of Experimental Social Psychology* 43, no. 6 (2007): 964–71.

Fischhoff, B., P. Slovic, S. Lichtenstein, S. Read, and B. Combs. "How Safe Is Safe Enough? A Psychometric Study of Attitudes towards Technological Risks and Benefits." *Policy Sciences* 9 (1978): 127–52.

Fischhoff, B., R. M. Gonzalez, D. A. Small, and J. S. Lerner. "Judged Terror Risk and Proximity to the World Trade Center." *Journal of Risk and Uncertainty* 26, no. 2 (2003): 137–51.

Fishbein, Martin, and Icek Ajzen. *Belief, Attitude, Intention, and Behavior.* Reading, MA: Addison-Wesley, 1975.

Ford, C. A., J. R. Udry, K. Gleiter, and K. Chantala. "Reactions of Young Adults to September 11, 2001." *Archives of Pediatrics and Adolescent Medicine* 157 (2003): 572–78.

Gaines, Brian J. "Where's the Rally? Approval and Trust of the President, Cabinet, Congress, and Government Since September 11." *PS: Political Science and Politics* 35, no. 3 (2002): 530–36.

Gamson, William A. *Talking Politics.* New York: Cambridge University Press, 1992.

————, D. Croteau, W. Hoynes, and T. Sasson. "Media Images and the Social Construction of Reality." *Annual Review of Sociology* 18 (1992): 373–93.

Gamson, William A., and Andre Modigliani. "Media Discourse and Public Opinion on Nuclear Power: A Constructionist Approach." *American Journal of Sociology* 95, no. 1 (1989): 1–37.

Gans, Herbert J. *Deciding What's News: A Study of CBS Evening News, NBC Nightly News, Newsweek, and Time.* New York: Pantheon Books, 1979.

————. "Reopening the Black Box: Toward a Limited Effects Theory." *Journal of Communication* 43, no. 4 (1993): 29–35.

Gitlin, Todd. *The Whole World Is Watching: Mass Media in the Making & Unmaking of the New Left.* Berkeley: University of California Press, 1980.

Glassner, Barry. *The Culture of Fear: Why Americans Are Afraid of the Wrong Things.* New York: Basic Books, 1999.

Goffman, Erving. *Frame Analysis: An Essay on the Organization of the Experience.* New York: Harper Colophon, 1974.

Gottdiener, Mark. *Postmodern Semiotics: Material Culture and the Forms of Postmodern Life.* Oxford: Blackwell, 1995.

Greenberg, J., T. Pyszczynski, S. Solomon, A. Rosenblatt, M. Veeder, S. Kirkland, and D. Lyon. "Evidence for Terror Management Theory II: The Effects of Mortality Salience on Reactions to Those Who Threaten or Bolster the Cultural Worldview." *Journal of Personality and Social Psychology* 58 (1990): 308–18.

Greenberg, J., S. Solomon, and T. Pyszczynski. "Terror Management Theory of Self-Esteem and Cultural Worldviews: Empirical Assessments and Conceptual Refinements." *Advances in Experimental Social Psychology,* vol. 29. Edited by Mark P. Zanna. San Diego: Academic Press, 1997.

Greenberg, Stanley B. "'We'—not 'me.'" *American Prospect* 12, no. 22 (2001): 25–27.

Gross, Kimberly, Sean Aday, and Paul R. Brewer. "A Panel Study of Media Effects on Political and Social Trust after September 11, 2001." *Harvard International Journal of Press/Politics* 9, no. 4 (2004): 49–73.

Hall, Stuart. "The Rediscovery of 'Ideology': Return of the Repressed in Media Studies." *Culture, Society, and the Media.* Edited by Michael Gurevitch, Tony Bennett, James Curran, and Janet Woollacott. London: Methuen, 1982.

Hallin, Daniel C., and Paolo Mancini. *Comparing Media Systems: Three Models of Media and Politics.* Cambridge, UK; New York: Cambridge University Press, 2004.

Heider, Fritz. *The Psychology of Interpersonal Relations.* New York: Wiley, 1958.

Herman, E. S., and Noam Chomsky. *Manufacturing Consent: The Political Economy of the Mass Media.* New York: Pantheon Books, 2002.

Hoffman, Bruce. *Inside Terrorism.* New York: Columbia University Press, 2006.

Hollander, Paul *Anti-Americanism: Critiques at Home and Abroad, 1965–1990.* Oxford: Oxford University Press, 1992.

Hooks, Gregory, and Clayton Mosher. "Outrages against Personal Dignity: Rationalizing Abuse and Torture in the War on Terror." *Social Forces* 83, no. 4 (2005): 1627–45.

Huddy, Leonie, Nadia Khatib, and Theresa Capelos. "Trends: Reactions to the Terrorist Attacks of September 11, 2001." *Public Opinion Quarterly* 66, no. 3 (2002): 418–50.

Huddy, Leonie, Stanley Feldman, Charles Tabar, and Gallya Lahav. "Threat, Anxiety, and Support of Antiterrorism Policies." *American Journal of Political Science* 49, no. 3 (2005): 593–608.

Huddy, Leonie, Stanley Feldman, Gallya Lahav, and Charles Taber. "Fear and Terrorism: Psychological Reactions to 9/11." *Framing Terrorism: The News Media, the Government, and the Public.* Edited by Pippa Norris, Montague Kern, and Marion Just. New York: Routledge, 2003.

Huntington, Samuel P. *The Clash of Civilizations and the Remaking of the World.* New York: Simon & Schuster, 2003.

Johnson, C. A. *Blowback: The Costs and Consequences of American Empire.* New York: Metropolitan Books, 2000.

Kahneman, D., and A. Tversky. "Choices, Values, and Frames." *American Psychologist* 39 (1984): 73–103.

King, Erika G., and Mary deYoung. "Imag(in)ing September 11: Ward Churchill, Frame Contestation, and Media Hegemony." *Journal of Communication Inquiry* 32, no. 2 (2008): 123–39.

Kuzma, Lynn M. "Trends: Terrorism in the United States." *Public Opinion Quarterly* 64, no. 1 (2000): 90–105.

Lakoff, George. *Don't Think of An Elephant!* White River Junction, VT: Chelsea Green, 2004.

Landau, M. J., S. Solomon, J. Greenberg, F. Cohen, T. Pyszczynski, J. Arndt, C. H. Miller, D. M. Ogilvie, and A. Cook. "Deliver Us From Evil: The Effects of Mortality Salience and Reminders of 9/11 on Support for President George W. Bush." *Personality and Social Psychology Bulletin* 30 (2004): 1136–50.

Levin, Jack, and Jim Nolan. *The Violence of Hate: Confronting Racism, Anti-Semitism, and Other Forms of Bigotry.* Boston: Pearson Allyn and Bacon, 2010.

Maney, Gregory M., Lynne M. Woehrle, and Patrick G. Coy. "Harnessing and Challenging Hegemony: The U.S. Peace Movement after 9/11." *Sociological Perspectives* 48, no. 3 (2005): 338–57.

Mayer, Jane. *The Dark Side: The Inside Story of How the War on Terror Turned into a War on American Ideals.* New York: Doubleday, 2008.

McQuail, Denis. *Mass Communication Theory.* London; Thousand Oaks, CA: Sage, 2000.

Merolla, Jennifer L., and Elizabeth J. Zechmeister. *Democracy at Risk: How Terrorist Threats Affect the Public.* Chicago: University of Chicago Press, 2009.

Molotch, H., and M. Lester. "News as Purposive Behavior: On the Strategic Use of Routine Events, Accidents and Scandals." *American Sociological Review* 39 (1974): 101–12.

Moore, Kathleen M. "'United We Stand': American Attitudes toward (Muslim) Immigration Post-September 11th." *Muslim World* 92, nos. 1–2 (2002): 39–57.

Moskalenko, Sophia, Clark McCauley, and Paul Rozin. "Group Identification under Conditions of Threat: College Students' Attachment to Country, Family, Ethnicity, Religion and University Before and After September 11, 2001." *Political Psychology* 27, no. 1 (2006): 77–97.

Mueller, John. *Overblown.* New York: Free Press, 2006.

———. "Simplicity and Spook: Terrorism and the Dynamics of Threat Exaggeration." *International Studies Perspectives* 6, no. 2 (2005): 208–34.

Nacos, Brigitte L. *Terrorism and the Media: From the Iran Hostage Crisis to the World Trade Center Bombing.* New York: Columbia University Press, 1994.

Newcomb, T. M. *The Acquaintance Process.* New York: Holt, Rinehart and Winston, 1961.

Norris, Pippa, Montague Kern, and Marion Just, eds. *Framing Terrorism: The News Media, the Government, and the Public.* New York: Routledge, 2003.

Nye, Joseph S. "The Decline of America's Soft Power: Why Washington Should Worry." *Foreign Affairs* 83, no. 3 (2004): 16–20.

Olivas-Luján, Miguel R., Anne-Wil Harzing, and Scott McCoy. "September 11, 2001: Two Quasi-Experiments on the Influence of Threats on Cultural Values and Cosmopolitanism." *International Journal of Cross Cultural Management* 4, no. 2 (2004): 211–28.

Panagopoulos, Costas. "The Polls—Trends: Arab and Muslim Americans and Islam in the aftermath of 9/11." *Public Opinion Quarterly* 70, no. 4 (2006): 608–24.

Pape, Robert. *Dying to Win: The Strategic Logic of Suicide Terrorism.* New York: Random House, 2005.

Parenti, Michael. *Inventing Reality: Politics and the Mass Media.* New York: St. Martin's Press, 1986.

Perrin, Andrew J. "National Threat and Political Culture: Authoritarianism, Antiauthoritarianism, and the September 11 Attacks." *Political Psychology* 26, no. 2 (2005): 167–94.

———, and S. J. Smolek. "Who Trusts? Race, Gender, and the September 11 Rally Effect." *Social Science Research* 38, no. 1 (2009): 134–45.

Peterson, C., and Martin E. P. Seligman. "Character Strengths Before and After September 11." *Psychological Science* 14, no. 4 (2003): 381–84.

Petty, Richard E., and John T. Cacioppo. *Communication and Persuasion: Central and Peripheral Routes to Attitude Change.* New York: Springer-Verlag, 1986.

Prior, Markus. "Political Knowledge after September 11." *PS: Political Science and Politics* 35, no. 3 (2002): 523–29.

Putnam, Robert D. *Bowling Alone: The Collapse and Revival of American Community.* New York: Simon & Schuster, 2000.

———. "Bowling Together." *American Prospect,* February 11, 2002.

Pyszczynski, Thomas A., A. Abdollahi, S. Solomon, J. Greenberg, F. Cohen, and D. Weise. "Mortality Salience, Martyrdom, and Military Might: The Great Satan versus the Axis of Evil." *Personality and Social Psychology Bulletin* 32 (2006): 525–37.

Pyszczynski, Thomas A., Jeff Greenberg, and Sheldon Solomon. *In the Wake of 9/11: The Psychology of Terror.* Washington, DC: American Psychological Association, 2003.

"Remains of a Day." *Time,* September 9, 2002.

Sander, Thomas H., and Robert D. Putnam. "Still Bowling Alone? The Post-9/11 Split." *Journal of Democracy* 21, no. 1 (2010): 9–16.

Sardar, Z., and M. W. Davies. *Why Do People Hate America?* New York: Disinformation Company, 2003.

Scheufele, D. A. "Framing as a Theory of Media Effects." *Journal of Communication* 49 (1999): 103–19.

Schuman, Howard, and Willard L. Rodgers. "Cohorts, Chronology, and Collective Memories." *Public Opinion Quarterly* 68, no. 2 (2004): 217–54.

Shaheen, Jack G. "Reel Bad Arabs: How Hollywood Vilifies a People." *Annals of the American Academy of Political and Social Science* 588, no. 1 (2003): 171–93.

Shlapentokh, Vladimir, Joshua Woods, and Eric Shiraev, eds. *America: Sovereign Defender or Cowboy Nation?* Aldershot, UK; Burlington, VT: Ashgate, 2005.

Shoemaker, Pamela J., and Stephen D. Reese. *Mediating the Message: Theories of Influences on Mass Media Content.* White Plains, NY: Longman, 1996.

Siebert, Fred. S., Theodore Peterson, and Wilbur Schramm. *Four Theories of the Press: The Authoritarian, Libertarian, Social Responsibility, and Soviet Communist Concepts of What the Press Should Be and Do.* Urbana: University of Illinois Press, 1956.

Simmel, Georg. *The Sociology of Georg Simmel.* Glencoe, IL: Free Press, 1950.

Sjöberg, Lennart. "The Perceived Risk of Terrorism." *Risk Management: An International Journal* 7 (2005): 43–61.

Skitka, Linda J. "Patriotism or Nationalism? Understanding Post–September 11, 2001, Flag-Display Behavior." *Journal of Applied Social Psychology* 35, no. 10 (2005): 1995–2011.

————, C. W. Bauman, and E. Mullen. "Political Tolerance and Coming to Psychological Closure Following the September 11, 2001, Terrorist Attacks: An Integrative Approach." *Personality and Social Psychology Bulletin* 30, no. 6 (2004): 743–56.

Skocpol, Theda. "Will 9/11 and the War on Terror Revitalize American Civic Democracy?" *PS: Political Science and Politics* 35, no. 3 (2002): 537–40.

Slater, Philip. *The Pursuit of Loneliness.* Boston: Beacon Press, 1970.

Slovic, Paul. *The Perception of Risk.* London; Sterling, VA: Earthscan, 2004.

————. "Terrorism as Hazard: A New Species of Trouble." *Risk Analysis* 22, no. 3 (2002): 425–26.

————, M. L. Finucane, E. Peters, and D. G. McGregor. "The Affect Heuristic: Rational Actors or Rational Fools? Implications of the Affect Heuristic for Behavioral Economics." *Heuristics and Biases: The Psychology of Intuitive Judgment.* Edited by Thomas Gilovich, Dale W. Griffin, and Daniel Kahneman. Cambridge, UK: Cambridge University Press, 2002.

Smelser, Neil J. "Epilogue: September 11, 2001, as Cultural Trauma." *Cultural Trauma and Collective Identity.* Edited by Jeffrey Alexander, Ron Eyerman, Bernhard Giesen, Neil J. Smelser, and Piotr Sztompka. Berkeley: University of California Press, 2004.

Smith, Tom W., Kenneth A. Rasinski, and Marianna Toce. *America Rebounds: A National Study of Public Response to the September 11th Terrorist Attacks: Preliminary Findings.* Chicago: National Opinion Research Center, 2001.

Sniderman, P. M., and S. M. Theriault. "The Structure of Political Argument and the Logic of Issue Framing." *Studies in Public Opinion: Attitudes, Nonattitudes, Measurement Error, and Change.* Edited by Willem. E. Saris and Paul M. Sniderman. Princeton: Princeton University Press, 2004.

Snow, David A., and Scott C. Byrd. "Ideology, Framing and the Islamic Terrorist Movement." *Mobilization: An International Quarterly Review* 12, no. 1 (2007): 119–36.

Solomon, S., J. Greenberg, and T. Pyszczynski. "A Terror Management Theory of Social Behavior: The Psychological Functions of Self-Esteem and Cultural Worldviews." *Advances in Experimental Social Psychology.* Edited by Leonard Berkowitz. New York: Academic Press, 1991.

Steinberg, Marc. "The Talk and Back Talk of Collective Action: A Dialogic Analysis of Repertoires of Discourse among Nineteenth-Century English Cotton Spinners." *American Journal of Sociology* 105, no. 3 (1999): 736–80.

Stewart, Jon, Ben Karlin, and David Javerbaum. *America (The Book): A Citizen's Guide to Democracy Inaction.* New York: Warner Books, 2004.

Sunstein, Cass. "Fear and Liberty." *Social Research* 71, no. 4 (2004): 976–96.

————. "Terrorism and Probability Neglect." *Journal of Risk and Uncertainty* 26, nos. 2/3 (2003): 121–36.

Tajfel, Henri. "Social Psychology of Intergroup Relations." *Annual Review of Psychology* 33 (1982): 1–39.

————, and J. C. Turner. "An Integrative Theory of Intergroup Conflict." *The Social Psychology of Intergroup Relations.* Edited by William G. Austin and Stephen Worchel. Monterey, CA: Brooks/Cole, 1979.

Ten Eyck, Toby A., and M. Williment. "The National Media and Things Genetic." *Science Communication* 25, no. 2 (2003): 129–52.

Tichenor, Phillip J. *Community Conflict and the Press.* Beverly Hills, CA: Sage, 1980.

Tocqueville, Alexis de. *Democracy in America.* Translated by George Lawrence. New York: Harper & Row, 1966.

Traugott, Michael W., and Ted Brader. "Explaining 9/11." *Framing Terrorism: The News Media, the Government, and the Public.* Edited by Pippa Norris, Montague Kern, and Marion Just. New York: Routledge, 2003.

Tuchman, Gaye. *Making News: A Study in the Construction of Reality.* New York: Free Press, 1978.

Tversky, Amos, and Daniel Kahneman. "Judgment under Uncertainty: Heuristics and Biases." *Science* 185 (1974): 1124–31.

Williams, Kristian. *American Methods: Torture and the Logic of Domination.* Cambridge, MA: South End Press, 2006.

Williams, Rhys H. "From the 'Beloved Community' to 'Family Values': Religious Language, Symbolic Repertories, and Democratic Culture." *Social Movements: Identity, Culture, and the State.* Edited by David S. Meyer, Nancy Whittier, and Belinda Robnett. New York: Oxford University Press, 2002.

Woehrle, Lynne, Patrick Coy, and Gregory Maney. *Contesting Patriotism: Culture, Power and Strategy in the Peace Movement.* New York: Rowman & Littlefield, 2008.

Woods, Joshua. "America: The Archipelago of Almost Fame." Midwest Quarterly 48, no. 3 (2007): 359–75.

———. "The Common Enemy Rationale: An Attempt to Apply Concepts of Cognitive Consistency to the Portrayals of the United States in the Foreign Press." *Global Media Journal* 4, no. 7 (2005) (available online at http://lass.calumet.purdue.edu/cca/gmj/fa05/gmj-fa05-woods.htm).

———. "Democracy and the Press: A Comparative Analysis of Pluralism in the International Print Media." *Social Science Journal* 44, no. 2 (2007): 213–30.

———. "What We Talk about When We Talk about Terrorism: Elite Press Coverage of Terrorism Risk from 1997 to 2005." *Harvard International Journal of Press/Politics* 12, no. 3 (2007): 3–20.

———, Toby A. Ten Eyck, Stan A. Kaplowitz, and Vladimir Shlapentokh. "Terrorism Risk Perceptions and Proximity to Primary Terrorist Targets: How Close Is Too Close?" *Human Ecology Review* 15, no. 1 (2008): 63–70.

Yum, Young-Ok, and William Schenck-Hamlin. "Reactions to 9/11 as a Function of Terror Management and Perspective Taking." *Journal of Social Psychology* 145, no. 3 (2005): 265–86.

Zajonc, Robert B. "Feeling and Thinking: Preferences Need No Inferences." *American Psychologist* 35 (1980): 151–75.

Zaller, John R. *The Nature and Origins of Mass Opinion.* New York: Cambridge University Press, 1992.

Zhao, Yuezhi. *Media, Market, and Democracy in China: Between the Party Line and the Bottom Line.* Urbana: University of Illinois Press, 1998.

Zimbardo, Philip, and Bruce Kluger. "Phantom Menace: Is Washington Terrorizing Us More than Al Qaeda?" *Psychology Today* 36, no. 3 (2003): 34–36.

Zoch, L. M., and J. V. Turk. "Women Making News: Gender as a Variable in Source Selection and Use." *Journalism and Mass Communication Quarterly* 75 (1998): 762–75.

INDEX

ABOUT THE AUTHOR

Joshua Woods is an assistant professor of sociology at West Virginia University, where he teaches courses on social psychology, media and society, the sociology of organizations, and social research methods. His previous books include *Feudal America: Elements of the Middle Ages in Contemporary Society* and *America: Sovereign Defender or Cowboy Nation?* Woods has also written numerous journal articles, as well as opinion pieces in national and international newspapers.